WHAT TEST-TAKERS ARE SAYING ABOUT LEARNINGEXPRESS PREPARATION GUIDES

"The information from the last two study guides I ordered from your company was invaluable. . . . Better than the $200 6-week study courses being offered. . . . After studying from dozens of books I would choose yours over any of the other companies."

S. Frosch

"Excellent . . . It was like having the test in advance!"

J. Kennedy

"Without this book, I wouldn't have understood the test."

R. Diaz

"Told me everything that was going to be on the test [and] gave me a good understanding of the whole process, too."

J. Molinari

"The best test-prep book I've used!"

H. Hernandez

"I felt 100% prepared when I took the Suffolk County exam this past June. I scored a 96 on it. I had taken it previously in 1992 and only scored an 82. Your guide helped me add 14 points to my score!"

R. Morrell

BUS
OPERATOR
EXAM

LEARNINGEXPRESS
NEW YORK

Copyright © 1997 Learning Express, LLC.

...nal and Pan-American Copyright Conventions. Published in the United
...w York.

...rk City Transit Authority. Reprinted with permission. Neither the
...ority nor the Transit Authority endorse or have any responsibility for this
publication.

Library of Congress Cataloging-in-Publication Data

Bus operator exam : national edition. — 1st ed.
     p.   cm. — (The LearningExpress civil service library)
  ISBN 1-57685-046-3
  1. Bus driving—United States—Examinations—Study guides. 2. Bus driving—
Vocational guidance—United States.   3. Bus drivers—Licenses—United States.
  I. Series.
  TL232.3.B8757   1997
  629.28'333'0973—dc21
                                                      97-25469
                                                          CIP

Printed in the United States of America
9 8 7 6 5 4 3 2 1
First Edition

Regarding the Information in this Book

We attempt to verify the information presented in our books prior to publication. It is always a good idea, however, to double-check such important information as minimum requirements, application and testing procedures, and deadlines with your local hiring agency, as such information can change from time to time.

For Further Information

For information on LearningExpress, other LearningExpress products, or bulk sales, please call or write to us at:
    LearningExpress®
    900 Broadway
    Suite 604
    New York, NY 10003
    212-995-2566

LearningExpress is an affiliated company of Random House, Inc.
Distributed to the retail trade by Random House, Inc., as agent for LearningExpress, LLC.
Visit LearningExpress on the Web at http://www.learnx.com/

ISBN 1-57685-046-3

7 85555 85046 0

CONTENTS

LIST OF CONTRIBUTORS

The following individuals contributed to the content of this book.

Jan Gallagher, Ph.D., is a test-development specialist, editor, and teacher living in Jersey City, New Jersey.

Mary Hesalroad, a former police officer for the Austin, Texas, Police Department, consults with police departments on recruiting efforts and is a freelance writer now living in San Marcos, Texas.

Judith F. Olson, M.A., is chairperson of the language arts department at Valley High School in West Des Moines, Iowa, where she also conducts test preparation workshops.

Judith Robinovitz is an independent educational consultant and director of Score At the Top, a comprehensive test preparation program in Vero Beach, Florida.

Jo Lynn Southard is a writer and editor living in Portland, Maine.

The following LearningExpress staff members also contributed to the writing and researching of this book: **Jean Eckhoff** and **Edward Grossman**.

C·H·A·P·T·E·R 1

HOW TO BECOME A BUS OPERATOR

CHAPTER SUMMARY

If you're looking for a challenging career in a growing field, becoming a bus operator may be just the ticket. But the job involves much more than simply turning a steering wheel and opening the door. To find out what it takes to become a bus operator and to learn more about what will be expected of you on the job, read this chapter.

Would you enjoy working outdoors—yet safe from the rain and snow? Do you like talking to people and helping them solve problems? Are you able to work independently, without a supervisor watching over your shoulder? Would you like to work flexible hours—for great pay? Do you appreciate job security but want to work at a job that is different every day? If you answered yes to these questions, you should consider becoming a bus operator.

As suburbs sprawl farther and farther from downtown areas, as more and more of these suburban areas add manufacturing and retail establishments, and as people become more aware of the environmental pollution and personal stress caused by driving a private automobile, the number of transit systems, the number of buses, and the number of bus operators will continue to grow. In fact, the number of bus drivers in the United States has increased every year since 1990. According to the American Public Transit Association (APTA), there are about 2,250 transit systems in the U.S. that operate 67,000 buses, which are driven by over 89,500 drivers, and these transit systems employ the same number of people again in non-driving jobs.

> **BUS STOP 1**
>
> The American Public Transit Association is an organization of bus, rapid transit and commuter rail systems. In fact, if you ride a bus in the U.S. or Canada, chances are it belongs to an APTA member, since 95% of all passengers are carried by APTA members. For more information, APTA's address is:
> 1201 New York Ave, NW
> Suite 400
> Washington D.C. 20005
> 202-898-4000
> http://www.apta.com
>
> The Community Transportation Association of America (CTAA) is an association of organizations and individuals working to provide transportation options in locations where mass transit is not available. The CTAA's address is:
> 1440 New York Ave, N.W.
> Suite 440
> Washington, D.C. 20005
> 202-628-1480
> http://www.ctaa.org

As we rely more on public transit in general and on buses in particular, the job of bus operator will become more attractive. Most bus operators work for the city or county and, therefore, receive good wages and benefits. Also, as transit continues to grow, jobs become more secure and more jobs open up.

THE PRIVATE SECTOR

While this book focuses on operating a bus for a city, county, or regional transit system, there are a variety of other bus driving opportunities. Greyhound and other interstate bus services employ bus drivers, as do tour companies and local private companies, like those that provide airport transportation. Bus drivers are also needed to drive school buses. In addition, becoming a bus driver can be the starting point for other career opportunities, such as becoming a bus dispatcher or line supervisor. And in areas that have a variety of modes of transit, subway, street car, trolley, and paratransit operators are often hired from the ranks of bus drivers. ("Paratransit" is transportation for passengers whose disabilities preclude them from using the fixed route bus system. The Americans with Disabilities Act of 1990 required that disabled individuals have accessible transportation comparable to the transit system in the area.)

> **BUS STOP 2**
>
> Private companies such as Greyhound Lines, Inc. and the regional interstate bus companies provide a different kind of bus driving experience—so-called "over the road" driving. In many areas of the country, tour companies—which may operate locally or long distance—provide another opportunity for those interested in a career in bus operation.
>
> If you would like more information on these kinds of driving experiences, check your Yellow Pages under "Buses" and "Sightseeing Tours." And don't forget to look for information on the World Wide Web. You can even file an application online with Greyhound at www.greyhound.com.
>
> Finally, if you are interested in becoming a school bus operator, check with your local school district, which may operate its own fleet or can at least tell you whom they contract with to provide transportation.

HOW THE BUS OPERATOR HIRING PROCESS WORKS

Transit systems are generally operated by local governments, that is, cities and counties. Some municipalities contract with a private firm to provide bus service, but they still play a role in determining the standards for hiring bus operators. In some areas, applications for new bus operators are accepted continually and simply kept on file until an opening arises. In many other areas, applications are accepted only when jobs are open or training classes are scheduled to begin. Transit openings are usually advertised in the paper, and most cities have bulletin boards and telephone job lines that announce job openings. Be sure to also check any state-run employment agencies.

You should be aware that bus operators often do not work nine to five. This may be one of the things that attracts you to being a bus operator; but before you proceed too far in the hiring process, make sure that you know what kind of hours you will be expected to work and whether they fit your schedule. Also find out what the training schedule will be. It may be different from your regular driving schedule and you will need to arrange to attend all training sessions.

BUS STOP 3

The World Wide Web provides a wealth of information about local transit companies. Check your favorite search engine, like Yahoo or Altavista, to see if the city you are interested in is on the Web. The Web sites for the APTA and CTAA (www.apta.com and www.ctaa.org) can also lead you to other Web sites. And if you just love buses, check out "The Bus Spot" at www.members.aol.com/busspot/main.html. This site has photographs of buses from all over the world and even a "Bus of the Month."

PART-TIME VS. FULL-TIME

The hiring trends in transit indicate that most new bus operators will initially be hired part-time. In fact, 40% of all bus drivers (including school bus drivers) work part-time. If you are looking for a full-time job, however, don't give up on bus driving. Once you are hired, you will probably have the opportunity to "move up" to a full-time position. This may take a few months or a few years, depending on the rate of turnover a system experiences. The transit human resources office or city personnel office can tell you how long it usually takes to be offered a full-time job.

On the other hand, a part-time position may be just what you are looking for. It can be a perfect schedule for students and retirees, as well as for people who have other part-time jobs. If the transit system you are interested in is hiring for a full-time opening, you may be expected to work a split-shift, that is, during the morning rush hour and the evening one. Since transit systems may operate 24 hours a day, it is important to know what kind of schedule you will be expected to keep if you are hired.

MINIMUM QUALIFICATIONS

Most transit systems have minimum qualifications that you must meet in order to even apply to be a bus operator. Usually, you must be 21 years of age in order to drive a city bus, although in a few places the age limit is 18. Sometimes the age requirement is higher. For example, in order to be hired in Milwaukee, Wisconsin, and Jacksonville, Florida, you must be 23. In San Francisco, you must be over 25!

Many transit systems require that you have a high school diploma or GED in order to apply to be a bus operator. In many other cases, however, you must simply demonstrate the ability to communicate in English, verbally and in writing. Usually you must also hold a valid driver's license, although you don't need to have a commercial driver's license to apply.

It is imperative, though, that you have a good driving record. Sometimes this is spelled out in detail, especially in states that have a "point system" for reporting traffic violations. If you have more than a certain number of points, you will not be considered for the job. In other places, the transit system requires that you have an "acceptable" or "clean" driving record, and the details are left to the transit manager. If you have doubts about your driving record, it is best to talk with the transit human resources office.

> ### BUS STOP 4
> Hollywood has given us some famous bus drivers—including Jackie Gleason as Ralph Kramden in *The Honeymooners* and Sandra Bullock as Annie in *Speed*. Jackie Gleason even has a bus depot named after him in Brooklyn. Perhaps Los Angeles will soon open the "Sandra Bullock Transit Garage"!

Once you've determined that you meet the minimum qualifications for the bus operator opening, you will need to fill out a job application. These can be obtained from the transit division human resources office or city personnel office. Generally, these are standard applications that ask about your education and employment history. (See Chapter 3 for advice on how to fill out a civil service application.)

In addition, you will often be responsible for supplying an official copy of your driving record. The transit division can tell you how to obtain this; most often you simply contact the state Department of Transportation or Division of Motor Vehicles. Even if you don't have to supply a copy of your driving record, you will no doubt be asked to indicate any moving violations you have had on your application.

THE EXAM

In most cases, you will be required to take an exam as the second step of the transit hiring process. Generally, you will run into one or more of three kinds of test: a personality survey, a decision-making test, and a general aptitude test.

The most common personality survey currently in use is the Bus Operator Selection Survey, or the BOSS. This is not a test of your knowledge of Bruce Springsteen! Instead, the point of the BOSS is to identify applicants whose personalities are particularly suited to being a bus operator.

Remember that the BOSS is a survey and not a test. It contains 77 multiple-choice questions that ask about your feelings and attitudes. If you are asked to take the BOSS, relax and answer the questions honestly. Don't waste time trying to figure out what the transit manager wants you to say. Even if you manage to fool everyone at this stage, if you don't have the personality to be a bus operator, it will become apparent soon enough.

In addition to giving your potential employer some insight into your personality, the BOSS helps them prepare the questions they want to ask you during your oral interview. The oral interview is discussed in the next section.

The most popular decision-making test currently in use is the Seattle Metro Video Bus Operator Test. Although this test, usually just called the Seattle test, is on video, it is not designed to test your knowledge of the television show *Frasier*!

The Seattle test is designed to determine how well you deal with common situations that bus operators face. The videotape that you will watch has 66 scenarios, depicted by actors, that represent typical situations bus drivers deal with every day. Before the completion of each scenario, the words "The operator should . . ." appear on the screen along with several possible answers. You then choose what you think is the best answer.

Typical situations that an operator might face that may be depicted in the Seattle test include unruly and difficult passengers, lost and confused passengers, and dealing with lost and found items. You then use your common sense to choose the most logical, most ethical, and most practical answer to the situation.

BUS STOP 5

Hollywood has also given us some famous bus passengers—Dustin Hoffman and Katherine Ross in The Graduate, for example. Later, Dustin Hoffman rode the bus with Jon Voight in Midnight Cowboy. By the time he was in Rain Man with Tom Cruise, Hoffman traded in his bus for a classic car. More recently, Spike Lee brought us Get On The Bus!, whose passengers included Ossie Davis, Andre Braugher and Richard Belzer.

Instead of, or in addition to, one or both of these exams, you may be given a general aptitude test. Most often this will be a multiple-choice test designed to test your reading comprehension and basic math skills. In addition, this test may contain bus operator-specific material, such as testing your ability to read maps and bus schedules. Consult Chapter 2 of this book to see if the major city transit system you are interested in is listed and then look at the exam information for that city. If it is not listed, human resources or personnel offices will often give you some information about the test—including its format (multiple choice, fill in the blank, etc.), length, and the skills it is designed to evaluate. The three practice exams and instructional chapters in this book provide excellent preparation for this type of basic skills exam.

In some cases, you may not be required to take a written or video-based exam. Whether you do or not, you will usually have an interview with the transit director, or perhaps a panel of interviewers, before you can be hired as a bus operator.

THE ORAL INTERVIEW

As noted, if you take the BOSS, the exam itself is just the first step. The results of that test are used to formulate the questions you will be asked in an oral interview. Of course, interviewers are not required to ask only the questions provided by the BOSS. Whatever test you take—or even if you don't take one—you will most likely have at least one face-to-face interview before you are hired to train as a bus operator.

It might seem as though it is impossible to prepare for a job interview. After all, you don't have any idea what questions you will be asked. Or do you? You can be pretty certain that if you have ever been fired from a job, quit a job after a short period of time, or have a large gap in your employment history, you will be asked about it in the job interview. When you are interviewing to be a bus operator, your driving record is fair game as well.

Don't let any "blemishes" on your record throw you. Nobody's record is perfect. Just be prepared to answer the question and don't act surprised that they want an explanation before they hire you. When they say, "Why did you get a ticket for speeding four years ago?" it's better to say, "Because I didn't know what the speed limit was there" than, "Oh, you found out about that, huh? I was mad, and I always drive fast when I'm mad." Don't lie, just use your common sense and be prepared for the questions you know they will ask.

BUS STOP 6

History's most famous bus passenger is Rosa Parks who, on December 1, 1955, refused to move to the back of a Montgomery, Alabama, bus and so became the mother of the Civil Rights Movement. In March, 1997, the American Public Transit Association presented her with its first-ever Lifetime Achievement Award.

TRAINING

After you are hired as a bus operator, you will be trained by the transit system for which you are going to work. While there will often be a classroom component to this training, where you will learn about the bus routes, how to read the bus schedules, and how to complete any paperwork required of bus operators in this particular system, the training consists largely of learning to drive a bus. Prior to driving the bus, you will need to acquire a Commercial Driver's License or, in some states, a Commercial Driver's Permit, which allows you to drive as long as a commercially licensed driver is with you.

THE COMMERCIAL DRIVER'S LICENSE

If you don't have a Commercial Driver's License (CDL) at the time you apply to become a bus operator, don't worry. And don't get one until you are hired. It's not required in order to apply for the job and can be quite expensive—$40 or $50 is common, but it can be more than twice that much. Not only would it be a waste of money to get the license before you apply—especially if you don't get the job—but in many cases employers will train you for the test. In some cases they can give you the test, and in some places, they even pay part of the cost!

In most cases, you will receive anywhere from two to eight weeks of training, both in the classroom and "behind the wheel." In class, you will learn general safety rules and rules specific to your particular system. You will also become familiar with the routes and schedules you will be driving. Classroom and on-the-road training also gives you an opportunity to learn about common situations that arise for bus operators and to get experienced guidance on the best way to deal with these situations. As noted, no matter what kind of schedule you will be working, training may very well be Monday through Friday from 8 to 5. You will need to be available during these hours in order to complete your training.

Initially, you will drive the bus on a closed course, practicing turning, backing up, and other maneuvers. Your first trips out onto city streets will probably be during times when the traffic is light and, as you become more and more accustomed to driving the bus, you will drive in heavier traffic. Also during your first trips on the road, you will drive a training vehicle without passengers. By the end of your training, you will be driving a regular route, accompanied by an experienced driver.

ON THE JOB

Forty percent of bus drivers nationwide are part-time; so, in most cases, your initial assignment will be as a part-time bus operator. Also, it is likely that, after completing your training, you will be on probation for anywhere from 30 days to 6 months. After completing your probation, you will be eligible to apply for any full-time openings that arise.

Bus drivers are usually assigned their routes by a lottery. In this process, you choose the routes and schedules you prefer to drive. The routes are then assigned based on seniority. This means that until you acquire some seniority, you will most likely drive the "bad" routes. But, remember, what is bad to one person is not necessarily bad to another. For example, late night and early morning routes are generally considered undesirable, but you might prefer these hours. At any rate, the lottery is usually held more than once a year, sometimes every quarter, and even, in some places, as each new semester starts at the local university, so that drivers who are students can arrange their schedules.

BUS STOP 7
Bus operators in the United States and Canada are largely represented by two unions—the Transport Workers Union of America (TWU) and the Amalgamated Transit Union (ATU). Their addresses are:

TWU
80 West End Ave
New York NY 10023
212-873-6000

ATU
5025 Wisconsin Ave N.W.
Washington, D.C. 20016
202-537-1645

On a normal workday, you will report to your assigned terminal to pick up your bus. There, you will also receive any transfers, tickets, or forms you will need during the course of the day. Before you leave, you will check over your bus, making sure that tires, brakes, windshield wipers, and lights are in working order. In addition, you will want to be certain that you have enough fuel and that all safety equipment, like the fire extinguisher, is working.

Once on the road, the job of bus operator involves much more than driving a pre-set route. You will pick up and drop off passengers at bus stops, collect fares and issue transfers, and answer questions about routes and schedules. It is imperative that you can do all this while, at the same time, keeping your route on schedule and remaining pleasant and efficient in your dealings with your passengers.

At the end of your shift, you will return your bus to your assigned terminal and complete any paperwork that is required by the transit system. Usually, you will need to fill out some kind of daily report that lists the fares you received, as well as report any damage to or malfunction of the bus itself. In addition, if anything unusual happens during the course of your shift, like an accident or an injury to one of your passengers, you will need to complete an incident report.

SALARY AND BENEFITS

Bus operator wages vary depending on the area in which they work. According to the Occupational Outlook Handbook, prepared by the U.S. Bureau of Labor Statistics, in large metropolitan areas—with populations over two million—the median wage for bus drivers is about $15.50 an hour. As the size of the system and the number of people it is serving decreases, so does the median wage, down to about $12 an hour. In addition, you will usually be paid less during the time you are training. The chart on the next page shows the training wage and starting wage for a few transit systems.

Remember when you compare these wages to the median wages above, that these are *starting* wages. For example, in San Jose, California, trainees are paid $10 an hour and then receive $11.80 when they begin driving on their own. However, the most senior drivers are paid $19.78 an hour. Just as the cost of living varies in different geographic locations, so does the pay received by bus operators, but they are generally well-paying jobs.

Fringe benefits also vary greatly by transit system, but it would be typical to receive health, dental, and life insurance, some paid vacation time and sick leave, and access to a pension plan. If you are required to wear a uniform at work—and you probably will be—you will receive a uniform allowance to pay for the minimum number of uniforms you need. Because most transit systems are unionized, most bus operators receive good fringe benefits and salaries as well as having secure jobs. One fringe benefit that is unique to bus operators is that you will probably be able to ride the bus anywhere in your system for free!

WHAT BUS OPERATORS EARN

Transit System	Hourly Salary/ Training	Starting Hourly Salary
Metropolitan Boston Transit Authority	$6.00	$12.99
Chicago Transit Authority	$4.75	$12.38
Detroit Department of Transportation	$7.60	$10.25 ($14.35 after 6 months)
Los Angeles Metropolitan Transit Authority	$9.57	$11.45
Miami–Metro Dade Transit Authority	$5.00	$10.06–11.24
New York Metropolitan Transportation Authority	$4.60	$13.73
San Antonio VIA Metropolitan Transportation Authority	$4.75	$8.88
San Diego Transit Corporation	min wage	$8.11
Santa Clara Valley Transportation Authority (San Jose, CA)	$10.00	$11.80
Department of Transportation of King County (Seattle)	$5.10	$12.96
Washington D.C. Metro Area Transit Authority	$4.75	$11.34

WHAT DOES IT TAKE TO BE A BUS DRIVER?

1. Even Temperament—Dealing with the public can be the most enjoyable part of the job; it can also be the most annoying. A bus operator needs to maintain his or her good humor.
2. Ability to Work on Your Own—After your training is complete, you will be driving your route without another driver along for the ride. Good bus operators are able to run their routes and take care of their passengers without supervision.
3. Attention to Detail—The safety of the 40 or 50 people on your bus is, quite literally, in your hands. A safe bus operator is continually aware of weather and traffic conditions and able to adjust to any changes that occur.
4. Excellent Driving Skills—Every movement that an operator makes with a bus is potentially many times more dangerous than the same maneuver in a car. Slamming on the brakes, swerving, and sudden acceleration can all cause injury to bus passengers. A good bus operator is a good driver, one who is serious about the rules of the road.

LOOKING AHEAD

The future for bus operators looks good. Many transit systems are expanding and many experience high rates of turnover, meaning jobs are frequently available. The greatest expansion will occur in urban areas with growing populations. Some experts predict that the greatest need in the future will be for school bus drivers, so remember to check on those opportunities. Another growing market is the paratransit system. It is expected that the need for bus operators for intracity transit systems will grow over the next several years as well.

You are most likely to get hired as a bus operator if you have a clean driving record and are willing to work part-time, split-shifts, or other "odd" hours. However, a few months or years of working these kinds of shifts will position you for full-time employment at more regular hours.

Driving a bus can be stressful—you will be dealing with passengers and, often, heavy traffic, while keeping one eye on the clock to make sure you are running on schedule. On the other hand, most bus operators appreciate the opportunity to work on their own without direct supervision and enjoy the responsibility they have for their bus and its passengers. The pay and fringe benefits for bus operators are good and, while some may dislike the hours initially, if you are willing to work odd hours, being a bus operator is an attractive and fulfilling occupation.

> **BUS STOP 8**
> Mass transit continues as an important item on the political agenda. In June, 1997, Vice President Al Gore announced a program whereby the federal government would provide $150 million in seed money for states to use for road, bridge, and transit projects.

C·H·A·P·T·E·R 2

HIRING PROCEDURES FOR MAJOR U.S. CITIES

CHAPTER SUMMARY

This chapter presents a goldmine of information: minimum requirements and hiring procedures for bus operators at top cities around the country. Use the information presented in these profiles to get the specific information you need to apply for a job in these cities—or just generally to find out what's likely to be required of you to get a bus operator job in your city.

One of the keys to becoming a bus operator is knowing what the minimum requirements are and how the hiring process works. Just keeping on top of those basics will help you stand out from the crowd and win the job you want.

The following pages present a rundown of important information on how bus operators are hired in 34 major cities in the U.S. Even if your city isn't among those listed, chances are its hiring procedures will be similar to those listed here. Be sure to contact the personnel department of your local transit company for all the particulars, though. The cities listed here are presented in alphabetical order.

ATLANTA, GEORGIA

Hiring Agency

Metropolitan Atlanta Rapid Transit Authority
(MARTA)
2424 Piedmont Road
Atlanta, GA 30324
(404) 848-5544

Requirements

- Over age 25
- High School Diploma or GED
- CDL Class A or B Driver's License with P endorsement
- Experience in city driving

Applicants must provide:

- Clean motor vehicle record for 7 years. No DWI; fewer than 2 moving violations for 2 years
- DD 214 Military Discharge (if applicable)
- Birth Certificate

Procedures

Current job openings are posted each Monday on Job Hot Line (404) 848-5000.

1. Instructions given on Hot Line to go to GA Department of Labor for interview and test schedule.
2. Background check, physical, and DEA screening done.
3. Successful applicant receives conditional offer of employment letter.
4. There is a 30-day training period at minimum wage.
5. Part-time operators start at $10.75/hr.

Notes

MARTA is a state-funded regional authority. Employees are not civil service, but belong to a union.

There are two classifications: part-time and full-time.

Candidates take the Seattle Test: 66 questions plus video section.

Eligibility list is not held over.

Applicants (1996): 3,600*

New Hires (1995): 500

*Last few years skewed by Olympics.

AUSTIN, TEXAS

Hiring Agency

Capital Metropolitan Transportation Authority
(CMTA)
2910 E. 5th Street
Austin, TX 78702
(512) 389-7400

Operating Contractor

Star Tran, Inc.
106 E. 8th Street
Austin, TX 78702

Requirements

- At least 21 years of age
- Have possessed a valid driver's license for at least the past two years
- Have no more than 2 moving violations in the previous 5 years and no conviction of a serious traffic violation (i.e., DWI, driving with a suspended license) in the past 7 years
- Demonstrate a stable work history
- Pass Department of Transportation (DOT) physical examination, which includes drug and alcohol screen

Note: Applicants with a High School diploma or GED will be given first consideration.

Additional Requirements

- Possess interpersonal skills to effectively and sensitively communicate with all levels of supervisory and non-supervisory employees, customers, public, and others both inside and outside CMTA; must be able to communicate in English (oral and in writing).
- Have the physical ability to pass an agility test and operate CMTA vehicles safely.
- Obtain, at minimum, a Class B Learner's Permit and pass the following written portions of the Commercial Driver's License (CDL) test by the date of hire: Driving Safely, Transporting Passengers, Air Brakes, and Special Requirements for Texas Commercial Motor Vehicles.
- Available to train after 6 P.M. Monday through Friday and all day Saturday, Sunday, and Holidays.
- Complete a 5 to 6-week part-time training program (training pay is $7.50/hr).

Procedures

Vacancies advertised on Hot Line (512) 389-7450, in newspapers, and via postings in job centers.

1. Completed applications are reviewed for minimum qualifications; eligibles are notified about interview site, date, and time.
2. Background, driving, criminal record, drug/alcohol checks made of successful interviewees.
3. Eligibles are given job offer in training program.

Notes

Capital Metro is a member of APTA.
Test used is the Seattle test; eligibility determined by cut-off score.
Employees are not civil service; they work for Star Tran.

Texas is a right-to-work state; voluntary union membership is in ATU.
All new hires are part-time; full-time offers by seniority.
Eligibility list lasts through one training class (exceptions may be made to extend list if highly qualified trainees are not hired initially).
Applicants (1996): 300-400
New Hires (1996): 100
Anticipated Vacancies (1997-8): 100

BALTIMORE, MARYLAND
Hiring Agency

Mass Transit Administration (MTA)
6 Saint Paul Street, 5th Floor
Baltimore, MD 21202
(410) 767-3860

Requirements

- Over 21 years of age
- Driver's License with good record
- Eligible for CDL Class D with P endorsement (must be obtained before beginning employment)

Procedures

Vacancies advertised in newspapers.

1. Applications picked up at Headquarters or mailed, returned within 2 weeks.
2. Application review and screening.
3. Eligibles scheduled for APTA test.
4. Successful candidates interviewed by panel.
5. Ranked list created; selections in order.

Notes

The MTA is an agency of the state Department of Transportation.
Employees are not civil service.
MTA has its own pension plan.

Bus operators belong to the Transport Workers Union.

The eligible list can be terminated by the agency at any time.

Applicants (1996): 1,200 (unscreened)

New Hires (1996): less than 100

Early retirement incentive has created vacancies.

BOSTON, MASSACHUSETTS

Hiring Agency

Metropolitan Boston Transit Authority (MBTA)

10 Park Plaza, 4th Floor

Boston, MA 02116

(617) 222-5000

Requirements

- Over 18 years of age
- In possession of a valid Driver's License
- Eligible for a CDL Class B with AB and P endorsements
- Good driving record:
    DWI in past 5 years equals disqualification
    Moving violations in past 3 years equals disqualification
- U.S. citizen
- High School diploma or GED

Procedures

Vacancies are advertised in all local newspapers; advertisement has a clip-out coupon to return.

1. Consulting firm places all names in a data base and selects candidates in a random method that amounts to a lottery.
2. Applicants are scheduled for 2 exams:
    Seattle Working With The Public Exam
    Employee Productivity Index (McGraw Hill)
3. Eligibles are notified to report for interview with documents:

Proof of no parking violations

Proof of paid-up taxes

Birth certificate or Naturalization Papers

4. Physical exam administered, including drug & alcohol screening.
5. Background check for criminal record and job references.
6. Those who pass are given a job offer and begin training.

Notes

MBTA is a quasi-governmental state authority; member of APTA.

Employees are not civil service.

Employees are union members: Amalgamated Transit Workers.

All new hires are part-time; full-time jobs by seniority.

Eligibility list lasts until exhausted.

MBTA has the highest cut-off score in the nation for the Seattle test.

Last call from lottery was 14,000.

CHICAGO, ILLINOIS

Hiring Agency

Chicago Transit Authority (CTA)

222 West Bank Drive

Chicago, IL 60654-0555

312-664-7200

Requirements

- High School Diploma or GED
- Illinois Driver's License
- No felony convictions

Procedures

1. File resume with the CTA.
2. CTA conducts background check and creates a file of acceptable candidates.

3. When vacancies are declared, names are picked at random from the candidate file for interview.
4. Exams are given when there is a large number of openings.

Notes
Employees are not considered civil service. Current procedures are an interim arrangement. The CTA is planning to return to an exam system. Exam format is currently under review, and details are unobtainable at this time.
Applicants (1996): 500
New Hires (1996): 200

CLEVELAND, OHIO
Hiring Agency
Regional Transit Authority (RTA)
Department of Personnel, 10th Floor
Cleveland, OH 44113
(216) 621-9500

Requirements
- Two years of High School or GED
- Driver's License for vehicles with air brakes
- 5 years' good driving record

Procedures
Openings and application information are posted on the Job Hot Line (216) 566-5284.
1. Applications checked; candidates notified within 2 weeks.
2. Results are ranked; list chosen in order of score.
3. Selected candidates must successfully complete orientation course.

Notes
Eligibility list lasts for 1–2 years, but may be extended.

Employees are not civil service.
Employees belong to a union.

COLUMBUS, OHIO
Hiring Agency
Central Ohio Transportation Authority (COTA)
1600 McKinley Avenue
Columbus, OH 43222
(614) 275-5800
www.coda.com

Requirements
- At least 21 years old
- High School Diploma or GED
- Ohio Driver's License (at time of application)
- License for job: Ohio CDL, Class B with P endorsement
- U.S. citizen
- Must have own transportation
- No relatives working as bus operators
- Resident of Franklin County
- Not be a former employee
- No moving violations for 1 year; fewer than 2 in past 3 years; no license suspension in past 5 years

Procedures
Vacancies are advertised in Ohio newspapers and at job fairs.
1. Advertisements posted every other month or as needed.
2. Applicants send in resumes, which are screened; telephone interview to pre-screen references and make recommendations.
3. Candidate is called to come in and complete formal application and submit to 1st interview, for informational purposes.

4. Selected eligibles are called for 2nd interview with manager or director of department.
5. More are sent for training than will ultimately get a job. Top of the training class is chosen.

Training program 6-8 weeks full-time.

Notes

COTA is a member of APTA.

Test used is the Seattle Metro test.

Employees are not civil service.

Voluntary union membership is in TWU.

All employees are full-time.

Recently, the entire list has been hired within the life of the list (1 year).

Applicants (1996): 175

New Hires (1996): 27

Anticipated vacancies (1997-8): more than in recent years (buy-out in progress).

DALLAS, TEXAS

Hiring Agency

Dallas Area Rapid Transit (DART)
1401 Pacific
Dallas, TX 75202
(214) 749-3257

Requirements

- Must be over 21 years of age
- In possession of Commercial Driver's License
- Be eligible for a CDL with P endorsement
- No DWI for last 5 years
- No more than one DWI in entire driving record

Procedures

Vacancies are posted in the DART building on Tuesdays & Thursdays.

1. Applications are picked up, completed, and submitted.

2. Applications are reviewed for meeting criteria.
3. Eligibles are notified by letter to report for testing.
4. Tests are administered and graded.
5. Candidates are notified to report for interview, medical, and background check.
6. Job offer made; hired as trainee.

Notes

DART is a member of APTA.

Testing is:

1. Basic Skills test
2. Bus Operator Selection Survey from APTA

Employees are not civil service.

Union membership (ATWU) is voluntary.

Employment classifications: 1) trainee 2) operator

Applicants (1996): 600

New Hires (1996): 35

Turnover is high; trainee classes begin every 6 weeks.

Current workforce: 800

DENVER, COLORADO

Hiring Agency

Regional Transportation District
1600 Blake
Denver, CO 80202-1399
(303) 628-9000

Requirements

- Over 21 years of age
- Able to speak and understand English
- High School Diploma not required
- Current Driver's License with good record
- Eligible for CDL Class D with P endorsement (must be obtained before beginning employment)

Procedures

Vacancies posted at Headquarters and advertised

in papers

1. Applications must be completed and filed within time limit, followed by evaluation and screening.
2. Applicants given a qualifying test: map reading, following directions.
3. Eligibles placed on non-ranked list.
4. Random selection from list followed by interview, then job offer.

Notes

Employees are not civil service.
Classification: part-time/full-time
Applicants (1996): 1,200 (unscreened)
New Hires (1994-6): 300

DETROIT, MICHIGAN
Hiring Agency

Detroit Department of Transportation
1301 Warren Avenue
Detroit, MI 48207
(313) 935-4910

Requirements

- Minimum Age: 18
- "Sufficient education" to perform the job (High School Diploma not required)
- For application: Driver's License
- For employment: Current Driver's License with P endorsement
- "Reasonably good" driving record: less than 5 points

Procedures

Openings are advertised on the bulletin board at City/County Hall and on TV (NOT in newspapers). There is a hot line for all public employment: (313) 224-6928.

1. Applications are picked up from City Hall and must be submitted within one week.
2. Notification of testing date comes within 3-4 weeks.
3. Written test administered and graded, list created in ranked order of score.
4. Eligibles notified; background checks conducted (8 weeks).
5. As openings occur, candidates are selected from top of list for 6-8 week training program.

Notes

The exam is created by the Test Development Unit of the department.
DOT is a municipal agency.
Employees are civil service.
Bus operators belong to the Amalgamated Transport Union.
All operators are full-time, but new hires work split shifts.
The eligibility list lasts for 1 year, but may be extended.
Applicants (1996): 969
New Hires (1996): 265

EL PASO, TEXAS
Hiring Agency

Sun-Metro
700A San Francisco
El Paso, TX 79901
(915) 533-3333

Requirements

- Valid Driver's License
- U.S. citizen
- Must have completed 10th Grade

Procedures

Openings are announced on the Information Number: (915) 541-4905.

1. Pick up application, complete, and submit with copies of: Proof of citizenship, Driver's License, and proof of Military Service (if applicable).
2. After screening, eligables are notified by mail of test dates and locations.
3. Successful candidates are placed on a ranked list.

Notes

Sun-Metro is a municipal agency.

Some employees are civil service.

The duration of the eligibility list is 18 months.

Sun-Metro is a member of APTA.

Testing is part of a new project: Landy Jacobs Test of skills (rules of the road), abilities (dexterity), and traits (personality inventory).

Number of Applicants (1996): 400

Number of New Hires (1996): 100

FORT WORTH, TEXAS

Hiring Agency

Fort Worth Transportation Authority ("The T")
2304 Pine Street
Fort Worth, TX 76102
(817) 871-6200

Requirements

- Minimum age: 21
- Minimum Education: High School Diploma or GED
- Legal U.S. resident with work card
- Decent driving record: less than 1 violation last year.
- License required for application: TX CDL Learner's Permit; icense required for job: TX CDL/P endorsement

Procedures

Vacancies are advertised in Dallas-Fort Worth area newspapers, listed with employment agencies, and announced on the job hot line: (817) 871-6220.

1. Candidates can submit completed applications or resumes.
2. Supervisors select candidates for interviews.
3. General background, criminal record, and driving history checks are made.
4. Eligibles are scheduled for physical exam; D&A test given at clinic.
5. Job offers are made, beginning with a 6 week training program.
6. All successful candidates begin as part-time operators.

Notes

The T is a municipal agency that has been turned over to a private operating company.

The T is a member of APTA.

There is no formal examination given.

Employees are not civil service.

Texas is a right-to-work state; voluntary union membership is in Teamster Local 997.

There is no lasting eligibility list.

Full-time employment is offered by seniority as jobs become available.

Mail inquiries should be sent to:
> P.O. Box 1477
> Fort Worth, TX 76101-1477

HOUSTON, TEXAS

Hiring Agency

Metropolitan Transit Authority of Harris County
1201 Louisiana
Houston, TX 77022
(713) 739-4000

Requirements

- Minimum Age: 21
- Minimum education: High School Diploma or GED
- Five years' commercial driving experience with customer service.
- Disqualification for:
    More than 2 moving violations
    DWI conviction
    Criminal record
    Inability to pass a drug and alcohol screen

Procedures

Vacancies are announced in newspapers and on the hot line (717) 739-4046.

1. Applications and required documents submitted
2. Test date and site notification
3. Eligibles go before interview panel
4. Performance evaluation (on-road)
5. Background check through DOT, physical, D/E screen
6. Applications for CDL Learner's Permit
7. Job offer

Notes

MTA is a member of APTA.

Tests used are *Bus Operator Selection Survey* and the Seattle test.

Employees are not civil service.

Texas is a right-to-work state. Union is TWU Local 260.

All new hires are part-time. Application for full-time work is internal.

There are more vacancies than applicants at the moment. (Hiring is going on now.)

Applicants (1996): 1,500

New Hires (1996): 100

INDIANAPOLIS, INDIANA

Hiring Agency

Indiana Public Transit Corporation (Metro Bus)*
1501 West Washington
Indianapolis, IN 46222
(317) 635-2100

Requirements

- Minimum Age: 21
- Minimum Education: High School Diploma or GED
- License at application: IN DL, CDL from another state or IN CDL Learner's Permit
- License for job: IN CDL, Class B/P
- Clean driving record: No preventable accidents last 3 years; fewer than 2 moving violations last 3 years; no felony convictions; no convictions for "moral turpitude"
- Summary disqualification: DUI, DWI

Procedures

Vacancies are advertised in newspapers, at unemployment offices, and on college bulletin boards.

1. Applications submitted with references and a copy of driver's license.
2. Applications are reviewed; criminal background and DMV record are checked.
3. Eligibles scheduled for interview with Human Resources; selections are made.
4. Candidates' records sent to Transportation Division for review and recommendation.
5. Job offer made subject to physical and D&A. CDL Learner's Permit acquired if necessary.
6. Training Program: 5 weeks

Notes

Metro is a member of APTA.

Metro is a quasi-government agency and is in a

transitional period at the moment.

Employees are not civil service.

Bus operators union: ATU

Job levels: part-time, full-time. Average period before full-time employment: 1 year

Up to last month, Metro used the Seattle test, but may develop their own or contact APTA for another.

Applications (1996): 250

New Hires: 35–40

*A name change is being considered with the acronym INDIGO

Current number of bus operators: 211

JACKSONVILLE, FLORIDA
Hiring Agency
Jacksonville Transportation Authority

100 North Myrtle Avenue

Jacksonville, FL 32204

(904) 630-3181

Requirements
- Minimum Age: 23
- Minimum Education: High School Diploma or GED
- Driving record review: Eligibles are chosen in order from best driving record, defined as "no violations in past seven years."
- Legal Resident of U.S. with work permit

Procedures
1. Apply at Headquarters. Advertisements are occasionally placed in local newspapers.
2. No applications may be submitted until a driving record check is completed.
3. After application is reviewed, interview is arranged.
4. Eligibles take physical and D&A test.
5. If successful, candidates enter into a 5 week training program.

Notes
No formal exam is given for applicants.

Certification is obtained through training program.

The JTA is a state-charted quasi-public service for the City of Jacksonville and Duval County.

Employees are not civil service.

Union membership for operators: ATU

There is no eligibility list; at the moment, there is little turnover, but a large number of operators are scheduled to retire in the next few years.

Number of applicants (1996): 300

New Hires (1996): 30

Anticipated vacancies (1997-8): 30

LOS ANGELES, CALIFORNIA
Hiring Agency
Metropolitan Transit Authority

1 Gateway Plaza

Los Angeles, CA 90012

(213) 626-4455

Requirements
- Must be over 21 years of age
- Minimum 6 months' experience in "public contact" employment
- Valid CA Class C Driver's License
- Good driving record for past 5 years

Procedures
1. Vacancies are announced every 2 years or as needed.
2. Applicants submit completed application.

3. Application reviewed; testing information sent.
4. Candidates take written exam created and administered by Authority.
5. Successful candidates are interviewed and position offered to those who pass.
6. Physical examination given.

Notes

LA Transit is a private company with a public service franchise.

Employees are not civil service.

Employees are members of the UTA union.

There are two classifications: part-time and full-time.

The written exam consists of between 50 and 75 multiple choice questions. There is a "narrative" part, which is a typical report of an accident.

Last exam given: July, 1996

Number of applicants (1996): 350 (last exam)

New Hires 200

Anticipated vacancies: (1997-8): 450

Website: *www.mta.net*

It is anticipated that LA Metro Transit will enter the list of 10 largest systems in the U.S. in 1997 or 1998.

MEMPHIS, TENNESSEE
Hiring Agency

Memphis Area Transit Authority (MATA)
1370 Levee Road
Memphis, TN 38108
(901) 722-7100

Requirements

- Minimum Age: none
- Minimum Education: High School Diploma or GED
- License at Application: DL (any state)
- License at job: TN CDL/P

Procedures

Vacancies are posted on job board at Headquarters and announced on hot line:
(901) 722-7135

1. Applicant applies.
2. Applications are reviewed.
3. Best qualified of the pool are called for interviews.
4. Best candidate is called and offered a position.

Notes

MATA is a private agency with some city and government funding.

Employees are not civil service.

Optional union membership: Amalgamated Transit Union, Local 713

Standardized test used for 2nd tier and Trolley Bus Operators: Personnel Labs Selection Inventory (PSI-3S)

Hired in as full-time: 40 hours per week.

Eligibility list remains valid 90 days.

Bus operators currently employed by MATA: 258 (246 Bus Division; 12 Trolley Division)

Number of applicants (1996): 425-430

Number of New Hires (1996): 75-77

MIAMI, FLORIDA
Hiring Agency

Metro Dade Transit Authority
3300 NW 32d Avenue
Miami, FL 33142
(305) 638-6700

Requirements

- Over 18 years of age
- Commercial Driver's License
- Fewer than 3 points on license in past 3 years

Procedures

Advertisements posted in *Miami Herald* when there are between 60 and 70 vacancies.

1. Applications picked up in person.
2. After review of application and background check, applicants are notified of testing.
3. Applicants take test created and administered by the County Personnel Department.
4. Eligibles must score 70 or higher on the test.
5. Candidates are selected from the list in rank order, and are interviewed prior to job offer.

Notes

MDTA is a county agency.

Employees are considered civil service.

There are two classifications: part-time and full-time.

The examination consists of a written and a practical part. Points of emphasis: geographical knowledge and customer relations.

The eligibility list lasts for 1 year.

Applications in 1996: 500

New Hires: 200

MILWAUKEE, WISCONSIN

Hiring Agency

1942 N. 17th Street

Milwaukee, WI 53205

(414) 344-4550

Requirements

- Minimum Age: 23
- License required for application: Valid WI Driver's License
- License required for training: WI CDL Permit of License

- Clean Driving record for one year prior to application
- No criminal convictions

Procedures

Vacancies advertised monthly in major papers, at biennial job fairs, and in community outreach programs. Hot Line: (414) 937-0471.

1. Candidates submit resumes; 2–3 week review period.
2. Letters sent with test date/site information.
3. First two tests administered.
4. Third test given to eligibles who passed first two
5. Eligibles complete formal application.
6. Background check completed; interview is then scheduled.
7. After successful interview, physical test is administered.
8. Eligible list created, job offers in rank order.
9. Training class for 3 weeks (6–10 in a class).
10. Job offer: part time.

Notes

MCT is a private company, franchised by the county.

Official name: Milwaukee Transit System, Inc.

Employees are not civil service.

Union membership is in ATU.

MCT is a member of APTA.

Tests given: 1-Wonderlic General Knowledge (London House); 2-Seattle video test (soon to be replaced by BOSS test); 3-Personnel Inventory (all APTA sponsored tests).

Full-time job offer after 1 1/2 to 2 years of part-time work.

Eligible list does not terminate, but physical tests

must be re-done after 6 months without a job offer.
Applicants (1996): 400-500
New Hires (1996): 50-70
Anticipated Vacancies (1997-8): 30-40

NASHVILLE, TENNESSEE
Hiring Agency
Metro Transit Authority
130 Nestor Street
Nashville, TN 37210
(615) 862-5969

Requirements
- Minimum Age: 21
- Minimum Education: High School Diploma or GED
- License when applying: TN CDL or completed paperwork
- License for job: TN CDL with P endorsement
- INS proof of legal residence and work status
- Clean driving record for 3 years
- Verifiable references covering last 7 years

Procedures
Vacancies advertised in newspapers and busses
1. Applications submitted
2. Training course for required license
3. Road test
Process takes 2 weeks

Notes
Metro Transit is a member of APTA.
Municipal service operated by a management company.
Employees are not civil service.
Union membership: UTA

Metro Transit hires in 3 categories (in order of increasing pay scale): trolley driver, excess (handicapped van) driver, and bus operator. Bus operator vacancies are almost always filled from the other categories through the bargaining unit. *There is rarely a direct opening.*
New hires (1996): less than 7

NEW ORLEANS, LOUISIANA
Hiring Agency
Regional Transit Authority (RTA)
6700 Plaza Drive
New Orleans, LA 70127
(504) 242-2600

Requirements
- Minimum Age: 21
- Minimum Education: High School Diploma or GED
- License at application: LA CDL, Class B or completed application
- License for job: LA CDL, Class B, with P endorsement
- U.S. citizen or legal resident with work permit
- Fewer than 2 violations in past 2 years (evaluated at interview)

Procedures
Vacancies are advertised in newspapers and sent to hiring agencies. Notices are posted only when openings exist.
1. Applications must be filed before announced deadline.
2. Applications are reviewed and eligibles are notified of date and site of pre-employment test.
3. Eligibles must bring all required documentation to first interview with recruiter.

4. Those that pass are scheduled for a 2nd interview and skills test by the Department of Transportation.
5. Candidates complete physical and D/A testing.
6. Process takes 4-6 weeks if all paperwork is in order.
7. Training program commences.

Notes
RTA is a member of APTA.
RTA is a municipal service.
Employees are not civil service.
Union membership is voluntary in ATU.
Currently, 2 tests produced by London House are used.
All new hires are full-time.
Eligibility test duration: 6 months
Applicants/New Hires (1996): About 30 new operators were hired, but they came from other job titles. There were no advertisements placed for bus operators in 1996.

NORTHERN NEW JERSEY
Hiring Agency
New Jersey Transit
180 Boyden Avenue
Maplewood, NJ 07040
(201) 378- 6300

Requirements
- Minimum age: 21
- Minimum education: High School Diploma or GED
- Legal resident of U.S.; in possession of work permit
- License required at application:
  NJ residents must qualify for a CDL with P and AB endorsements.

Out-of-state residents must have DCL with P endorsement from their jurisdiction of residence.
- Good driving record
- Drug and alcohol free

Procedures
Vacancies are advertised in local newspapers (NY & NJ) at least once every quarter (sometimes more often).
1. Applications are available at Maplewood or Newark Headquarters.
2. Completed applications are checked, and candidates are notified within 3 weeks of test date and site.
3. Eligibles are scheduled for interview; NJ residents are prepared for NJ CDL test.
4. Medical and physical test administered.
5. Successful candidates enter training program (5–7 weeks).
6. Jobs offered as near to residence as possible.

Notes
NJ Transit is a member of APTA.
The test used is the Bus Operator Selection Service (an APTA test).
NJ Transit is a quasi-public corporation, chartered by the state. It technically consists of several formerly private bus companies.
Employees are not civil service.
Union membership is TWU, ATU, or UTU, depending on old company's contract.
All new hires are part-time; full-time job offer after 500 hours of successful driving.
Job offers are made according to residence location and seniority; union status and contract depend on this factor.
Number of Applicants (1996): 500-600

New Hires (1996): 300
Anticipated Vacancies (1997-8): 280-350

OKLAHOMA CITY, OKLAHOMA
Hiring Agency
Central Oklahoma Transportation and Parking
Authority
Metro Transit Bus System
300 SW Seventh
Oklahoma City, OK 73109
(405) 297-3808

Requirements
- Minimum age: 18
- Minimum Education: none
- License at application: OK CDL with P endorsement (may be waived for employees of other divisions or when there is an insufficient pool of applicants)
- License at job: see above
- Clean driving record (penalties for each point on license)
- Transit experience (school bus, other passenger service)
- Legal residence in Oklahoma

Procedures
Vacancies advertised in Oklahoma City
newspapers, unemployment offices, and in-house
bulletins. Advertisements are generally made each
quarter.
1. Applications are received and screened.
2. Eligibles are scheduled for testing.
3. Scores are set in ranked order with bonuses and deductions.
4. Candidates selected for first interview by route supervisor and 2 department managers.
5. List of top choices created to attend a second interview with personnel supervisor.
6. Conditional offer of job made, pending DOT, criminal record, drug/alcohol test, and physical exam.

Notes
Metro Transit is a member of APTA.
Tests used: Seattle, in-house test of math skills,
and accident report writing.
Metro Transit is a regional public trust agency.
Employees are not civil service.
Union membership is in ATU, Local 993.
All new hires are part-time. Other categories:
full-time, para-transport
Eligibility list lasts 1 year.
Applicants (1996): 260
New Hires (1996): 20
Anticipated Vacancies (1997-8): 10-20
There have been enough candidates to fill all
vacancies in recent years.

PHILADELPHIA, PENNSYLVANIA
Hiring Agency
Southeast Pennsylvania Public Transit Authority
(SEPTA)
1234 Market Street
Philadelphia, PA 19107
(215) 580-4000

Requirements
- High School Diploma
- Driver's License for 5 years
- No moving violations for 2 years

Procedures

- Bus Operator openings are advertised in the *Sunday Inquirer*.
- Candidates mail resume and wait for instruction in response.

Notes

SEPTA is a quasi-public city agency.
Employees are not considered civil service.
There are two job levels: trainee and operator.
University of Seattle test has been administered since 1989.
Applicants (1995): 2,400
Last exam: 1995

PHOENIX, ARIZONA
Hiring Agency

Phoenix Public Transit
P.O. Box 4275
Phoenix, AZ 85030-4275
(602) 262-7191

Requirements

- High School Diploma
- CDL Permit
- Paid License Fee

Procedures

Openings are advertised quarterly. Day and evening application hours are available.
1. Applications evaluated
2. Background check made
3. Physical exam administered at Central Medical Center
4. Interviews conducted
5. New hires chosen from list of eligibles

Notes

PPT is a municipal agency.
Employees are considered civil service.
There is no exam at this time. Currently the program is being evaluated, and a decision will be made in the near future as to whether or not to resume examinations .
The eligibility list lasts for 3 months.
There are an average of 15 openings when vacancies are announced.

PITTSBURGH, PENNSYLVANIA
Hiring Agency

Port Authority Transit (PAT)
2235 Beaver Avenue
Pittsburgh, PA 15233
(412) 237-7000

Requirements

- Minimum Age: 23
- Minimum Education: no requirement
- License at Application: PA CD/P
- Fewer than 3 points on DL in past 3 years
- No convictions (DWI, etc.) for past 3 years
- No accidents for past 3 years (reviewed at interview)

Procedures

1. Applications are picked up at Pennsylvania Job Service in Pittsburgh.
2. PAT contacts Job Service when vacancies occur; applications are forwarded in chronological order of receipt.
3. Test is administered; successful candidates go through 2 interviews.
4. Concurrent with interviews: DMV, criminal record, health, and D/A checks made.

5. Eligibles are offered place in training program: 9 weeks.

Notes

PTA is a member of APTA.

PAT does not advertise; all vacancies are filled through the PA Job Service.

PA Job Service accepts applications continuously.

PAT is a State Authority; employees are not considered civil service.

Union membership is in ATU.

All new hires are full-time.

Hiring procedures preclude any eligibility lists.

Exam given: Passenger Relations Test

PAT currently employs 1,400 bus operators.

There were 41 new hires in 1996.

Approximately 15% of applicants are successful.

Anticipated Vacancies (1997-8): 30-50

PORTLAND, OREGON

Hiring Agency

Tri-County Metropolitan Transportation District of Portland (TRI-MET)
4012 SE 17th Avenue
Portland, OR 97202
(503) 238-4840

Requirements

- Minimum Age: 21
- License at Application: Driver's License (any U.S. jurisdiction)
- License for job: OR CDL with P endorsement
- Two or more years customer service experience
- No criminal record
- Good driving record

Procedures

Vacancies are sent to all newspapers, minority outreach programs, community centers, dislocated workers' organizations, and state employment offices. Job fairs are held regularly.

Applications can be picked up at headquarters, garages, community college job offices, and Urban League Headquarters.

1. Completed applications are reviewed with a recruiter.
2. Eligibles are scheduled for testing.
3. Candidates undergo an interview; a background check and DMV record review is conducted.
4. Criminal record is checked along with references.*
5. Medical and Drug/Alcohol screening. Required by FTA.
6. Successful candidate applies for CDL Permit.
7. Job offer: 1 month full-time training course.

Notes

Tri-Met is a member of APTA.

The tests used are the "Report Test" and a job-related physical aptitude test—both are created internally.

Tri-Met is a municipal service.

Employees are civil service.

Union membership is in ATU.

New Hires are part-time. Full-time offered after 16–24 months.

Operators must renew their medical qualifications every 2 years.

Number of Applicants (1996): 600

New Hires (1996): 100

Anticipated Vacancies (1997-8): 300-400

The system is growing rapidly; there are more vacancies than applicants, and recruitment is ongoing.

*Process is suspended at this point if there are no vacancies.

SALT LAKE CITY, UTAH

Hiring Agency

Utah Transit Authority
3600 S. 700 W.
Salt Lake City, UT 84119
(801) 287-4636

Requirements

- Minimum Age: 21
- Minimum Education: High School Diploma or GED
- License at Application: Operator, CH, or CDL of any state
- License for job: UT CDL with P endorsement
- Familiarity with Salt Lake City vicinity
- Legal resident of U.S. with work permit
- Driving record: fewer than 2 moving violations in past 3 years; no DWI in past 7 years
- Ability to pass DOT physical and complete training program

Procedures

Openings are advertised in area newspapers, in in-house organizations, and at 109 community-based organizations.

1. Completed applications are assessed, scanned, and collated once a week.
2. A basic test-questionnaire is part of the application.
3. Scores are ranked and a list is created under the supervision of a "generalist" and a department supervisor.
4. Candidates are selected from the list for interviews by generalist and supervisor.
5. A decision is made whether to extend an offer for training.
6. A Human Resources coordinator explains the testing procedure; all applicants are given a token and asked to ride the bus to confirm their desire for the job.
7. Criminal, MVR, physical checks completed.
8. Training class begins: 7 weeks, including DOT certification.

Notes

UTA is an award-winning member of APTA.
UTA is funded by the City, County, and State.
There is an independent Board of Directors.
Employees are not civil service.
Union membership is voluntary in ATU.
The eligibility list stays alive for 1 year.
Job classifications: Operator for handicapped bus; bus operator. All new hires are full-time.

SAN ANTONIO, TEXAS

Hiring Agency

VIA Metropolitan Transportation Authority
800 West Myrtle
San Antonio, TX 78212
(210) 362-2000

Requirements

- More than 21 years of age
- High School Diploma or GED
- For application: Valid TX Driver's License or eligibility through other jurisdiction
- For employment: Valid TX CDL with P endorsement
- Good driving record
- Able to read and follow detailed instructions about routes
- Complete list of requirements included in the application

Procedures

Positions advertised in local newspapers and at employment centers as vacancies occur.

Information obtainable on hot line: (201) 362-2002

1. Applications are submitted, and are subject to a 2–3 week background check.
2. First interview conducted to complete application.
3. Eligibles are notified about 2nd interview.
4. Eligibles who are successful at 2nd interview are given job offer.
5. Candidates attend a 5 week training course.
6. Qualifying exam given at end of course.

Notes

VIA is a member of APTA.

VIA is a regional authority funded by government grants.

Employees are not civil service.

Union membership is optional.

All new hires are part-time. Part-time employment is a probationary period. Full-time employees must successfully complete part-time period.

There is no eligibility list. All who complete the training course are hired.

Current number of part-time employees: 203

Current number of full-time employees: 607

SAN DIEGO, CALIFORNIA

Hiring Agency

San Diego Transit Corporation
100 16th Street
San Diego, CA 92101
(619) 238-0100

Requirements

- Minimum Age: 21
- Minimum Education: none
- License at application: CA Driver License
- License for job: CA Class B CDL with P endorsement

- Proof of legal residency
- Driving record disqualifications:
  DWI conviction
  "Failure to appear" citation
  Conviction of negligence or careless driving
  More than 3 moving violations
  Note: accident record will be reviewed.

Procedures

Vacancies advertised in newspapers and on return postcards

1. Completed applications submitted with driving record.
2. Applicants notified of test dates and sites.
3. Eligibles listed after testing and scheduled for interview.
4. Background check and interview.
5. Physical exam, including drug and alcohol testing.
6. Job offer made.

Notes

SDTC is a member of APTA.

The test used is the Seattle Validated Customer Relations Test.

SDTC is a quasi-government corporation.

Employees are not civil service.

Union membership is in ATU.

There is a full-time training program for 3 weeks.

Full-time positions are offered as they become available.

There is a high turnover; the list has rarely lasted for more than 6 months.

SAN FRANCISCO, CALIFORNIA
Hiring Agency
San Francisco Municipal Railway
949 Presidio Avenue
San Francisco, CA 94115
(415) 923-5212

Requirements
- Over 25 years of age
- High School Diploma
- Drug and alcohol free
- Class C (regular Driver License); must have Class B with P endorsement by time of employment
- Fewer than 2 moving violations in last 5 years

Procedures
Vacancies are announced in newspapers. San Francisco has an active community outreach and recruitment program.

1. Applicants received, processed, and entered into data base.
2. Applicants selected randomly for testing; all are tested.
3. Eligibles listed in ranked order of score.
4. Criminal history background check, including fingerprints.
5. Candidates are selected from top of list for training program.

Notes
San Francisco Municipal Railway is a municipal service.
Employees are civil service.
Employees belong to the TWU.
The test is comprised of elements from APTA exams.
The list lasts 2 years or until exhausted.
Job categories: part-time, full-time.

Number of applicants (1996): 420
Number of new hires (1996): 200+
Anticipated vacancies (1997–8): there are presently 100
Last test: January 1997
Successful candidates may also apply for training in the cable car system.

SAN JOSE, CALIFORNIA
Hiring Agency
Santa Clara Valley Transportation Authority (VTA)
3331 North 1st Street
San Jose, CA 95134
(408) 321-2300

Requirements
- Minimum Age: 18
- Minimum Education: none
- For application: Valid CA Driver License
- For employment: CA Class B CDL with P endorsement
- Driving record free of violations involving carelessness or lack of responsibility

Procedures
Positions advertised via job bulletins sent to 300 locations, including active outreach to minority population. Advertisements are continuous.

1. Completed applications screened; applicants notified of exam date and site.
2. Qualifying exam given; then Seattle test.
3. DMV printout, fingerprint and criminal record check.*
4. Eligibles called for interview.
5. Job offer as trainee (6–8 week training course)

Entire process takes 6 months.

Notes

VTA is an independent public utility under the Public Utility Commission. Its status relative to the city and county government is currently under review.

Employees are not civil service; a merit system is in place.

Operators belong to ATU.

All new hires are part-time. Every quarter there is an open bidding for preferred full-time routes using a system of seniority and merit.

The qualifying test consists of map reading, basic common sense, and fundamental math (making change, etc.).

*In the future, candidates will have to bring in their own DMV printout and criminal record check.

Hot Line: (408) 321-5565

Website: *www.vta.com*

SEATTLE, WASHINGTON

Hiring Agency

Department of Transportation of King County
Metro Transit Division (METRO TRANSIT)
821 2nd Avenue
Seattle, WA 98104
(206) 296-7340
Metro Transit website: *www.metrokc.gov*
For job information:
www.metrokc.gov/ohrm/openings

Requirements

- Minimum Age: 21
- Minimum Education: none
- License required at application: WA Driver License
- License required for job: WA CDL, Class B with P endorsement
- Legal resident of the U.S. with work permit
- Acceptable driving record
- Means for reporting to work
- Oral and written communication skills

Procedure

Vacancies are advertised in county newspapers, and through a community outreach program. Applications are available at Metro Headquarters and the King County Human Resources office.

1. After completing application, applicant calls to reserve space for test (date and site on application cover).
2. Classes are formed, orientation given, test administered.
3. WA criminal background check completed (with fingerprinting).
4. Reading comprehension test administered; employment references checked.
5. CDL orientation session; on-bus practical test.
6. Job offer to successful candidates.

Notes

Metro Transit is a member of APTA.

Advertisements are usually weekly. Only 50% of applicants qualify and there is heavy attrition.

Strong minority community outreach program.

The test given is the Seattle *Working With The Public* exam, along with a 2-paragraph document writing test.

Qualification score: over 200 (40-50 percentile) on Seattle Test.

Employees are not civil service.

Union membership is in ATU, Local 587.

All new hires are part-time; full-time job offers by seniority after 4 years.

Number of applicants (1996): 300

New Hires (1996): 250

Anticipated Vacancies: (1997-8): 150

WASHINGTON, DC

Hiring Agency

Washington Metro Area Transit Authority
(WMATA)
600 5th Street NW
Washington, DC 20001
(202) 962-1071

Requirements

- Over 21 years of age
- Valid Driver's License from any jurisdiction
- CDL permit with passenger and air brake endorsement (prior to testing)
- Clean driving record for past 36 months (no points on license)
- Experience with driving large vehicles (preferred)

Procedures

Vacancies are announced in *Washington Post* every two weeks.
Applications are available at the Metro Building our at selected bus driver information sites.

1. Applications are reviewed.
2. Accepted applicants are scheduled for pre-employment exam.
3. Hiring is done from successful exam candidates.

Notes

WMATA is a quasi-government municipal service, funded by regional jurisdictions and the Federal government.
Employees are not civil service.
Employees belong to a union.
WMATA is a member of APTA.
Priority given to applications accompanied by documented traffic record.
Pre-employment test is PSI-7ST (London House-McGraw Hill). Test consists of reading and math evaluation, and personality inventory.
Presently, there is no eligibility list; all successful candidates in recent test have been hired.
Vacancies exist at this time.

FILLING OUT A CIVIL SERVICE APPLICATION

CHAPTER SUMMARY

Filling out an application is usually the first step in applying for a job working for local government. It's your first (and maybe your last!) chance to make a good impression. This chapter shows you how to avoid common application mistakes while putting your best foot forward so that you come out a step ahead.

magine this. You work in the personnel department of a huge city transit company. You've just been handed 100 applications for the position of bus operator and your boss asks you to check through them to make sure each applicant meets the minimum qualifications for the job. Oh. And there's 2,900 more where that came from, so when you're done . . . .

This situation was *not* make-believe for human resource specialists in a large transit operation in the state of Washington in 1996. They had to examine over 3,000 applications before the field was narrowed down to the 250 people they hired that year. It's overwhelming to even imagine reading that much material—almost as overwhelming as thinking about *your* application being one of 3,000 someone has to read. How on earth can you compete against all those people?

THE REAL ENEMY

Here's a secret . . . you aren't competing against anyone but yourself at this stage of the game. It might surprise you to hear that in the example mentioned above, over 50% of the applications submitted were rejected before the applicant reached the interview stage. They weren't rejected because another applicant beat them out, but because they didn't meet the minimum qualifications for applying in the first place *and/or* because their applications weren't properly completed.

According to personnel specialists from many of the major transit companies nationwide, all applications are screened first to see if the applicant meets minimum qualifications. For example, if the company requires all applicants to have a valid state commercial license and you do not have one then your application will most likely see the reject pile. Save yourself a bit of disappointment by carefully checking the requirements for bus operator <u>before</u> you fill out the application. And don't be afraid to ask questions if you have doubts about whether you meet the requirements.

You might not have much control over whether or not you meet minimum requirements at the time you apply for bus operator, but you have 100% control over the first impression you make on your potential employer. That first impression will be made, in most cases, with the written application.

Let's face it, paperwork is tedious and most people believe that no one reads their applications or resumes anyway. This is the Sirens' call for the unsuccessful—don't listen! Not only will companies thoroughly scrutinize your written application for bus operator, this document will be judged and assigned a point value in many of the hiring systems in use nationwide. The written application is a fantastic opportunity for you to earn brownie points and build up a solid reputation with your potential employer.

Here are some tips from the biggest bus operator employers across the nation for turning in a winning application.

READ THE DIRECTIONS FIRST

It may sound silly, but failure to follow the directions for filling out the application is something that will eventually cause disqualification for many applicants. Before you set pen to paper read the form from beginning to end, no matter if the form has more pages than the last novel you read. Make a list of questions that may come up as you read. If you still have questions by the time you've completely read over the application you should call the personnel office and get the answers. Better to ask "How do I do this?" now than "Why was my application thrown out?" down the road.

You'd also be wise to consider asking for more than one application so that you can use a copy for practice purposes. If you can't get more than one, then copy the one you do have and use it for a practice sheet. Practice even if the application is a "simple" one-pager.

TYPEWRITER VS. HANDWRITING

Always, always, always *type* your application if this option is available. A neatly typewritten document is an eye-catcher and immediately sends the message that you care enough to go the extra mile. It also makes the reader's job easier and more pleasant and that can only be a good thing!

Sometimes typing is not an option. You may be asked to fill out a brief application on site and may not have the opportunity to take it home. If this happens then make sure you read the directions carefully, take your time writing, and print *legibly*.

Even if you are permitted to take the application home to fill it out you may be asked to complete it in your own handwriting. Some companies like to use this as an opportunity to judge your handwriting—yet another reason to read the directions! If the directions don't specify how you fill out the application then don't be shy—add this to your list of questions for that phone call you'll make to the Personnel Office.

Your application should be tidy for yet another reason—accuracy. You sure don't want the company background investigator to call up your last job and ask to speak to "Mr. Dork" instead of "Mr. York" all because she can't read your penmanship. Of course if the person investigating your background can't read what you wrote then maybe she'll take the time to call you, go over each and every item on your application that she can't read, and then rewrite it for you. And then there's the one about the Tooth Fairy . . . .

DOTTING *ALL* I'S AND T'S

Without exception, the biggest pet peeve most hiring entities express about the written applications they receive is *lack of completeness.* Amazing as it might seem, many applicants fail to simply fill in all the blanks—especially when it comes to the job history portion of the application. The job history section is not the place to forget about attention to detail. When potential employers see gaps in time on your job history they have the opportunity to use their imaginations to fill them in. Here's a few of their most likely thoughts:

- Hmmm. Wonder what this applicant did for six months after that first job. Something must've happened that she doesn't want us to know about.
- Wonder if this guy is just lazy? He can't even be bothered to follow the directions on the application that tell him to fill in *all* of the blanks. Bet he's likely to be a lazy employee.
- Wonder why he didn't mention the job we know he had one summer as a construction worker? Maybe he got fired and doesn't want us to know!

Employers have another complaint about incomplete job history sections on written applications—vague dates and times. If the application calls for the month, day, and year you started and ended a job then that is exactly what needs to appear in the appropriate blanks. That can be a daunting task if you have a lengthy employment history, but you need to come as close as possible to providing the information that is requested.

GETTING IT RIGHT

While we're on the subject of job history, there's nothing wrong with picking up the phone and calling your ex-employers to make sure that the correct information appears in this section. Nothing is more impressive than seeing a neat, complete, detailed, *accurate* listing of information. It won't take long for the person who conducts your background investigation to realize that you are serious enough about this career opportunity to take the time to verify dates and hunt up current phone numbers for old employers and co-workers. You've made their job a breeze and as a result you'll see the right ears come to a point in your hiring process.

Leaving other blanks in your application can prove equally as risky as leaving gaps in your job history. For example, most applications ask for references. Of course you'll want to list the people who know you best and who can give you glowing recommendations. No matter how much your friends may want to glow for you, however, they won't be able to help much if you don't list *daytime* phone numbers where they can be reached. Most personnel specialists work during traditional daytime office hours. Listing a home number for your personal reference who is never at home during the day is not going to win brownie points for your application.

WINDING UP

Even after these tips there's probably a few of you left who still feel the pressures of competition. This last piece of advice from a personnel specialist who helped hire the 250 bus operators mentioned at the beginning of this chapter is for you. "Do the best job you can on the written application. The truth is, if you turn in an application that has plenty of detail, is filled out completely, and leaves no stone unturned, then you are already ahead of half of the people who apply for this job."

The following page presents a sample Employment Application from Metro-Dade County (which covers metropolitan Miami, Florida) to give you an idea of the type of information you'll be asked to provide when you apply for a job as a bus operator.

PLEASE PRINT - DO NOT WRITE IN SHADED AREAS

① SOCIAL SECURITY NUMBER ___ — ___ — ___

DATE ACCEPTED

METRO-DADE

PERSONNEL DEPARTMENT
PERSONNEL SERVICES DIVISION
140 WEST FLAGLER STREET - SUITE 105
MIAMI, FLORIDA 33130
EMPLOYMENT APPLICATION

METRO-DADE COUNTY PROVIDES EQUAL ACCESS OPPORTUNITY IN EMPLOYMENT AND SERVICES FOR MINORITIES / FEMALES / APPLICANTS WITH DISABILITIES
JOB INFORMATION HOTLINE 375-1871   HEARING IMPAIRED CALL TDD-TTY 375-5645

POSITIONS APPLIED FOR

TITLE _____ (Q) _____ (DNQ) _____   TITLE _____ (Q) _____ (DNQ) _____
OCC CODE _____ DATE _____   OCC CODE _____ DATE _____

TITLE _____ (Q) _____ (DNQ) _____   TITLE _____ (Q) _____ (DNQ) _____
OCC CODE _____ DATE _____   OCC CODE _____ DATE _____

TITLE _____ (Q) _____ (DNQ) _____   TITLE _____ (Q) _____ (DNQ) _____
OCC CODE _____ DATE _____   OCC CODE _____ DATE _____

TITLE _____ (Q) _____ (DNQ) _____   TITLE _____ (Q) _____ (DNQ) _____
OCC CODE _____ DATE _____   OCC CODE _____ DATE _____

TITLE _____ (Q) _____ (DNQ) _____   TITLE _____ (Q) _____ (DNQ) _____
OCC CODE _____ DATE _____   OCC CODE _____ DATE _____

LAST NAME   **FIRST NAME**   **MIDDLE INITIAL**

ADDRESS   CITY   STATE   ZIP CODE

HOME PHONE #   **WORK PHONE #**

Dade County will use information concerning ethnicity, sex, age and disability for affirmative action purposes only, consistent with and pursuant to its obligation under federal law. Answers to these questions are voluntary, and will be kept confidential.

ARE YOU CURRENTLY A COUNTY EMPLOYEE? _____ (Yes) _____ (No)

DATE OF BIRTH _____

IN THE PAST FIVE YEARS, HAVE YOU BEEN CONVICTED OF A FELONY? _____ (Yes) _____ (No)

MALE (M) _____ **FEMALE (F)** _____

ARE YOU A VETERAN OF THE UNITED STATES ARMED FORCES?
_____ (Yes) _____ (No)   (IF YES, ATTACH DD214)
FROM _____ TO _____

ETHNIC GROUP WITH WHICH YOU WANT TO BE IDENTIFIED
(A) WHITE / NON HISPANIC   (B) BLACK / NON HISPANIC
(C) HISPANIC   (D) ASIAN OR PACIFIC ISLANDER
(E) AMERICAN INDIAN OR ALASKAN NATIVE

VETERAN'S PREFERENCE _____ (NONE) _____ (5 PTS) _____ (10PTS) _____ (30%DIS)

LANGUAGES OTHER THAN ENGLISH _____

DRIVER LICENSE
☐ OPERATOR'S CLASS E   ☐ CHAUFFEUR'S CLASS D   ☐ COMMERCIAL CLASS

COL ENDORSEMENTS _____

CERTIFICATIONS / LICENSES _____

HAS LICENSE EVER BEEN SUSPENDED? _____ (Yes) _____ (No)

IF YES, GIVE DETAILS _____

EDUCATION

SCHOOL NAME AND CITY AND STATE WHERE LOCATED	DATES OF ATTENDANCE FROM	TO	SEMESTER OR CREDIT HOURS (NUMBER)	COURSE TITLES OR MAJOR FIELD	DEGREE OR CERTIFICATE RECEIVED
High School, If "High School equivalent", give date and source					
College or University					

EMPLOYMENT RECORD

LIST PREVIOUS EMPLOYMENT HISTORY. START WITH YOUR PRESENT EMPLOYMENT, OR IF UNEMPLOYED, YOUR MOST RECENT EMPLOYMENT, AND LIST YOUR WORK RECORD IN REVERSE ORDER. IF YOU HAVE HELD MORE THAN ONE POSITION WITH THE SAME ORGANIZATION, LIST EACH POSITION AS A SEPARATE PERIOD OF EMPLOYMENT. BE SURE TO SHOW WHERE EMPLOYMENT MAY BE VERIFIED. INCLUDE VOLUNTEER AND PAID TEMPORARY OR PART-TIME WORK AND MILITARY EXPERIENCE.

TYPE

MOST RECENT JOB EMPLOYER _____ ADDRESS _____ PHONE # _____

FROM _____ TO _____ JOB TITLE _____ SUPERVISOR'S NAME _____

DESCRIBE YOUR WORK _____

2nd MOST RECENT JOB EMPLOYER _____ ADDRESS _____ PHONE # _____

FROM _____ TO _____ JOB TITLE _____ SUPERVISOR'S NAME _____

DESCRIBE YOUR WORK _____

3RD MOST RECENT JOB EMPLOYER _____ ADDRESS _____ PHONE # _____

FROM _____ TO _____ JOB TITLE _____ SUPERVISOR'S NAME _____

DESCRIBE YOUR WORK _____

4TH MOST RECENT JOB EMPLOYER _____ ADDRESS _____ PHONE # _____

FROM _____ TO _____ JOB TITLE _____ SUPERVISOR'S NAME _____

DESCRIBE YOUR WORK _____

IT IS THE POLICY OF METROPOLITAN DADE COUNTY THAT HIRING DECISIONS WILL BE MADE CONTINGENT UPON THE RESULTS OF A PHYSICAL EXAMINATION, INCLUDING ALCOHOL AND DRUG SCREENING. PRIOR TO EMPLOYMENT, YOUR FINGERPRINTS WILL BE TAKEN FOR ROUTINE CHECK.

CERTIFICATION: I hereby certify that all statements made on this form are true to the best of my knowledge. I realize that should an investigation disclose any misrepresentation, I may be subject to dismissal. In accordance with the provisions of Ordinance No. 77-39, I hereby certify that I am presently a resident of Dade County, or if not a resident, I hereby agree to establish my residence within Dade County within (6) six months of employment by the County. I further understand that my failure to comply with the provisions of said ordinance may result in my automatic termination from County employment.

Date _____ Signature _____

METRO DADE

EASYSMART TEST PREPARATION SYSTEM

CHAPTER SUMMARY

Taking a Bus Operator Exam can be tough. It demands a lot of preparation if you want to achieve a top score. If your city uses your written exam score to determine your rank on the eligibility list, your chances of being hired depend on how well you do on the exam. The EasySmart Test Preparation System, developed exclusively for LearningExpress by leading test experts, gives you the discipline and attitude you need to be a winner.

F irst, the bad news: Taking the Bus Operator Exam is no picnic, and neither is getting ready for it. Your future career as a bus operator depends on your getting a high score, but there are all sorts of pitfalls that can keep you from doing your best on this all-important exam. Here are some of the obstacles that can stand in the way of your success:

- Being unfamiliar with the format of the exam
- Being paralyzed by test anxiety
- Leaving your preparation to the last minute
- Not preparing at all!
- Not knowing vital test-taking skills: how to pace yourself through the exam, how to use the process of elimination, and when to guess

- Not being in tip-top mental and physical shape
- Messing up on test day by arriving late at the test site, having to work on an empty stomach, or shivering through the exam because the room is cold

What's the common denominator in all these test-taking pitfalls? One word: *control*. Who's in control, you or the exam?

Now the good news: The EasySmart Test Preparation System puts *you* in control. In just nine easy-to-follow steps, you will learn everything you need to know to make sure that *you* are in charge of your preparation and your performance on the exam. *Other* test-takers may let the test get the better of them; *other* test-takers may be unprepared or out of shape, but not *you*. *You* will have taken all the steps you need to take to get a high score on the Bus Operator Exam.

Here's how the EasySmart Test Preparation System works: Nine easy steps lead you through everything you need to know and do to get ready to master your exam. Each of the steps listed below includes both reading about the step and one or more activities. It's important that you do the activities along with the reading, or you won't be getting the full benefit of the system. Each step tells you approximately how much time that step will take you to complete.

Step 1. Get Information	60 minutes
Step 2. Conquer Test Anxiety	20 minutes
Step 3. Make a Plan	25 minutes
Step 4. Learn to Manage Your Time	10 minutes
Step 5. Learn to Use the Process of Elimination	20 minutes
Step 6. Know When to Guess	20 minutes
Step 7. Reach Your Peak Performance Zone	10 minutes
Step 8. Get Your Act Together	10 minutes
Step 9. Do It!	5 minutes
Total	**3 hours**

We estimate that working through the entire system will take you approximately three hours, though it's perfectly OK if you work faster or slower than the time estimates assume. If you can take a whole afternoon or evening, you can work through the whole EasySmart Test Preparation System in one sitting. Otherwise, you can break it up, and do just one or two steps a day for the next several days. It's up to you—remember, *you're* in control.

STEP 1: GET INFORMATION

Time to complete: 60 minutes
Activities: Use the suggestions listed here to find out about the content of your exam.

Knowledge is power. The first step in the EasySmart Test Preparation System is finding out everything you can about the Bus Operator Exam. Once you have your information, the next steps in the EasySmart Test Preparation System will show you what to do about it.

Part A: Straight Talk About Civil Service Exams

Why do you have to take this exam, anyway? The fact is that way too many people want a secure job with the city, far more than can ever be hired—far more, in fact, than the city can even afford to process in a conventional application-resume-interview process. The city needs a way to dramatically cut the number of applicants they have to consider. That's where the exam comes in.

Like any civil service test, the Bus Operator Exam is a screening device. It enables the city to rank candidates according to their exam score and then to pull only from the top of that list to get applicants to go through the rest of the selection process. Since the exam assesses job-related skills—abilities you actually have to have to be a good bus operator—there's a rough correlation between how well a person does on the test and how good an employee that person will make. But it's only a rough correlation. There are all sorts of things a written exam like this can't test: whether you can get along with the public, fellow employees, and supervisors; whether you're likely to show up on time or call in sick a lot; and so on. But those kinds of things are hard to evaluate, while whether or not you fill in the right circle on a bubble answer sheet is easy to evaluate. So most cities use an exam simply to cut the number of applicants they have to deal with.

This information should help you keep some perspective on the exam and what it means. Don't make the mistake of thinking that your score determines who you are or how smart you are or whether you'll make a good employee, with the city or elsewhere. All it shows is whether you can fill in the little circles correctly. Of course, whether you can fill in the little circles correctly is still vitally important to you! After all, your chances of being hired depend on your getting a top score. And that's why you're here—using the EasySmart Test Preparation System to achieve control over your exam.

Part B: What's on the Test

If you haven't already done so, stop here and read the first three chapters of this book, which give you vital information on becoming a bus operator, hiring procedures for major U.S. cities, and filling out a civil service application.

Bus operator exams vary from city to city. Most test the skills in the practice exams in this book—reading, verbal expression (writing), judgment and common sense, knowledge of the rules of the road, courtesy to passengers, and the like. Some exams, however, are given in a different format—and you need to know what *your* exam will be like.

How best to get that information also varies from city to city. Here are some avenues to try:

- **Go to the public library,** which may have information on jobs available in your city. Ask the librarian at the reference desk for help.
- **Call the Bus Department,** Department of Transportation, or whatever it's called in your city. You can find the number in the blue (government) pages of your phone book.
- **Call the city's Department of Personnel.** This department may be called "Civil Service" or "Human Resources." This number is also in the blue pages of the phone book, or you may be referred to this department by the Department of Buses.
- **Ask around.** Friends or relatives who already work for the city—better yet, for the Bus Department—may have inside information that hasn't yet been released to the public.

If an exam has been scheduled in your city, or if your city conducts ongoing exams, one of these steps should give you an exam announcement or similar document that outlines the content of your test. If no exam is scheduled, you may simply have to wait—and put your name on a notification list, if the department keeps one. In the meantime, however, you can still go through the rest of the steps in the EasySmart Test Preparation System and work through the rest of this book, to make sure you're prepared when the exam is announced.

STEP 2: CONQUER TEST ANXIETY

Time to complete: 20 minutes
Activity: Take the Test Stress Test
Having complete information about the exam is the first step in getting control of the exam. Next, you have to overcome one of the biggest obstacles to test success: test anxiety. Test anxiety can not only impair your performance on the exam itself; it can even keep you from preparing! In Step 2, you'll learn stress management techniques that will help you succeed on your exam. Learn these strategies now, and practice them as you work through the exams in this book, so they'll be second nature to you by exam day.

COMBATING TEST ANXIETY

The first thing you need to know is that a little test anxiety is a good thing. Everyone gets nervous before a big exam—and if that nervousness motivates you to prepare thoroughly, so much the better. It's said that Sir Laurence Olivier, one of the foremost British actors of this century, threw up before every performance. His stage fright didn't impair his performance; in fact, it probably gave him a little extra edge—just the kind of edge you need to do well, whether on a stage or in an examination room.

On the next page is the Test Stress Test. Stop here and answer the questions on that page, to find out whether your level of test anxiety is something you should worry about.

Test Stress Test

You only need to worry about test anxiety if it is extreme enough to impair your performance. The following questionnaire will provide a diagnosis of your level of test anxiety. In the blank before each statement, write the number that most accurately describes your experience.

0 = Never   1 = Once or twice   2 = Sometimes   3 = Often

_____ I have gotten so nervous before an exam that I simply put down the books and didn't study for it.

_____ I have experienced disabling physical symptoms such as vomiting and severe headaches because I was nervous about an exam.

_____ I have simply not showed up for an exam because I was scared to take it.

_____ I have experienced dizziness and disorientation while taking an exam.

_____ I have had trouble filling in the little circles because my hands were shaking too hard.

_____ I have failed an exam because I was too nervous to complete it.

_____ **Total: Add up the numbers in the blanks above.**

Your Test Stress Score

Here are the steps you should take, depending on your score. If you scored:

- **Below 3,** your level of test anxiety is nothing to worry about; it's probably just enough to give you that little extra edge.
- **Between 3 and 6,** your test anxiety may be enough to impair your performance, and you should practice the stress management techniques listed in this section to try to bring your test anxiety down to manageable levels.
- **Above 6,** your level of test anxiety is a serious concern. In addition to practicing the stress management techniques listed in this section, you may want to seek additional, personal help. Call your local high school or community college and ask for the academic counselor. Tell the counselor that you have a level of test anxiety that sometimes keeps you from being able to take the exam. The counselor may be willing to help you or may suggest someone else you should talk to.

Stress Management Before the Test

If you feel your level of anxiety getting the best of you in the weeks before the test, here is what you need to do to bring the level down again:

- **Get prepared.** There's nothing like knowing what to expect and being prepared for it to put you in control of test anxiety. That's why you're reading this book. Use it faithfully, and remind yourself that you're better prepared than most of the people taking the test.
- **Practice self-confidence.** A positive attitude is a great way to combat test anxiety. This is no time to be humble or shy. Stand in front of the mirror and say to your reflection, "I'm prepared. I'm full of self-confidence. I'm going to ace this test. I know I can do it." Say it into a tape recorder and play it back once a day. If you hear it often enough, you'll believe it.
- **Fight negative messages.** Every time someone starts telling you how hard the exam is or how it's almost impossible to get a high score, start telling them your self-confidence messages above. If the someone with the negative messages is *you*, telling yourself *you don't do well on exams, you just can't do this*, don't listen. Turn on your tape recorder and listen to your self-confidence messages.
- **Visualize.** Imagine yourself driving your route and collecting fares as a bus operator. Think of yourself coming home with your first paycheck as a city employee and taking your family or friends out to celebrate. Visualizing success can help make it happen—and it reminds you of why you're going to all this work in preparing for the exam.
- **Exercise.** Physical activity helps calm your body down and focus your mind. Besides, being in good physical shape can actually help you do well on the exam. Go for a run, lift weights, go swimming—and do it regularly.

Stress Management on Test Day

There are several ways you can bring down your level of test anxiety on test day. They'll work best if you practice them in the weeks before the test, so you know which ones work best for you.

- **Deep breathing.** Take a deep breath while you count to five. Hold it for a count of one, then let it out on a count of five. Repeat several times.
- **Move your body.** Try rolling your head in a circle. Rotate your shoulders. Shake your hands from the wrist. Many people find these movements very relaxing.
- **Visualize again.** Think of the place where you are most relaxed: lying on the beach in the sun, walking through the park, or whatever. Now close your eyes and imagine you're actually there. If you practice in advance, you'll find that you only need a few seconds of this exercise to experience a significant increase in your sense of well-being.

When anxiety threatens to overwhelm you right there during the exam, there are still things you can do to manage the stress level:

- **Repeat your self-confidence messages.** You should have them memorized by now. Say them quietly to yourself, and believe them!
- **Visualize one more time.** This time, visualize yourself moving smoothly and quickly through the test answering every question right and finishing just before time is up. Like most visualization techniques, this one works best if you've practiced it ahead of time.
- **Find an easy question.** Skim over the test until you find an easy question, and answer it. Getting even one circle filled in gets you into the test-taking groove.
- **Take a mental break.** Everyone loses concentration once in a while during a long test. It's normal, so you shouldn't worry about it. Instead, accept what has happened. Say to yourself, "Hey, I lost it there for a minute. My brain is taking a break." Put down your pencil, close your eyes, and do some deep breathing for a few seconds. Then you're ready to go back to work.

Try these techniques ahead of time, and see if they don't work for you!

STEP 3: MAKE A PLAN

Time to complete: 25 minutes

Activity: Construct a study plan

Maybe the most important thing you can do to get control of yourself and your exam is to make a study plan. Too many people fail to prepare simply because they fail to plan. Spending hours on the day before the exam poring over sample test questions not only raises your level of test anxiety, it also is simply no substitute for careful preparation and practice over time.

Don't fall into the cram trap. Take control of your preparation time by mapping out a study schedule. On the following pages are four sample schedules, based on the amount of time you have before the Bus Operator Exam. If you're the kind of person who needs deadlines and assignments to motivate you for a project, here they are. If you're the kind of person who doesn't like to follow other people's plans, you can use the suggested schedules here to construct your own.

Even more important than making a plan is making a commitment. You can't improve your reading and judgment skills overnight. You have to set aside some time every day for study and practice. Try for at least 20 minutes a day. Twenty minutes daily will do you much more good than two hours on Saturday.

If you have months before the exam, you're lucky. Don't put off your study until the week before the exam. Start now. A few minutes a day, with half an hour or more on weekends, can make a big difference in your score—and in your chances of getting the job!

SCHEDULE A: THE LEISURE PLAN

If you have six months or more in which to prepare, you're lucky! Make the most of your time.

Time	Preparation
Exam minus 6 months	Take the first practice exam in Chapter 5. Use your score to help you decide on <u>one</u> area to concentrate on this month, and read the corresponding chapter. When you get to that chapter in this plan, review it.
Exam minus 5 months	Read Chapter 6 and work through the exercises. Get a driver's license manual and study it. Find other people who are preparing for the test and form a study group.
Exam minus 4 months	Read Chapter 7 and work through the exercises. Set aside some time every day for some serious reading—books and magazines, not comic books.
Exam minus 3 months	Read Chapter 8 and work through the exercises. Take some bus rides and watch how the operators handle difficult situations.
Exam minus 2 months	Read Chapter 9 and work through the exercises. Practice your math skills in everyday situations.
Exam minus 1 month	Take the second practice test in Chapter 10. Use your score to help you decide where to concentrate your efforts. Review the relevant chapters, and get the help of a friend or teacher.
Exam minus 1 week	Take the third practice test, and again review the areas that give you the most trouble.
Exam minus 1 day	Relax. Do something unrelated to the exam. Eat a good meal and go to bed at your usual time.

SCHEDULE B: THE JUST-ENOUGH-TIME PLAN

If you have three to five months before the exam, that should be enough time to prepare for the written test. This schedule assumes four months; stretch it out or compress it if you have more or less time.

Time	Preparation
Exam minus 4 months	Take the first practice test in Chapter 5. Then read Chapter 6 and work through the exercises. Get a driver's license manual and study it.
Exam minus 3 months	Read Chapter 7 and work through the exercises. Start a program of serious reading to improve your reading comprehension.
Exam minus 2 months	Read Chapters 8 and 9 and work through the exercises. Take some bus rides to see how operators handle difficult situations, and work on your math skills in everyday situations.
Exam minus 1 month	Take the second practice test in Chapter 10. Use your score to help you decide where to concentrate your efforts this month. Review the relevant chapters, and get the help of a friend or teacher.
Exam minus 1 week	Take the third practice test. See how much you've learned in the past months? Review the chapter on the <u>one</u> area that gives you the most trouble.
Exam minus 1 day	Relax. Do something unrelated to the exam. Eat a good meal and go to bed at your usual time.

SCHEDULE C: MORE STUDY IN LESS TIME

If you have one to three months before the exam, you still have enough time for some concentrated study that will help you improve your score. This schedule is built around a two-month timeframe. If you have only one month, spend an extra couple of hours a week to get all these steps in. If you have three months, take some of the steps from Schedule B and fit them in.

Time	Preparation
Exam minus 8 weeks	Take the first practice test in Chapter 5. Evaluate your performance to find one or two areas you're weakest in. Choose one or two chapter(s) from among Chapters 6–9 to read in these two weeks. When you get to those chapters in this plan, review them.
Exam minus 6 weeks	Read Chapters 6 and 7 and work through the exercises.
Exam minus 4 weeks	Read Chapters 8 and 9 and work through the exercises.
Exam minus 2 weeks	Take the second practice test in Chapter 10. Then score it and read the answer explanations until you're sure you understand them. Review the areas where your score is lowest.
Exam minus 1 week	Take the third practice test in Chapter 11. Review chapters 6–9, concentrating on the areas where a little work can help the most.
Exam minus 1 day	Relax. Do something unrelated to the exam. Eat a good meal and go to bed at your usual time.

SCHEDULE D: THE CRAM PLAN

If you have three weeks or less before the exam, you really have your work cut out for you. Carve half an hour out of your day, *every day,* for study. This schedule assumes you have the whole three weeks to prepare in; if you have less time, you'll have to compress the schedule accordingly.

Time	Preparation
Exam minus 3 weeks	Take the first practice test in Chapter 5. Read Chapters 6 and 7 and work through the exercises.
Exam minus 2 weeks	Read Chapters 8 and 9 and work through the exercises. Take the second practice test in Chapter 10.
Exam minus 1 week	Take the third practice test in Chapter 11. Evaluate your performance on the second and third practice tests. Review the parts of Chapters 6–9 that you had the most trouble with. Get a friend or teacher to help you with the section you had the most difficulty with.
Exam minus 2 days	Review all three tests. Make sure you understand the answer explanations.
Exam minus 1 day	Relax. Do something unrelated to the exam. Eat a good meal and go to bed at your usual time.

STEP 4: LEARN TO MANAGE YOUR TIME

Time to complete: 10 minutes to read, many hours of practice!

Activities: Practice these strategies as you take the sample tests in this book

Steps 4, 5, and 6 of the EasySmart Test Preparation System put you in charge of your exam by showing you test-taking strategies that work. Practice these strategies as you take the sample tests in this book, and then you'll be ready to use them on test day.

First, you'll take control of your time on the exam. Most civil service exams have a time limit, which may give you more than enough time to complete all the questions—or may not. It's a terrible feeling to hear the examiner say, "Five minutes left," when you're only three-quarters of the way through the test. Here are some tips to keep that from happening to *you.*

- **Follow directions.** If the directions are given orally, listen to them. If they're written on the exam booklet, read them carefully. Ask questions *before* the exam begins if there's anything you don't understand. If you're allowed to write in your exam booklet, write down the beginning time and the ending time of the exam.
- **Pace yourself.** Glance at your watch every ten or fifteen minutes, and compare the time to how far you've gotten in the exam. When one-quarter of the time has elapsed, you should be a quarter of the way through the exam, and so on. If you're falling behind, pick up the pace a bit.
- **Keep moving.** Don't dither around on one question. If you don't know the answer, skip the question and move on. Circle the number of the question in your test booklet in case you have time to come back to it later.
- **Keep track of your place on the answer sheet.** If you skip a question, make sure you skip on the answer sheet too. Check yourself every 5–10 questions to make sure the question number and the answer sheet number are still the same.
- **Don't rush.** Though you should keep moving, rushing won't help. Try to keep calm and work methodically and quickly.

STEP 5: LEARN TO USE THE PROCESS OF ELIMINATION

Time to complete: 20 minutes

Activity: Complete worksheet on Using the Process of Elimination

After time management, your next most important tool for taking control of your exam is using the process of elimination wisely. It's standard test-taking wisdom that you should always read all the answer choices before choosing your answer. This helps you find the right answer by eliminating wrong answer choices. And, sure enough, that standard wisdom applies to your exam, too.

Let's say you're facing a vocabulary question that goes like this:

13. "Biology uses a <u>binomial</u> system of classification." In this sentence, the word <u>binomial</u> most nearly means

   a. understanding the law

   b. having two names

   c. scientifically sound

   d. having a double meaning

If you happen to know what *binomial* means, of course, you don't need to use the process of elimination, but let's assume that, like most people, you don't. So you look at the answer choices. "Understanding the law" sure doesn't sound very likely for something having to do with biology. So you eliminate choice **a**—and now you only have three answer choices to deal with. Mark an X next to choice **a** so you never have to read it again.

On to the other answer choices. If you know that the prefix *bi-* means *two,* as in *bicycle,* you'll flag answer **b** as a possible answer. Mark a check mark beside it, meaning "good answer, I might use this one."

Choice **c,** "scientifically sound," is a possibility. At least it's about science, not law. It could work here, though, when you think about it, having a "scientifically sound" classification system in a scientific field is kind of redundant. You remember the *bi* thing in *binomial,* and probably continue to like answer **b** better. But you're not sure, so you put a question mark next to **c,** meaning "well, maybe."

Now, choice **d,** "having a double meaning." You're still keeping in mind that *bi-* means *two,* so this one looks possible at first. But then you look again at the sentence the word belongs in, and you think, "Why would biology want a system of classification that has two meanings? That wouldn't work very well!" If you're really taken with the idea that *bi* means *two,* you might put a question mark here. But if you're feeling a little more confident, you'll put an X. You've already got a better answer picked out.

Now your question looks like this:

13. "Biology uses a <u>binomial</u> system of classification." In this sentence, the word <u>binomial</u> most nearly means

  ✕ **a.** understanding the law

  ✔ **b.** having two names

   ? **c.** scientifically sound

   ? **d.** having a double meaning

You've got just one check mark, for a good answer. If you're pressed for time, you should simply mark answer **b** on your answer sheet. If you've got the time to be extra careful, you could compare your check-mark answer to your question-mark answers to make sure that it's better. (It is: the *binomial* system in biology is the one that gives a two-part genus and species name like *homo sapiens.*)

It's good to have a system for marking good, bad, and maybe answers. We're recommending this one:

  ✕ = bad

  ✔ = good

  ? = maybe

If you don't like these marks, devise your own system. Just make sure you do it long before test day—while you're working through the practice exams in this book—so you won't have to worry about it during the test.

Even when you think you're absolutely clueless about a question, you can often use process of elimination to get rid of one answer choice. If so, you're better prepared to make an educated guess, as you'll see in Step 6. More often, the process of elimination allows you to get down to only *two* possibly right answers. Then you're in a strong position to guess. And sometimes, even though you don't know the right answer, you find it simply by getting rid of the wrong ones, as you did in the example above.

Try using your powers of elimination on the questions in the worksheet Using the Process of Elimination beginning on this page. The answer explanations there show one possible way you might use the process to arrive at the right answer.

The process of elimination is your tool for the next step, which is knowing when to guess.

Using the Process of Elimination

Use the process of elimination to answer the following questions. (These questions are extra difficult to force you to use elimination. Don't worry; the questions on your exam won't be this hard!)

1. Ilsa is as old as Meghan will be in five years. The difference between Ed's age and Meghan's age is twice the difference between Ilsa's age and Meghan's age. Ed is 29. How old is Ilsa?
    a. 4
    b. 10
    c. 19
    d. 24

2. "All drivers of commercial vehicles must carry a valid commercial driver's license whenever operating a commercial vehicle." According to this sentence, which of the following people need NOT carry a commercial driver's license?
    a. a truck driver idling his engine while waiting to be directed to a loading dock
    b. a bus operator backing her bus out of the way of another bus in the bus lot
    c. a taxi driver driving his personal car to the grocery store
    d. a limousine driver taking the limousine to her home after dropping off her last passenger of the evening

3. Smoking tobacco has been linked to
    a. increased risk of stroke and heart attack
    b. all forms of respiratory disease
    c. increasing mortality rates over the past ten years
    d. juvenile delinquency

4. Which of the following words is spelled correctly?
   a. incorrigible
   b. outragous
   c. domestickated
   d. understandible

Answers

Here are the answers, as well as some suggestions as to how you might have used the process of elimination to find them.

1. **d.** You should have eliminated answer **a** off the bat. Ilsa can't be four years old if Meghan is going to be Ilsa's age in five years. The best way to eliminate other answer choices is to try plugging them in to the information given in the problem. For instance, for answer **b,** if Ilsa is 10, then Meghan must be 5. The difference in their ages is 5. The difference between Ed's age, 29, and Meghan's age, 5, is 24. Is 24 two times 5? No. Then answer **b** is wrong. You could eliminate answer **c** in the same way and be left with answer **d.**

2. **c.** Note the word *not* in the question, and go through the answers one by one. Is the truck driver in choice **a** "operating a commericial vehicle"? Yes, idling counts as "operating," so he needs to have a commercial driver's license. Likewise, the bus operator in answer **b** is operating a commercial vehicle; the question doesn't say the operator has to be on the street. The limo driver in **d** is operating a commercial vehicle, even if it doesn't have passenger in it. However, the cabbie in answer **c** is *not* operating a commercial vehicle, but his own private car.

3. **a.** You could eliminate answer **b** simply because of the presence of the word *all.* Such absolutes hardly ever appear in correct answer choices. Choice **c** looks attractive until you think a little about what you know—aren't *fewer* people smoking these days, rather than more? So how could smoking be responsible for a higher mortality rate? (If you didn't know that *mortality rate* means the rate at which people die, you might keep this choice as a possibility, but you'd still be able to eliminate two answers and have only two to choose from.) And choice **d** is plain silly, so you could eliminate that one, too. And you're left with the correct choice, **a.**

4. **a.** How you used the process of elimination here depends on which words you recognized as being spelled incorrectly. If you knew that the correct spellings were *outrageous, domesticated,* and *understandable,* then you were home free. Surely you knew that at least one of those words was wrong!

STEP 6: KNOW WHEN TO GUESS

Time to complete: 20 minutes

Activity: Complete worksheet on Your Guessing Ability

Armed with the process of elimination, you're ready to take control of one of the big questions in test-taking: Should I guess? The first and main answer is Yes. Unless the exam has a so-called "guessing penalty," you have nothing to lose and everything to gain from guessing. The more complicated answer depends both on the exam and on you—your personality and your "guessing intuition."

Most civil service exams don't use a guessing penalty. The number of questions you answer correctly yields your score, and there's no penalty for wrong answers. So most of the time, you don't have to worry—simply go ahead and guess. But if you find that your exam does have a "guessing penalty," you should read the section below to find out what that means to you.

How the "Guessing Penalty" Works

A "guessing penalty" really only works against *random* guessing—filling in the little circles to make a nice pattern on your answer sheet. If you can eliminate one or more answer choices, as outlined above, you're better off taking a guess than leaving the answer blank, even on the sections that have a penalty.

Here's how a "guessing penalty" works: Depending on the number of answer choices in a given exam, some proportion of the number of questions you get wrong is subtracted from the total number of questions you got right. For instance, if there are four answer choices, typically the "guessing penalty" is one-third of your wrong answers. Suppose you took a test of 100 questions. You answered 88 of them right and 12 wrong.

If there's no guessing penalty, your score is simply 88. But if there's a one-third point guessing penalty, the scorers take your 12 wrong answers and divide by 3 to come up with 4. Then they *subtract* that 4 from your correct-answer score of 88 to leave you with a score of 84. Thus, you would have been better off if you had simply not answered those 12 questions that you weren't sure of. Then your total score would still be 88, because there wouldn't be anything to subtract.

What You Should Do About the Guessing Penalty

That's how a guessing penalty works. The first thing this means for you is that marking your answer sheet at random doesn't pay. If you're running out of time on an exam that has a guessing penalty, you should not use your remaining seconds to mark a pretty pattern on your answer sheet. Take those few seconds to try to answer one more question right.

But as soon as you get out of the realm of random guessing, the "guessing penalty" no longer works against you. If you can use the process of elimination to get rid of even one wrong answer choice, the odds stop being against you and start working in your favor.

Sticking with our example of an exam that has four answer choices, eliminating just one wrong answer makes your odds of choosing the correct answer one in three. That's the same as the one-out-of-three guessing

(continued on page 20)

Your Guessing Ability

The following are ten really hard questions. You're not supposed to know the answers. Rather, this is an assessment of your ability to guess when you don't have a clue. Read each question carefully, just as if you did expect to answer it. If you have any knowledge at all of the subject of the question, use that knowledge to help you eliminate wrong answer choices. Use this answer grid to fill in your answers to the questions.

ANSWER GRID

1. Ⓐ Ⓑ Ⓒ Ⓓ   5. Ⓐ Ⓑ Ⓒ Ⓓ   9. Ⓐ Ⓑ Ⓒ Ⓓ
2. Ⓐ Ⓑ Ⓒ Ⓓ   6. Ⓐ Ⓑ Ⓒ Ⓓ   10. Ⓐ Ⓑ Ⓒ Ⓓ
3. Ⓐ Ⓑ Ⓒ Ⓓ   7. Ⓐ Ⓑ Ⓒ Ⓓ
4. Ⓐ Ⓑ Ⓒ Ⓓ   8. Ⓐ Ⓑ Ⓒ Ⓓ

1. September 7 is Independence Day in
   A. India
   B. Costa Rica
   C. Brazil
   D. Australia

2. Which of the following is the formula for determining the momentum of an object?
   A. $p = mv$
   B. $F = ma$
   C. $P = IV$
   D. $E = mc^2$

3. Because of the expansion of the universe, the stars and other celestial bodies are all moving away from each other. This phenomenon is known as
   A. Newton's first law
   B. the big bang
   C. gravitational collapse
   D. Hubble flow

4. American author Gertrude Stein was born in
   A. 1713
   B. 1830
   C. 1874
   D. 1901

5. Which of the following is NOT one of the Five Classics attributed to Confucius?
   A. the I Ching
   B. the Book of Holiness
   C. the Spring and Autumn Annals
   D. the Book of History

6. The religious and philosophical doctrine that holds that the universe is constantly in a struggle between good and evil is known as
   A. Pelagianism
   B. Manichaeanism
   C. neo-Hegelianism
   D. Epicureanism

7. The third Chief Justice of the U.S. Supreme Court was
   A. John Blair
   B. William Cushing
   C. James Wilson
   D. John Jay

8. Which of the following is the poisonous portion of a daffodil?
   A. the bulb
   B. the leaves
   C. the stem
   D. the flowers

9. The winner of the Masters golf tournament in 1953 was
   A. Sam Snead
   B. Cary Middlecoff
   C. Arnold Palmer
   D. Ben Hogan

10. The state with the highest per capita personal income in 1980 was
    A. Alaska
    B. Connecticut
    C. New York
    D. Texas

Answers

Check your answers against the correct answers below.

1. C.	**5.** B.	**9.** D.
2. A.	**6.** B.	**10.** A.
3. D.	**7.** B.	
4. C.	**8.** A.	

How Did You Do?

You may have simply gotten lucky and actually known the answer to one or two questions. In addition, your guessing was more successful if you were able to use the process of elimination on any of the questions. Maybe you didn't know who the third Chief Justice was (question 7), but you knew that John Jay was the first. In that case, you would have eliminated answer **D** and therefore improved your odds of guessing right from one in four to one in three.

According to probability, you should get 2 1/2 answers correct, so getting either two or three right would be average. If you got four or more right, you may be a really terrific guesser. If you got one or none right, you may be a really bad guesser.

Keep in mind, though, that this is only a small sample. You should continue to keep track of your guessing ability as you work through the sample questions in this book. Circle the numbers of questions you guess on as you make your guess; or, if you don't have time while you take the practice tests, go back afterward and try to remember which questions you guessed at. Remember, on a test with four answer choices, your chances of getting a right answer is one in four. So keep a separate "guessing" score for each exam. How many questions did you guess on? How many did you get right? If the number you got right is at least one-fourth of the number of questions you guessed on, you are at least an average guesser, maybe better—and you should always go ahead and guess on the real exam. If the number you got right is significantly lower than one-fourth of the number you guessed on, you should not guess on exams where there is a guessing penalty unless you can eliminate a wrong answer. If there's no guessing penalty you would, frankly, be safe in guessing anyway, but maybe you'd feel more comfortable if you guessed only selectively, when you can eliminate a wrong answer or at least have a good feeling about one of the answer choices.

penalty—even odds. If you eliminate two answer choices, your odds are one in two—better than the guessing penalty. In either case, you should go ahead and choose one of the remaining answer choices.

WHEN THERE IS NO GUESSING PENALTY

As noted above, most civil service exams don't have a guessing penalty. That means that, all other things being equal, you should always go ahead and guess, even if you have no idea what the question means. Nothing can happen to you if you're wrong. But all other things aren't necessarily equal. The other factor in deciding whether or not to guess, besides the exam and whether or not it has a guessing penalty, is you. There are two things you need to know about yourself before you go into the exam:

- Are you a risk-taker?
- Are you a good guesser?

Your risk-taking temperament matters most on exams with a guessing penalty. Without a guessing penalty, even if you're a play-it-safe person, guessing is perfectly safe. Overcome your anxieties, and go ahead and mark an answer.

But what if you're not much of a risk-taker, *and* you think of yourself as the world's worst guesser? Complete the worksheet Your Guessing Ability to get an idea of how good your intuition is.

STEP 7: REACH YOUR PEAK PERFORMANCE ZONE

Time to complete: 10 minutes to read; weeks to complete!
Activity: Complete the Physical Preparation Checklist
To get ready for a challenge like a big exam, you have to take control of your physical, as well as your mental, state. Exercise, proper diet, and rest will ensure that your body works with, rather than against, your mind on test day, as well as during your preparation.

EXERCISE

If you don't already have a regular exercise program going, the time during which you're preparing for an exam is actually an excellent time to start one. And if you're already keeping fit—or trying to get that way—don't let the pressure of preparing for an exam fool you into quitting now. Exercise helps reduce stress by pumping wonderful good-feeling hormones called endorphins into your system. It also increases the oxygen supply throughout your body, including your brain, so you'll be at peak performance on test day.

A half hour of vigorous activity—enough to raise a sweat—every day should be your aim. If you're really pressed for time, every other day is OK. Choose an activity you like and get out there and do it. Jogging with a friend always makes the time go faster, or take a radio.

But don't overdo. You don't want to exhaust yourself. Moderation is the key.

Physical Preparation Checklist

For the week before the test, write down 1) what physical exercise you engaged in and for how long and 2) what you ate for each meal. Remember, you're trying for at least half an hour of exercise every other day (preferably every day) and a balanced diet that's light on junk food.

Exam minus 7 days
Exercise: _____ for _____ minutes
Breakfast: _____
Lunch: _____
Dinner: _____
Snacks: _____

Exam minus 6 days
Exercise: _____ for _____ minutes
Breakfast: _____
Lunch: _____
Dinner: _____
Snacks: _____

Exam minus 5 days
Exercise: _____ for _____ minutes
Breakfast: _____
Lunch: _____
Dinner: _____
Snacks: _____

Exam minus 4 days
Exercise: _____ for _____ minutes
Breakfast: _____
Lunch: _____
Dinner: _____
Snacks: _____

Exam minus 3 days
Exercise: _____ for _____ minutes
Breakfast: _____
Lunch: _____
Dinner: _____
Snacks: _____

Exam minus 2 days
Exercise: _____ for _____ minutes
Breakfast: _____
Lunch: _____
Dinner: _____
Snacks: _____

Exam minus 1 day
Exercise: _____ for _____ minutes
Breakfast: _____
Lunch: _____
Dinner: _____
Snacks: _____

DIET

First of all, cut out the junk. Go easy on caffeine and nicotine, and eliminate alcohol and any other drugs from your system at least two weeks before the exam. Promise yourself a binge the night after the exam, if need be.

What your body needs for peak performance is simply a balanced diet. Eat plenty of fruits and vegetables, along with protein and carbohydrates. Foods that are high in lecithin (an amino acid), such as fish and beans, are especially good "brain foods."

The night before the exam, you might "carbo-load" the way athletes do before a contest. Eat a big plate of spaghetti, rice and beans, or whatever your favorite carbohydrate is.

REST

You probably know how much sleep you need every night to be at your best, even if you don't always get it. Make sure you do get that much sleep, though, for at least a week before the exam. Moderation is important here, too. Extra sleep will just make you groggy.

If you're not a morning person and your exam will be given in the morning, you should reset your internal clock so that your body doesn't think you're taking an exam at 3 a.m. You have to start this process well before the exam. The way it works is to get up half an hour earlier each morning, and then go to bed half an hour earlier that night. Don't try it the other way around; you'll just toss and turn if you go to bed early without having gotten up early. The next morning, get up another half an hour earlier, and so on. How long you will have to do this depends on how late you're used to getting up.

STEP 8: GET YOUR ACT TOGETHER

Time to complete: 10 minutes to read; time to complete will vary
Activity: Complete Final Preparations worksheet
You're in control of your mind and body; you're in charge of test anxiety, your preparation, and your test-taking strategies. Now it's time to take charge of external factors, like the testing site and the materials you need to take the exam.

FIND OUT WHERE THE TEST IS AND MAKE A TRIAL RUN

The city will notify you when and where your exam is being held. Do you know how to get to the testing site? Do you know how long it will take to get there? If not, make a trial run, preferably on the same day of the week at the same time of day. Make note, on the worksheet Final Preparations, of the amount of time it will take you to get to the exam site. Plan on arriving 10–15 minutes early so you can get the lay of the land, use the bathroom, and calm down. Then figure out how early you will have to get up that morning, and make sure you get up that early every day for a week before the exam.

GATHER YOUR MATERIALS

The night before the exam, lay out the clothes you will wear and the materials you have to bring with you to the exam. Plan on dressing in layers; you won't have any control over the temperature of the examination room. Have a sweater or jacket you can take off if it's warm. Use the checklist on the worksheet Final Preparations to help you pull together what you'll need.

Don't Skip Breakfast

Even if you don't usually eat breakfast, do so on exam morning. A cup of coffee doesn't count. Don't do dough-nuts or other sweet foods, either. A sugar high will leave you with a sugar low in the middle of the exam. A mix of protein and carbohydrates is best: cereal with milk and just a little sugar, or eggs with toast, will do your body a world of good.

STEP 9: DO IT!

Time to complete: 5 minutes, plus test-taking time
Activity: Ace the Bus Operator Exam!
Fast forward to exam day. You're ready. You made a study plan and followed through. You practiced your test-taking strategies while working through this book. You're in control of your physical, mental, and emotional state. You know when and where to show up and what to bring with you. In other words, you're better prepared than most of the other people taking the Bus Operator Exam with you. You're psyched.

Just one more thing. When you're done with the Bus Operator exam, you will have earned a reward. Plan a celebration for exam night. Call up your friends and plan a party, or have a nice dinner for two—whatever your heart desires. Give yourself something to look forward to.

And then do it. Go into the Bus Operator Exam, full of confidence, armed with test-taking strategies you've practiced till they're second nature. You're in control of yourself, your environment, and your performance on the exam. You're ready to succeed. So do it. Go in there and ace the exam. And look forward to your future career as a bus operator!

Final Preparations

Getting to the Exam Site

Location of exam: _____

Date of exam: _____

Time of exam: _____

Do I know how to get to the exam site? Yes _____ No _____
If no, make a trial run.

Time it will take to get to exam site: _____

Things to lay out the night before the exam

Clothes I will wear _____

Sweater/jacket _____

Watch _____

Admission card _____

Photo ID _____

4 No. 2. pencils _____

_____ _____

_____ _____

C·H·A·P·T·E·R 5

BUS OPERATOR PRACTICE EXAM 1

CHAPTER SUMMARY

This is the first practice exam in this book based on the most commonly tested areas on bus operator written exams nationwide. Use this test to see how you would do if you had to take the exam today.

The skills tested on the exam that follows are those most often tested on bus operator exams across the country. Your exam may be somewhat different, but this exam will provide vital practice, since the exam includes actual job-related skills for a bus driver.

The practice exam consists of 70 multiple-choice questions in the following areas: reading schedules, bulletins, and route maps; rules of the road and safe driving; judgment and the ability to follow procedures in routine and emergency situations; and courtesy to passengers.

Normally you would have about two hours for a test like this, but for now, don't worry about timing. Just take the test in as relaxed a manner as you can. The answer sheet you should use for answering the questions is on the following page. Then comes the exam itself, and after that is the answer key, with each correct answer explained. The answer key is followed by a section on how to score your exam.

1.	ⓐ	ⓑ	ⓒ	ⓓ		25.	ⓐ	ⓑ	ⓒ	ⓓ		49.	ⓐ	ⓑ	ⓒ	ⓓ
2.	ⓐ	ⓑ	ⓒ	ⓓ		26.	ⓐ	ⓑ	ⓒ	ⓓ		50.	ⓐ	ⓑ	ⓒ	ⓓ
3.	ⓐ	ⓑ	ⓒ	ⓓ		27.	ⓐ	ⓑ	ⓒ	ⓓ		51.	ⓐ	ⓑ	ⓒ	ⓓ
4.	ⓐ	ⓑ	ⓒ	ⓓ		28.	ⓐ	ⓑ	ⓒ	ⓓ		52.	ⓐ	ⓑ	ⓒ	ⓓ
5.	ⓐ	ⓑ	ⓒ	ⓓ		29.	ⓐ	ⓑ	ⓒ	ⓓ		53.	ⓐ	ⓑ	ⓒ	ⓓ
6.	ⓐ	ⓑ	ⓒ	ⓓ		30.	ⓐ	ⓑ	ⓒ	ⓓ		54.	ⓐ	ⓑ	ⓒ	ⓓ
7.	ⓐ	ⓑ	ⓒ	ⓓ		31.	ⓐ	ⓑ	ⓒ	ⓓ		55.	ⓐ	ⓑ	ⓒ	ⓓ
8.	ⓐ	ⓑ	ⓒ	ⓓ		32.	ⓐ	ⓑ	ⓒ	ⓓ		56.	ⓐ	ⓑ	ⓒ	ⓓ
9.	ⓐ	ⓑ	ⓒ	ⓓ		33.	ⓐ	ⓑ	ⓒ	ⓓ		57.	ⓐ	ⓑ	ⓒ	ⓓ
10.	ⓐ	ⓑ	ⓒ	ⓓ		34.	ⓐ	ⓑ	ⓒ	ⓓ		58.	ⓐ	ⓑ	ⓒ	ⓓ
11.	ⓐ	ⓑ	ⓒ	ⓓ		35.	ⓐ	ⓑ	ⓒ	ⓓ		59.	ⓐ	ⓑ	ⓒ	ⓓ
12.	ⓐ	ⓑ	ⓒ	ⓓ		36.	ⓐ	ⓑ	ⓒ	ⓓ		60.	ⓐ	ⓑ	ⓒ	ⓓ
13.	ⓐ	ⓑ	ⓒ	ⓓ		37.	ⓐ	ⓑ	ⓒ	ⓓ		61.	ⓐ	ⓑ	ⓒ	ⓓ
14.	ⓐ	ⓑ	ⓒ	ⓓ		38.	ⓐ	ⓑ	ⓒ	ⓓ		62.	ⓐ	ⓑ	ⓒ	ⓓ
15.	ⓐ	ⓑ	ⓒ	ⓓ		39.	ⓐ	ⓑ	ⓒ	ⓓ		63.	ⓐ	ⓑ	ⓒ	ⓓ
16.	ⓐ	ⓑ	ⓒ	ⓓ		40.	ⓐ	ⓑ	ⓒ	ⓓ		64.	ⓐ	ⓑ	ⓒ	ⓓ
17.	ⓐ	ⓑ	ⓒ	ⓓ		41.	ⓐ	ⓑ	ⓒ	ⓓ		65.	ⓐ	ⓑ	ⓒ	ⓓ
18.	ⓐ	ⓑ	ⓒ	ⓓ		42.	ⓐ	ⓑ	ⓒ	ⓓ		66.	ⓐ	ⓑ	ⓒ	ⓓ
19.	ⓐ	ⓑ	ⓒ	ⓓ		43.	ⓐ	ⓑ	ⓒ	ⓓ		67.	ⓐ	ⓑ	ⓒ	ⓓ
20.	ⓐ	ⓑ	ⓒ	ⓓ		44.	ⓐ	ⓑ	ⓒ	ⓓ		68.	ⓐ	ⓑ	ⓒ	ⓓ
21.	ⓐ	ⓑ	ⓒ	ⓓ		45.	ⓐ	ⓑ	ⓒ	ⓓ		69.	ⓐ	ⓑ	ⓒ	ⓓ
22.	ⓐ	ⓑ	ⓒ	ⓓ		46.	ⓐ	ⓑ	ⓒ	ⓓ		70.	ⓐ	ⓑ	ⓒ	ⓓ
23.	ⓐ	ⓑ	ⓒ	ⓓ		47.	ⓐ	ⓑ	ⓒ	ⓓ						
24.	ⓐ	ⓑ	ⓒ	ⓓ		48.	ⓐ	ⓑ	ⓒ	ⓓ						

BUS OPERATOR PRACTICE EXAM 1

Questions 1 through 4 are based on the schedule for headway times shown below. Headway times are the intervals between two successive buses moving in the same direction on the same route.

HEADWAY IN MINUTES			
	Weekdays	**Saturdays**	**Sundays**
12:00 Midnight to 5:00 a.m.	30	30	30
5:00 a.m. to 6:30 a.m.	15	30	30
6:30 a.m. to 9:30 a.m.	5	15	30
9:30 a.m. to 2:30 p.m.	12	15	30
2:30 p.m. to 4:00 p.m.	10	15	30
4:00 p.m. to 7:00 p.m.	5	15	30
7:00 p.m. to 12:00 Midnight	15	15	30

Note: The Saturday schedule will be in effect on Presidents Day. The Sunday schedule will be in effect on all other holidays.

1. A bus leaves a stop at 2:45 p.m. on a Tuesday. If a woman arrives at the same stop at 2:50 p.m., how long will she wait for another bus to arrive?
   a. 3 minutes
   b. 5 minutes
   c. 7 minutes
   d. 12 minutes

2. What is the difference between the headway times at 7:00 a.m. on a Thursday and 7:00 a.m. on a Sunday?
   a. 10 minutes
   b. 15 minutes
   c. 25 minutes
   d. 30 minutes

3. A man knows that on weekdays there is a 9:30 a.m. bus at the stop nearest his home. One Friday, however, he cannot get to that stop until 9:55 a.m. When can he expect to board a bus?
   a. 10:00 a.m.
   b. 10:03 a.m.
   c. 10:06 a.m.
   d. 10:10 a.m.

4. If a woman arrives at a bus stop at 5:00 p.m. on Presidents Day, which is a Monday, what is the longest period of time she should have to wait before a bus arrives?
   a. 5 minutes
   b. 12 minutes
   c. 15 minutes
   d. 30 minutes

5. You pull up to the bus stop and open your doors to let passengers on. A man with a very large dog on a leash tries to board the bus, despite the sign saying "No Animals Allowed." The dog is barking and struggling to get away from the bus. Which of the following is the best action for you to take?
   a. overlook the rules this one time in the interest of good public relations
   b. ask someone in the crowd to help the man get his dog onto the bus
   c. exit the bus and help the man get the dog on board
   d. tell the man he cannot bring pets onto the bus and refuse to allow him to board

6. You are running ten minutes behind schedule. As you approach a busy intersection, you see a police officer directing traffic. Just as you reach the intersection, the officer blows her whistle and holds up her hand for you to stop, though the traffic light is still green. Which of the following actions should you take?
   a. stop when you get to where the police officer is standing
   b. stop before entering the intersection
   c. go on through the intersection as the green light gives you the right-of-way
   d. make a right turn and go around the block

7. At an intersection, the traffic light has just turned green, but the pedestrian sign still reads "Don't Walk." You are about to make a right turn when a man runs into the crosswalk in front of you. What should you do?
   a. honk the horn so the pedestrian will know he is doing something wrong
   b. turn wide, and carefully drive in front of the pedestrian to force him to wait
   c. edge the bus as close as possible to the pedestrian so that he will hurry
   d. wait until the pedestrian is out of the way and then make your turn

8. If a bus weighs 2.5 tons, how many pounds does it weigh? (1 ton = 2,000 pounds)
   a. 800
   b. 4,500
   c. 5,000
   d. 5,500

9. The light at the intersection in front of your bus turns green, and you begin to drive forward. A woman walking with a white cane and a guide dog suddenly steps into the crosswalk into your path. What should you do?
   a. honk so that she will know to get back onto the curb
   b. stop and wait for the next green light
   c. proceed if you are certain that you can drive through the crosswalk before she passes in front of your bus
   d. stop and wait for her to cross and then drive on

Questions 10 through 14 are based on the schedule on the next page. Running time is the time a bus takes to travel from one stop to the next. (For example, the running time from River Park Terminal to Washington & 1st is 6 minutes.) Recovery time is the time built into the schedule between the arrival of a bus at the terminal and the next departure.

RUNNING TIME		
Bus Stop	**Eastbound** (minutes)	**Westbound** (minutes)
River Park Terminal	(leaves)	6
Washington & 1st	6	4
Washington & 2nd	4	6
Washington & 4th	6	4
Washington & 5th	4	5
Market & Court	5	3
Church & Court	3	7
Madison & Court	7	5
Plaza Terminal	5	(leaves)

Note: If the bus is running on schedule, the recovery time is 15 minutes at both terminals.

10. If an eastbound bus leaves Washington and 5th at 8:02 a.m., at what time should it arrive at Plaza Terminal?
    a. 8:22 a.m.
    b. 8:23 a.m.
    c. 8:24 a.m.
    d. 8:26 a.m.

11. If an eastbound bus running two minutes late pulls into Plaza Terminal at 5:45 p.m., at what time will the bus depart on its westbound trip?
    a. 5:50 p.m.
    b. 5:58 p.m.
    c. 6:00 p.m.
    d. 6:02 p.m.

12. What is the running time in minutes from Church and Court westbound to River Park Terminal?
    a. 28
    b. 33
    c. 35
    d. 40

13. A bus is on schedule when it leaves Washington and 4th westbound at 12:19 p.m. If it arrives at River Park Terminal at 12:34 p.m., however, what will the recovery time be?
    a. 14 minutes
    b. 15 minutes
    c. 16 minutes
    d. 17 minutes

14. An eastbound passenger boards the bus at Washington and 1st at 8:35 a.m. If he departs at Madison & Court and the bus is on schedule, how many minutes was he on the bus?
    a. 27
    b. 29
    c. 35
    d. 40

15. A fire truck with lights and sirens on is approaching you in the opposite lane of a two-lane roadway. What is the proper action for you to take?
    a. keep going forward, but slow down so that you can stop quickly if necessary
    b. keep going forward at a normal speed, as the truck is in the opposite lane
    c. if a right turn is available, make a right turn to get out of the way
    d. pull over to the right and stop

16. You are driving out of the bus yard and want to make a right turn onto the street. A freight truck is approaching from your left. What is the appropriate action for you to take?
   a. stop and wait for the truck to pass
   b. get the other driver's attention and see if he'll let you make your turn
   c. pull out onto the street and force the truck to wait for you
   d. pull into the street, but move over close to the curb so that the truck can pass

17. It's rush hour, traffic is heavy, and your bus has reached maximum capacity. As you enter an intersection, the light turns yellow. What is the appropriate action for you to take?
   a. quickly apply the brakes and stop
   b. proceed with caution through the intersection
   c. make a sharp right turn to get out of the way of heavy oncoming traffic
   d. start honking the horn and pumping the brakes gently

18. It's snowing heavily and is extremely cold outside. You are at a terminal point and have several minutes left before your bus is scheduled to begin a run. Customers are standing outside waiting. Which of the following actions should you take?
   a. smile at the customers and tell them you'll allow them on board as soon as you are ready to get underway
   b. let older customers get on board so they will be safer and more comfortable while waiting
   c. begin your run early so that you can let everyone get on the bus and out of the cold immediately

   d. let everyone get on board so they can be safer and more comfortable while waiting

19. It's 11:30 p.m. At this hour, the time between buses on the route you're driving is 45 minutes. You're running almost five minutes behind schedule. As you are pulling up to a stop, you see a woman hurrying toward you from a block away and recognize her as a regular rider on your bus. What action should you take?
   a. move on to the next stop, but wave to the woman as you pass to apologize for leaving her behind
   b. wait for the woman and allow her to get on board
   c. wait for the woman, but chastise her, letting her know that she is causing you to be very late picking up other passengers
   d. because you are late, pretend you didn't see the woman and move on to the next stop

20. In order to pass a certain exam, candidates must answer 70% of the test questions correctly. If there are 70 questions on the exam, how many questions must be answered correctly in order to pass?
   a. 49
   b. 52
   c. 56
   d. 60

21. Of 150 residents polled, 105 said they rode the city bus at least 3 times per week. How many residents out of 100,000 could be expected to ride the city bus at least 3 times each week?
   a. 55,000
   b. 70,000
   c. 72,500
   d. 75,000

22. You pick up a passenger at the bus stop, and he walks to the back of the bus. Your bus has only ten passengers on board. The passenger stands in the stairwell leading to the back doors, and when he leans against the doors he activates the interlock safety device that automatically stops the bus. Which of the following actions is the best one for you to take?

a. ask the passenger to move, explaining that he cannot stand in the stairwell because he will set off this device

b. ask the passenger to get off the bus, because he is a danger to himself and the other passengers

c. walk to the back of the bus and, if necessary, physically remove the passenger from the stairwell

d. using the passenger as an example, explain to the other passengers why it is dangerous to stand in the stairwell

23. You are approaching a stop and see that the only passenger waiting to board the bus is a man in a wheelchair. You are already a little behind schedule, and you know that if you stop to pick him up it will take a few extra minutes to help him board. Which of the following is the best action for you to take?

a. point behind you as you pass, in order to indicate that the next bus will pick him up

b. stop the bus and explain to the man that you are running behind schedule and can't pick him up

c. stop and pick up the man but advise him to have someone else with him next time to help him on the bus

d. stop and help the man get on board the bus

Answer questions 24 through 26 on the basis of the following information.

Before taking a bus out on a run, bus operators are expected to perform a pre-trip inspection to determine whether or not the bus is safe and clean enough to carry passengers. All bus operators are expected to follow the procedures below:

1. Start the engine and turn on all inside and outside lights.

2. Exit the bus and walk completely around it, checking to make sure all outside lights are functioning, including turn signals and brake lights.

3. Check all tires for worn tread, bubbles, or foreign objects such as nails or glass.

4. Inspect the ground around the vehicle for evidence of fluid leaks. The engine should still be on while you are performing this inspection.

5. Enter the bus and walk up and down the aisles to check for trash and general cleanliness.

6. Check the windows to make sure they can swing open and shut, and then check the stairwells to make sure the lights are functioning so that customers can see all the steps.

7. Get back behind the wheel and check the windshield wipers, horn, fare box seals, and brakes.

8. Report any damage or mechanical failures to maintenance for immediate attention.

24. On a rainy Monday morning, Bus Operator Jamar Mohammed arrives at the yard late. He gets inside the bus and turns on the engine and all the lights. He runs outside and takes a quick look to see if all the lights are working and checks the tires. He then goes back inside the bus, figuring he won't be able to see evidence of fluid leaks on the ground in the rain. He makes a quick pass down the aisle looking for trash and broken windows or stairwell lights. Sliding into the driver's seat, he performs the behind-the-wheel checks and then pulls out onto the street. Mohammed's actions were
a. proper, because he performed all the checks he reasonably could perform
b. improper, because he wasn't outside long enough to really check the bus lights
c. proper, because he kept the engine running while he checked outside the bus
d. improper, because he did not report possible fuel leaks to maintenance

25. Bus Operator Jane Reynolds starts the engine on her bus and prepares for her pre-trip inspection. She turns on the lights, exits the bus and makes certain that all lights are operational, and then checks the tires for damage. She notices no evidence of fluid leaks and finds that the bus is free of trash and is clean. She checks the windows and notices that the light is out in the stairwell near the rear doors. She completes her check, writes herself a note to remember to tell maintenance about the stairwell light at the end of the day, and then begins her run. Reynolds' action were
a. improper, because she should have bought a light bulb for the stairwell
b. proper, because she recorded the fact that the light was out
c. improper, because she should have reported the defect immediately
d. proper, because she completed all phases of the pre-trip inspection

26. Bus Operator Ruben Fuentes arrives for his first day on the job. He walks around his new bus, carefully inspects the tires, and looks on the ground for evidence of escaped fluids. He finds no trash in the bus and declares it to be clean. The windows work well and all stairwells have adequate lighting. He gets behind the wheel, checks out the horn, windshield wipers, fare box seals, and brakes. He then pulls out onto the street to head for his first bus stop. Based on the passage Fuentes' actions were
a. proper, because he found nothing wrong with the bus
b. proper, because the main safety features of the bus were in good shape
c. improper, because he didn't have a supervisor with him the first day
d. improper, because he performed his inspection of the bus too quickly

Answer questions 27 through 29 on the basis of the information given below

REFRESHER TRAINING COURSES

During the next ten months, all bus operators with two or more years of service will be required to have completed twenty hours of refresher training on one of the Vehicle Maneuvering Training Buses. These buses are actually simulators that reproduce lifelike driving experiences. The simulators are linked by computer to a driving course. The driver sits in one room in a life-size replica of a real bus while a two-foot bus attached to the computer moves around the course in the next room, simulating the driving experience.

Instructors who have used this new technology report that trainees develop skills more quickly than with traditional training methods. In refresher training, this new system reinforces defensive driving skills and safe driving habits. Drivers can also check their reaction times and hand-eye coordination.

The city expects to save money with the simulators because the new system reduces the amount of training time in an actual bus, saving on parts, fuel, and other operating expenses.

27. All bus operators with two or more years of service are required to do which of the following?
   a. receive training in defensive driving and operating a computer
   b. complete ten months of refresher driver training
   c. train new drivers on how to operate a simulator
   d. complete twenty hours of training on a simulator

28. The main purpose of the refresher training course on the simulator is to
   a. make sure that all bus operators are maintaining proper driving habits
   b. give experienced bus operators an opportunity to learn new driving techniques
   c. help all bus operators to develop hand-eye coordination
   d. reduce the city's operating budget

29. The bulletin announcing the refresher training course is posted on April 1. If you are a bus operator with two or more years of service, this means you will be required to finish your training by the following
   a. January 31
   b. February 28
   c. March 31
   d. December 31

30. You are driving your bus in the right lane. A bicyclist traveling ahead of you in the same lane is riding close to the right curb. She signals with her left arm that she is about to make a legal left-hand turn and then starts to move over in front of you. Which of the following actions should you take?
   a. tap the horn and speed up so that you can pass before she makes her turn
   b. drive alongside her so that she will have to drop behind you to make her turn
   c. stay back until she safely completes her legal left turn
   d. honk so that she will know you are close behind her, giving her a chance to change her mind

31. You want to make a left turn at the next intersection. As you approach, you see that there is a red light above your lane of traffic, but there is a green arrow just beneath it pointing to the left. What should you do?
   a. stop, look both ways, and then proceed with the left-hand turn
   b. stop and wait for the arrow to flash
   c. stop and wait for the light itself to turn green
   d. make the left turn without stopping

32. You want to make a right-hand turn at the intersection where you are stopped. The traffic light ahead of you shows a green arrow pointing left, a green arrow pointing up, and a red arrow pointing right. What should you do?

a. make sure no traffic is coming from the left and make your right turn

b. wait until the right arrow turns green and then turn

c. go forward or to the left because a right turn is prohibited

d. wait for the flashing yellow arrow and turn cautiously

33. You have just finished making an announcement over the public address system telling the passengers that the next stop is Main Street. About ten seconds later a teenage boy who obviously wasn't listening asks you which stop is coming up next. Which of the following actions should you take?

a. hand the passenger a bus schedule so he can figure it out himself

b. tell the passenger that his question is distracting and that you are only required to make one announcement per stop

c. tell the passenger that the next stop is Main Street

d. let another passenger tell him so that you will not become unnecessarily distracted while driving

34. You are driving your bus and see four teenagers standing on the sidewalk near your next stop throwing tomatoes at passing vehicles, including the bus running in front of you. Which of the following actions should you take?

a. stop the bus, get out, and command the teenagers to stop

b. radio the problem in to the Command Center and let them handle the situation

c. speed up to make it harder for the teenagers to hit the bus as you pass

d. honk the horn and yell at the teenagers to stop or you'll call police

35. You are northbound in a lane of traffic. A green light shows at the next intersection. You notice that a southbound car in a lane of traffic at this intersection has on its left turn signal. What should you do?

a. stop and let the other car turn in front of you

b. keep moving, but wave the other car on, as long as you are sure it has time to turn before you reach the intersection

c. speed up through the intersection so that the car that is turning won't have to wait long to make its turn

d. proceed northbound through the intersection without stopping or yielding to the car that wants to turn

36. You are eastbound at a crowded intersection where you have waited through two light changes. You finally have a green light; however, as you start to enter the intersection, an ambulance headed northbound with flashing red lights and sirens blaring approaches the same intersection. What should you do?

a. stop and let the ambulance pass through the intersection

b. continue to pull cautiously toward the intersection but wait for the ambulance to pass

c. make a quick left turn to get out of the path of the ambulance

d. proceed through the intersection if you are certain you can do so before the ambulance reaches it

37. The city's bus system carries 1,200,000 people each day. How many people does the bus system carry each year? (1 year = 365 days)
- a. 4,380,000
- b. 43,800,000
- c. 438,000,000
- d. 4,380,000,000

38. You are trying to get through a crowded intersection during rush hour. The light is green, and the car in front of you pulls into the intersection but can't make it all the way through because traffic is backed up. What is the appropriate action for you to take?
- a. pull up as close behind the car in front of you as possible and wait for the traffic to move
- b. stop before entering the intersection and wait until you can enter the intersection without blocking it
- c. turn right, make a U-turn, and then come back to the intersection so that you make a right turn when the light turns green on the cross street
- d. honk your horn so the driver of the car in front of you will know to proceed

39. In the middle of your afternoon run on a two-way road, you see a school bus with flashing red lights stopped in the opposite lane of traffic. What action should you take?
- a. call in to the Command Center to report a stalled school bus
- b. slow down and watch for children crossing the street as you pass the bus
- c. come to a complete stop and then continue after you look both ways
- d. come to a complete stop until the school bus turns off the flashing red lights

40. During the month of June, Bus #B-461 used the following amounts of oil:
June 1—$3\frac{1}{2}$ quarts
June 19—$2\frac{3}{4}$ quarts
June 30—4 quarts

What is the total number of quarts used in June?
- a. $9\frac{3}{4}$
- b. 10
- c. $10\frac{1}{4}$
- d. $10\frac{1}{2}$

41. A man boards your bus one afternoon and begins talking quietly to an invisible companion. He pays the fare and walks to an empty seat, still talking aloud to someone who isn't there. What should you do?
- a. treat him like everyone else and continue on your route
- b. call the Command Center and ask them to send medical help for this passenger
- c. hit the emergency button and wait for help, as the man is unbalanced
- d. for the safety of your passengers, ask him get off of the bus at the next stop

Answer questions 42 through 44 on the basis of the information below.

CURBING AND KNEELING YOUR BUS

You are required to pull your bus over to the curb and open your front doors as close to the bus stop or shelter as possible. If there is an obstruction that prevents you from curbing—an illegally parked car, for example—you are required to kneel your bus.

Kneeling is a feature that allows the bus to tilt down toward the curb so that customers who must board in the middle of the street can step on more easily. You are required to kneel the bus whenever you are unable to pull into a stop or bus shelter and whenever a customer makes a request.

Even with a full load, you are obligated to kneel the bus. Although you may hear rumors to the contrary, a full load will not cause the kneeling feature to stick in the down position. If the feature is defective, be sure to document the defect on a "Vehicle Condition Report," and then make sure that your bus is repaired.

42. You are operating your bus during rush hour traffic. When you get to the Jefferson Street bus stop, you have four passengers getting off and three more waiting to get on. You see that an illegally parked car will not allow you to pull into the bus stop and curb your bus. Under the circumstances you should
   a. drive quickly to the next stop or shelter where you will be able to curb your bus
   b. pull behind the car, radio for a tow truck, and wait for the car to be towed
   c. stop the bus next to the car, keep the front doors closed, and have passengers use the back doors
   d. stop and kneel the bus as close to the stop as possible

43. You are operating your bus with a full load of passengers. You are five minutes behind schedule. At the stop on Jackson Street, you curb your bus at the shelter and open the front doors to let off two passengers. One of the passengers asks you to kneel the bus. Under the circumstances you should
   a. explain that you cannot kneel the bus because you are behind schedule
   b. explain that you cannot kneel the bus because you have too many passengers

   c. show the passenger that the bus has been curbed and does not need to be kneeled
   d. comply with the passenger's request and kneel the bus

44. You are required to fill out a "Vehicle Condition Report" whenever
   a. the kneeling feature on your bus is not operating properly
   b. an obstruction in the street prevents you from kneeling your bus
   c. you have a full load of passengers and cannot kneel the bus
   d. you kneel the bus due to a passenger request

45. As you pull away from your last stop, a 14-year-old boy runs after the bus, grabs onto the side mirror near the front door, and pulls his feet up so that he is hanging in the air. What is the best action for you to take?
   a. drive away carefully, keeping an eye on the boy until he lets go
   b. stop the bus immediately and make the boy get down
   c. let the boy get on the bus but charge him extra for causing the delay
   d. tap the brakes to jar the boy and scare him so he won't do it again

46. You are pulling into the next bus stop when you realize that the accelerator is sticking. You shift the bus into neutral and then work the pedal back and forth to see if you can correct the problem. The pedal is still sticking, but not as much as before. Which of the following actions should you take?
   a. continue with the run, since your brakes are working fine and can stop the bus if the accelerator pedal sticks again

b. radio the Command Center for assistance, and then let the passengers know there is a mechanical problem so that they can change buses

c. radio ahead for a bus mechanic to meet you at the next stop

d. since it seems a simple problem, stay at the stop, turn off the bus, get out your tools, and fix the sticking accelerator

Questions 47 through 51 are based on the accompanying portion of a bus route map (on the next page). This map has spaces and numbers along the bottom edge, and spaces and letters along the right edge. If the lines on the spaces and numbers and the lines on the spaces and letters were extended, they would form blocks, or quadrants. For example, Battery Park is in quadrant Q5. The Manhattan Bridge is in quadrant P7.

47. Which bus route goes from the corner of Canal and Bowery (quadrant P6) to Stuyvesant Square Park (quadrant N5)?

a. 1

b. 15

c. 101

d. 103

48. Which bus route goes from Union Square Park (quadrant N5) to Columbia Street (quadrant O7)?

a. 8

b. 9

c. 14

d. 21

49. Which bus route goes from the Vietnam Veteran's Memorial (quadrant Q5) to Peter Cooper Village (quadrant N6)?

a. 1

b. 15

c. 21

d. 103

50. Which bus route goes from the corner of West 14th Street and 7th Avenue (quadrant N4) to the World Trade Center (quadrant P4)?

a. 10

b. 34

c. 7

d. 1

51. Which bus route goes from the corner of Washington and Spring Streets (quadrant O4) to East 29th Street and 1st Avenue (quadrant M6)?

a. 103

b. 21

c. 16

d. 15

Answer questions 52 and 53 based on the following information.

If at any time a bus operator catches up to the bus running ahead, the operator will pass the lead bus when it stops at the next bus stop and take the bus stop after that to pick up passengers. The bus operator who is in the rear is responsible for notifying the Command Center of the bunching problem. Each bus is required to leapfrog the other in this manner until the situation is resolved by field supervisors.

52. Bus Operator Wendell Smith is driving along his route when he realizes that he has caught up to the bus in front of him. He sees that the lead bus is almost completely full of passengers. When the lead bus pulls into the next bus stop, Smith pulls in behind it and motions three waiting passengers to get on his bus instead of on the lead bus. After the lead bus pulls out, Smith falls in line behind it and drives on. Smith's actions were
    a. proper, because he followed the route and schedule assigned to him
    b. proper, because it is the Command Center's responsibility to take care of bunching problems
    c. improper, because he should not have invited the other bus's passengers to come aboard his bus
    d. improper, because he should have passed the lead bus when it stopped

53. Just as the afternoon rush hour begins, Bus Operator Lanie Jaworski sees that another bus is running close behind hers. When she pulls into a bus stop, she sees the bus pass her and move on to the next stop to take on passengers. She picks up her radio and calls in to complain to the Command Center dispatcher that the bus behind her has now taken the lead. Jaworski's actions were
    a. proper, because the bus in the rear is obviously ahead of schedule
    b. improper, because the bus in the rear is required to pass and move on to the next stop
    c. proper, because it's the lead bus operator's responsibility to report any bunching situation

d. improper, because she should have driven faster to keep the rear bus from catching up

54. You are approaching a lane control light and see a steady red X. What action should you take?
    a. stay in this lane
    b. do not drive in this lane
    c. move into this lane
    d. use this lane only for left turns

55. At the end of your shift you are headed back to the bus yard and want to make a right-hand turn at the next intersection. The light is green. A bicyclist is ahead of you riding close to the curb. You pull up beside the cyclist just as you both enter the intersection. What action should you take?
    a. if it is safe to do so, make your right turn, forcing the cyclist to turn with you
    b. honk and signal your intent so that the cyclist can get out of the way
    c. make your turn after the cyclist has passed through the intersection
    d. speed up if you feel certain you can turn in front of the cyclist without a collision

56. As you pull out of the bus yard, you hear an emergency siren getting closer, but you can't tell which direction the sound is coming from. What should you do?
    a. pull over to the right side of the road and stop
    b. keep driving until you are certain the emergency vehicle is close to you
    c. look to see exactly where the emergency vehicle is so you'll know how to proceed
    d. turn on your hazard lights

57. The bus running ahead of you has obviously fallen behind schedule, and as you get closer you notice that the lead bus has standing passengers. Your bus is half-empty and you know that the next stop will have lots of passengers waiting. Which of the following is the best action you can take?
a. pass the lead bus so that passengers at the next stop can board your half-empty bus first
b. let the lead bus take the next stop and drive past without stopping, so that you can be the first bus at the stop after that
c. let the driver of the lead bus take responsibility for his or her own problem and continue to follow along behind
d. slow down and drop back so that you will not become involved in a problem you can do nothing about

58. During morning rush hour, you are driving your bus in the designated bus lane when a lone driver pulls his car in front of you and drives on. What action should you take?
a. pull up as close as possible to the vehicle and begin honking your horn
b. bump the vehicle gently with the outside right corner of the bus
c. drive normally and let traffic enforcement personnel handle the situation
d. pull out of the bus lane and see if you can pass the vehicle on the right

Answer questions 59 through 62 on the basis of the following memo.

During the last fiscal year, the load factor on city buses was the lowest it has been since regular bus service began. On average, a city bus can carry 54 passengers; the average number of passengers actually riding last year was 32. These figures represent the lowest ratio that City Transit has ever experienced. In order to increase ridership, the following measures will be instituted over the next fiscal year.

1. City Transit will undertake an advertising campaign to encourage people to ride the bus.
2. City Transit will sponsor a "My Favorite Bus Operator" contest. Passengers can vote for their favorite driver on City Transit buses. The winning driver will receive an extra week of paid vacation.
3. Effective immediately, all passenger complaints about bus operators will be placed in the operator's permanent employment record. Employees may, of course, respond to these complaints in writing.
4. Conversely, any driver whose service is so outstanding as to motivate a passenger to contact City Transit to compliment a bus operator will receive a cash bonus at the end of the year. The amount of the bonus is determined by the number and nature of the compliments received.
5. It is important that each operator be as familiar as possible with the city's bus routes. The public reports confusion with the routes as the number two reason for not riding the bus. If the driver cannot answer a passenger's route question, he or she should direct the passenger to the proper person or material that can provide the

answer. At all times the driver must remain courteous.

59. The load factor is most likely
    a. the number of passengers a bus can carry
    b. the number of passengers on a bus at a given time
    c. the ratio of passengers riding a bus to the actual capacity of a bus
    d. the ratio of passengers riding a bus to stops made by the bus

60. The memo implies that a major problem faced by City Transit is
    a. passenger complaints about operators who are not helpful or not friendly
    b. lack of enough buses to adequately service the city
    c. operators arriving late for their shifts
    d. fuel efficiency and the cost of maintaining the buses

61. According to the memo, a goal for City Transit for the next fiscal year is
    a. to buy some new buses
    b. to increase bus ridership
    c. to decrease maintenance costs
    d. to replace several bus operators

62. Operator Slater is driving the number 78 route when a passenger asks which bus goes to the Municipal Building. Operator Slater is not sure and, therefore, should
    a. give the passenger a map that shows all the bus routes
    b. apologize and explain that every driver does not know every route
    c. make an educated guess as to which bus the passenger should take
    d. tell the passenger, "I don't know"

63. You have pulled up to a crowded bus stop, and you notice that a male attempting to board your bus smells strongly of alcohol and is trying to grab female passengers as they get on board. Which of the following actions should you take?
    a. let the man get on the bus so that you don't get behind schedule, but watch him carefully
    b. let the man board the bus only after all the female passengers have gotten on first, and tell him to sit down in front
    c. let the man on board, but ask the other passengers to wait for the next bus so that he doesn't have a chance to bother anyone else
    d. refuse to allow the man to board your bus

64. The stop you are pulling up to is crowded and you are running behind schedule. As the passengers come on board one man walks past you without paying the fare. You remind him how much the fare is, but he ignores you and keeps walking to the back of the bus. Which of the following actions should you take, given these circumstances?
    a. use the public address system to tell the man again to pay
    b. ask one of the passengers to walk to the back of the bus and get the man's money for you
    c. fill out appropriate paperwork documenting the failure to pay and continue with the run
    d. walk to the back of the bus and physically remove the man from the bus

65. A blind man boards your bus and tells you that he needs to get off at the 32nd Street stop. You announce this stop when you reach it, but the man does not get off. When you announce the next stop, the man suddenly realizes that he has missed his stop and accuses you of failing to let him know when to get off the bus as he requested. Which of the following actions is best for you to take?
  a. tell the passenger that you did announce the stop as requested, and offer to let him off at this stop with a transfer to get him back to 32nd Street
  b. explain to the passenger that it's not your fault that he wasn't listening and ask him to either get off at this stop or pick another one
  c. tell the passenger you did announce the stop and give him detailed directions for walking back to the 32nd Street stop
  d. tell the passenger he can wait for a taxi in the bus shelter if he wants a ride back to 32nd Street

66. As you get close to a busy intersection you notice that a police officer is directing traffic. You see that the light above the officer's head is red, but the officer is waving at you to proceed through the intersection. What action should you take?
  a. proceed cautiously through the intersection
  b. stop, and then proceed through the intersection
  c. pull over and let traffic behind you pass
  d. stop and wait for the green light

67. You come to an intersection controlled by a stop sign. There is no white stop line painted on the pavement, but there are two white parallel lines forming a crosswalk. What are you required to do at this intersection?
  a. stop and wait for a pedestrian to enter the crosswalk
  b. come to a complete stop behind the first of the parallel lines in the crosswalk, and then proceed if traffic is clear and there aren't any pedestrians in the crosswalk
  c. keep going through the intersection if traffic permits and there are no pedestrians in the crosswalk
  d. stop in the middle of the crosswalk so you can see more clearly, and look both ways

68. Your best friend is the first person to board your bus at one of the busiest stops. He wants to chat, so he sits behind you and starts talking to you as other passengers board the bus. Which of the following actions should you take?
  a. turn around and talk with your friend while the other passengers board the bus and then continue your run once everyone has boarded
  b. since you are allowed breaks, take your break now to chat with your friend for a few minutes, and then continue on your route
  c. listen to your friend, but just nod or give short answers in reply so that the other passengers won't feel that you are not paying attention to your driving
  d. let your friend know that you can't give him your full attention at the moment and then return your attention to your passengers and your driving

69. A flashing yellow "X" on an overhead lane-use control light means
   a. move into this lane
   b. move out of this lane
   c. use this lane for left turn only
   d. lane closed ahead

70. It's raining heavily, but you are running several minutes ahead of schedule. The stop you're approaching is crowded with dripping customers. Which of the following actions is the most appropriate for you to take?

   a. pull over before reaching the stop and wait until you are back on schedule
   b. pull into the stop but do not allow any passengers on or off for a few minutes
   c. pull into the stop, allow passengers to get off and waiting passengers to get on, but stay at the stop long enough to get back on schedule
   d. pull into the bus stop, let everyone off and on as quickly as possible, and then pull out so that you can finish your run early

ANSWERS

1. **b.** On weekdays between 2:30 p.m. and 4:00 p.m., buses come every 10 minutes. The woman arrived at the stop 5 minutes after one bus left, so she will only have to wait another 5 minutes.

2. **c.** On weekdays between 6:30 a.m. and 9:30 a.m., buses leave every 5 minutes; on Sundays, they leave every 30 minutes. The difference is 25 minutes.

3. **c.** On weekdays between 9:30 a.m. and 2:30 p.m., buses come every 12 minutes. If there is a bus at 9:30, there will also be buses at 9:42, 9:54, and 10:06. If the man cannot get to the stop until 9:55, the next bus will be at 10:06.

4. **c.** On Presidents Day, the Saturday schedule is in effect; between 4:00 p.m. and 7:00 p.m., buses arrive every 15 minutes.

5. **d.** Since the dog is struggling to get away from the bus and is probably frightened, it would not be safe to allow this animal on board even if transit rules allowed uncrated animals aboard buses.

6. **b.** State law says you must obey a traffic officer under these circumstances. It would be poor judgment to enter the intersection and drive to where the officer is actually standing, as in choice **a**.

7. **d.** Though the pedestrian is in the wrong, safety dictates that you let him cross now that he's already in front of you.

8. **c.** This is a simple multiplication problem. 2.5 times 2,000 is 5,000.

9. **d.** According to both law and common sense, you must give the right-of-way to blind pedestrians. Choice **b** is wrong because you need only wait until the pedestrian is through the crosswalk and may proceed if the light is still green. Regarding choice **c**, no matter how careful you are you cannot be sure you can make it through the crosswalk before the woman passes in front of your bus.

10. **a.** It takes 20 minutes to go from Washington and 5th to the Plaza Terminal, making the arrival time 8:22.

11. **b.** To find the answer, you must subtract 2 minutes from the recovery time of 15 minutes, giving 13 minutes of recovery time, and then add 13 minutes to the 5:45 arrival time.

12. **a.** Add the first six numbers in the westbound column to get the total running time.

13. **c.** The bus is scheduled to arrive in 16 minutes, at 12:35. Since it arrives a minute early, a minute is added to the normal recovery time.

14. **b.** To arrive at the answer, add 4, 6, 4, 5, 3, and 7 in the eastbound column.

15. **d.** A fire truck is an emergency vehicle. In order to yield right-of-way, the law says you must pull over to the right and stop because you cannot know when the vehicle might have to change direction.

16. **a.** The truck has the right-of-way, and you are not authorized to take the right-of-way from any vehicle or pedestrian, even if you judge that you can do it without causing an accident. Also, it would likely startle the driver of the truck if you pulled out, even if you move close to the curb, as in choice **d**.

17. **b.** Yellow lights on a traffic signal mean that you should proceed with caution. Since you are already in the intersection, you should not stop.

18. **d.** Letting the customers board early and wait in comfort is a kindness and does not interfere with the bus schedule.

19. **b.** Waiting for the woman will build good customer relations and is safer for the woman. It is not the bus operator's job to chastise customers as in choice **c**.

20. a. First change 70% to a decimal, which is 0.7. Then multiply. 70 times 0.7 is 49.

21. b. To find the percentage of people who said they rode at least 3 times a week, divide 105 by 150 to get 0.7, which is 70%. 0.7 times 100,000 is 70,000.

22. a. Your best option is to always start with the least confrontational approach for the safety of all concerned, as well as for your professional reputation. Embarrassing the man by using him as an example, as in choice **d**, would be unfair and bad for public relations.

23. d. It is important to pick up all passengers, even if you may run a little behind. Besides its being wrong to leave the man in the wheelchair sitting there, passing up passengers would likely cause customer complaints and bad public relations. The fact that there is a wheelchair lift indicates that there is no reason for the man to have someone with him when he boards the bus, as in choice **c**.

24. a. Mohammed performed all of the steps that were possible under the circumstances. He could not complete step 4 because the wet conditions kept him from doing so; however there is no indication there was a fuel leak (choice **d**).

25. c. According to step 8 of the list of procedures, Reynolds should notify maintenance immediately, not at the end of her shift.

26. d. Fuentes did not complete steps 1 and 2 on the list of procedures.

27. d. The first two sentences of the passage state that bus operators must have twenty hours of training on a simulator.

28. a. The second sentence in the second paragraph states that the simulator reinforces safe driving habits. Although choices **b**, **c**, and **d** are possible benefits of the program, these are not the main purpose of the refresher course.

29. a. The first line of the passage states that drivers must complete 20 hours of refresher training during the next ten months, which would be the end of the following January.

30. c. The bicyclist has the right-of-way and has given a legal hand signal. You do not have the right-of-way and should wait for her to turn. Except in emergency, never honk at cyclists, as in choice **d**, because you may startle them and cause them to swerve into your path.

31. d. The correct move with a green arrow is to make the left turn without stopping for the red light.

32. b. The red arrow means that you can't turn right until the arrow turns green. If right turns were prohibited altogether, as in choice **c**, this would be indicated by a sign, not by the traffic light.

33. c. As annoying as it might be to have to repeat yourself, there are many reasons why the passenger may not have heard you the first time. It's good public relations to answer the question. The fact that the passenger is a teenager should not be a consideration.

34. b. The teenagers present no immediate threat to the safety of the passengers. Therefore, you don't need to take any immediate action; instead, you should let the Command Center handle the situation. The other choices might escalate the situation.

35. d. You have the right-of-way in this circumstance. Never signal to other drivers that it is clear for them to go because the decision they make based on your information may not be the right one.

36. a. Always yield the right-of-way to an emergency vehicle by stopping when you hear or see it coming.

37. c. The easiest way to solve this problem is to multiply 365 by 12 and then add the five zeros. 365 times 12 is 4380. Add the zeros, for a total of 438,000,000.

38. b. Although it's commonly done, entering a blocked intersection, even with a green light, is illegal. Choice **c** is unnecessary and probably just as time-consuming as waiting for another green light. Honking at the other driver to hurry in heavy traffic is distracting and rude.

39. d. The law requires a driver to come to a complete stop before passing the school bus. It is illegal to move until the bus turns off its flashing red lights. Your driving experience would show you that it's unlikely the bus is stalled.

40. c. The simplest way to add these three numbers is to first add the whole numbers, then add the fractions. $3 + 2 + 4 = 9$. Then, $\frac{1}{2} + \frac{3}{4} = \frac{2}{4} + \frac{3}{4} = \frac{5}{4}$, or $1\frac{1}{4}$. Then, $9 + 1\frac{1}{4} = 10\frac{1}{4}$.

41. a. If this passenger is not a physical danger to others on the bus and is not disruptive, there's no reason not to allow him to ride. He does not appear to be in serious enough distress to warrant calling for medical help.

42. d. The last sentence of the second paragraph states that you must kneel the bus whenever you are unable to pull into a stop or shelter.

43. d. The last sentence of the second paragraph states that you must kneel the bus whenever a customer makes a request.

44. a. The third sentence in the last paragraph states that you must fill out the report when the kneeling feature is defective.

45. b. Stopping the bus and removing the boy is the safest choice for everyone concerned. Choices **a** and **d** would endanger the boy's safety. Choice **c**, letting the boy on the bus, might encourage the bad behavior, and charging him more than the usual fare would be unethical.

46. b. The safety of your passengers should always come first, and you would be putting your passengers at risk by driving an unsafe vehicle. It would not be appropriate or safe for you to try to fix the problem, as in choice **d**. It is not likely that the bus mechanic would make rounds to buses while they are on their routes.

47. d. Bus route 103 is the only route that goes from Little Italy to Stuyvesant Square Park.

48. c. Several bus routes leave Union Square Park, but route 14 is the only one that goes to Columbia Street.

49. b. Bus route 15 turns right at E. Broadway, and then leads directly to Peter Cooper Village.

50. a. The closest direct bus route would be route 10.

51. b. Bus route 21 is the only direct route between these two locations.

52. d. The rule requires the bus in the rear to pass the bus in the lead in this situation.

53. b. The rear bus is following the rule.

54. b. A lane control light showing a red X instructs drivers not to drive in this lane.

55. c. Since the bicycle is ahead of you, the cyclist has the right-of-way, so you must wait until the cyclist is out of the way before making your turn. Again, it is dangerous to honk at a cyclist, as in choice **b**.

56. a. You are required to pull over and stop when you hear emergency vehicle sirens, whether the direction the sound is coming from is obvious or not. Turning on your hazard lights, as in choice **d**, is unnecessary.

57. a. In this situation everyone, including your coworker driving the other bus, will appreciate your initiative to keep passenger riding conditions safe, reasonable, and comfortable.

58. c. None of the other choices are safe. Your driving and the safety of your passengers is the most important concern.

59. c. According to the first paragraph, the load factor is most likely the ratio of actual passengers to bus capacity.

60. a. At several points the memo addresses operator courtesy and helpfulness. None of the other issues are mentioned.

61. b. Sentence four of the memo reads: *In order to increase ridership, the following measures will be instituted over the next fiscal year.*

62. a. Step 5 of the memo states that if the driver can't answer a passenger's question, the driver *should direct the passenger to the proper . . . material that can provide the answer.*

63. d. It would create an unsafe environment for all concerned to allow the obviously intoxicated man to board the bus.

64. c. Using the public address system, as in choice a, is more likely to upset the other passengers than to make the man pay. It would be poor judgment to involve another passenger in a situation like this, as in choice b. Physically removing the man, as in choice d, would never be appropriate and would probably be illegal. Letting the man go but documenting his failure to pay is thus your best option.

65. a. It's good public relations to help the passenger out as much as possible, even if you do feel that he should have better listening skills.

66. a. The instructions of a police officer always overrule signal lights, so you should follow the officer's directions.

67. b. Intersections controlled by stop signs do not always have a single white line painted on the pavement to let you know where you should stop, but if crosswalk lines are present you should stop at the first white line. You should never go through a stop sign. Choice a, waiting for a pedestrian to come along, would make no sense.

68. d. It would be inappropriate to let a friend or any other distraction keep you from paying full attention to your responsibilities.

69. c. A flashing yellow lane use light means the lane is to be used for cautious left turns only.

70. c. It's important to keep to your schedule as closely as possible, but it's equally important to look after the safety and comfort of your passengers. You can accomplish both by letting people on while you lay over.

SCORING

In order to figure your total score on this exam, first find the number of questions you got right. Questions you skipped or got wrong don't count; just add up how many questions you got right out of the 70 questions on this exam. Then, in order to see how that score compares with a passing score, you'll have to convert that score to a percentage. Get out your calculator and divide your total score by 0.7 to find out what percentage of the questions you got right. The table below will help you check your work by giving you percentage equivalents for some possible scores.

Number of questions right	Approximate percentage
70	100%
65	93%
60	86%
55	79%
50	71%
45	64%
40	57%
35	50%

You need a score of 70 percent on most bus operator exams in order to pass. However, your rank on the eligibility list may well depend, in whole or in part, on your score on the written exam. If that's the case, then the higher your score, the more likely you are to be called to go through the rest of the selection process. And of course if you're not called, you won't get the job. So your goal is to score as high as you possibly can.

What's much more important than your total score, for now, is how you did on each of the kinds of question on the exam. You need to diagnose your strengths and weaknesses so that you can concentrate your efforts as you prepare for the exam. As you probably noticed, the various kinds of questions are all mixed up together on the exam. So take out your completed answer sheet and compare it to the table on this page. Find out which kinds of questions you did well in and which kinds gave you more trouble. Then you can plan to spend more of your preparation time on the chapters of this book that correspond to the questions you found hardest and less time on the chapters in areas in which you did well.

Even if you got a perfect score on a particular kind of question, you'll probably want to at least glance through the relevant chapter. On the other hand, you should spend a lot of time with the chapters on the question types that gave you the most difficulty. After you work through those chapters, take the second practice exam in Chapter 10 to see how much you've improved.

BUS OPERATOR EXAM 1		
Question Type	**Question numbers**	**Chapter**
Rules of the road and safe driving	6, 7, 9,15–17, 30–32, 35, 36, 38, 39, 54–56, 58, 66, 67, 69	6, "Safe Driving"
Reading bulletins, schedules, and route maps	1–4, 10–14, 27–29, 42–44, 47–51	7, "Reading Bulletins, Schedules, and Route Maps"
Judgment, application of procedures, and courtesy to passengers	5, 18, 19, 22–26, 33, 34, 41, 45, 46, 52, 53, 57, 59–62, 63–65, 68, 70	8, "Good Judgment and Common Sense"
Mathematics	8, 20–21, 37, 40	9, "Mathematics"

C·H·A·P·T·E·R 6
SAFE DRIVING

CHAPTER SUMMARY
The civil service exam for bus operators includes questions that test your knowledge of the rules of the road and safe driving skills. Armed with the tips in this chapter, as well as a little common sense and the basic knowledge you already have as a licensed driver, you can do well on driving questions.

I t doesn't stretch the imagination much to figure out that the Department of Buses is very interested in how much applicants for the position of bus operator know about the rules of good driving. Relax. No one is going to stop the civil service exam and take you out to the streets for a quick test of your driving skills—you won't have a road test till your training period after you're hired. You're not off the hook, though, because you *will* be tested on paper.

The multiple-choice questions on driving are similar to the situational judgment questions discussed in the chapter of this book called "Good Judgment and Common Sense." Although these questions are mostly designed to see what you know about the basic rules of the road, you'll also be revealing a lot about your common sense and good judgment.

WHAT SAFE DRIVING QUESTIONS ARE LIKE

The structure of driving questions is usually fairly simple. Here's an example:

1. You are driving on a one-way street. The traffic light at the next intersection is flashing yellow. What should you do?
    a. drive cautiously through the intersection
    b. stop, look both ways, and then drive through the intersection
    c. pull over and let traffic pass you
    d. yield to all traffic coming from your right at the intersection

The test maker wants to know if you know what a flashing yellow light means. If you know that a flashing yellow light means to drive with caution, then you will be able to eliminate option b immediately. A flashing yellow light does not mean you have to treat the intersection as if it had a stop sign. There's no reason for you to pull over to let traffic pass you, so option c can be eliminated with no problem. The same reasoning applies to choice d. Flashing yellow lights are not the same as yield signs. That leaves you with option a, the choice that probably leapt out at you in the first place.

HOW TO ANSWER SAFE DRIVING QUESTIONS

The first thing you want to do to get ready for driving questions on the exam is to refresh your memory. Whether you've had your driver's license for years and feel that you've forgotten more about driving than most people learn in a lifetime or you have only a few years of experience behind the wheel, do yourself a favor by brushing up on the rules of the road. Drop by the nearest Department of Motor Vehicles office and pick up a copy of the regular driver's manual. If you've applied for a commercial driver's licence, you probably already have that manual; if not, pick up the commercial driver's manual as well. Inside, you'll find the information you need to make sure these driving questions truly are as easy as they appear to be. Even if you're a very experienced driver, you'll probably find yourself saying, "I didn't know *that!*" more than once as you read through these books.

TEST-TAKING STRATEGIES THAT WORK

In addition to basic test-taking strategies you should always use—such as reading the question carefully and reading *all* the answer choices, using the process of elimination to find the *best* answer—two strategies are particularly useful for driving questions: visualization and keeping it simple.

Visualize

One of the best ways to approach driving questions is to create the scene in your mind as you read along. As you read sample question 2 below, try to visualize yourself driving on a two-way street and coming up on the intersection described.

2. You are on a two-way street driving northbound. Your route calls for you to make a left turn at the next intersection, which will put you onto another two-lane roadway. The light is flashing red in all four directions at this intersection. What action should you take?

a. come to a complete stop as if you were at a four-way stop sign and then turn left when it is your turn

b. come to a complete stop and do not move until the light turns green

c. come to a complete stop, make a right turn and then a U-turn, and go through the intersection without stopping

d. turn without stopping as long as no traffic is coming from the right or left

The question asks if you know that when a signal light is flashing red for all traffic, the rule is to treat this intersection as if it were controlled by a four-way stop sign. You probably know this rule, but you might not think about it as a rule. Instead, you simply do what you're supposed to when you're driving; it's second nature to you as a good driver. So use your basic driving instincts. As you read the question, visualize yourself driving at this intersection. Watch the flashing red light in your mind's eye. You should see yourself brake until your bus comes to a stop. Then you'll see vehicles at the intersection carefully taking their turn to go through the intersection as if a four-way stop sign were present. Then you'll drive on in your mind when it's your turn to go. If you visualized this way, you chose option **a** immediately.

But you also know that you should always read the other choices carefully, so you move on to option **b**. Since the light is probably flashing red for all directions because the light is malfunctioning, there's no telling how long you would have to camp out here before the light turns green. So option **b** is not the best answer. Option **c** is not also right for this situation. Even if it would be reasonable to assume that you could safely pull off these turns—which it isn't—you still couldn't go through the intersection without stopping. Remember, the lights are flashing red in all directions, so you have

to stop. That's why option **d** is also wrong; you have to stop for the light. So your first instinct was right: option **a** remains the best choice.

This example also shows why rushing through "easy" questions is a risky test-taking strategy. Reading questions carefully and accurately can mean the difference between a high exam score and a low one. For instance, if you read sample question 2 quickly and missed the part that says the light is *flashing* red, rather than being a steady red, you might have chosen option **b** as the right answer. And **b** *would* be the right answer under those circumstances. But the light *is* flashing in the question, so **b** is wrong. Read the question through once, and then read it again to form your mental image of the scene.

Keep It Simple

You must read the question carefully and use your imagination to help you answer it. But don't let your imagination run away with you and make the question harder than it really is. Think again about the first sample question in this chapter: "You are driving on a one-way street. The traffic light at the next intersection is flashing yellow. What should you do?" Do not sit there and torture yourself with *what ifs* like, "Well, if it's Saturday, there's probably not much traffic. . . ." The question doesn't say anything about how much traffic there is, so the amount of traffic isn't relevant. Just answer the question that you see; don't add to it. If you do, you'll just let the Anxiety Monster loose, and you don't need that kind of company on exam day.

BUS SAFETY

Driving a bus is different from driving a passenger car, of course. In driving a bus, you have to think about everything you would have to consider while driving your car, plus a lot of others—first and foremost, the safety and well-being of a busload of people! Questions on the exam are going to address these concerns, which is why it's best to consider a few basic safe bus-driving strategies before you take the exam.

Stopping and Starting

At the risk of overstating the obvious, a good bus operator would never slam on the brakes suddenly without good cause. Many bus passengers choose to stand rather than sit when riding the bus and aren't very comfortable with the idea of becoming high-speed projectiles. When you see choices for test questions that suggest you stop suddenly, look closely at the situation described. If it's not an emergency in which someone would be badly hurt if you *don't* stop in a hurry, you should reject slamming on the brakes and look for a better answer. Smooth, slow, and steady is the braking technique preferred by most good drivers.

The same goes for rapid starts. Buses aren't known for their ability to "peel out," but it is possible to accelerate too rapidly for the comfort and safety of passengers. Falling backwards isn't any more safe or desirable for passengers than falling forward. Watch out for answer choices that suggest you accelerate rapidly. Smooth, slow, and steady works as well for accelerating as it does for braking.

Length Considerations

Here's a news flash: buses are much longer than passenger cars. That means that, as a bus operator, you will have to be more patient than you might normally be behind the wheel of a car. When you are turning a bus, you have to allow enough room—and enough time—to get the entire vehicle through the intersection. If a test question suggests that you perform a maneuver that would be difficult, if not downright dangerous, in a bus, then it's more than likely not the right answer.

Backing Up

Driving in reverse is rarely a good idea, especially in a bus. You can't see what's directly behind you, nor can you tell how close you are to objects behind you. There are times, however, when there's no way around it; you have to back up. In that case, most safety experts strongly urge drivers of commercial vehicles to have a "spotter," someone who can stand outside of the vehicle and direct you safely as you back up.

Even with a spotter, backing up is a dangerous movement. Make sure that you do two things when you have to perform this maneuver:

- Move slowly and cautiously.
- Follow the directions of a spotter.

And don't be surprised when you see this information in the form of a civil service exam question. Generally, if the situation described doesn't absolutely *require* backing up, you should choose an answer choice that doesn't include that maneuver. And if the situation does require backing up, the option that involves using a spotter is most likely the right one.

Visibility

Seeing everything you need to see is more difficult in a bus than in a car. You may not have a rear-view mirror to let you see what's happening directly behind you any longer. You'll have side mirrors to tell you what is happening in the lanes next to you and behind you, but they don't cover the whole area behind you. Vehicles of this size have big "blind spots." And if that's not enough to worry about, sometimes the number of passengers on board your bus will make seeing to the sides and rear even more of a problem.

The best strategy for driving in low-visibility situations is *"Don't go if you don't know for sure."* Sometimes you simply have to wait until you know for certain what's in the lane next to you or what the traffic to your right is doing. If one of the choices to a test question suggests that you make a maneuver when your vision is obscured, you can eliminate that choice from consideration.

Hazardous Driving Conditions

Mother Nature will try to make your career as a bus operator a true challenge. She knows that you cannot drive the same way in snow or ice as you would on dry, clear pavement. The questions you'll see on the test expect you to recognize this also. If you see a scenario involving driving on ice, for example, you will be expected to know to drive slowly and be aware of the

traffic around you. Even in nothing more than a sudden rain shower, city streets become slick. And remember, visibility may be poor in bad weather—another reason to take it slow and easy. You shouldn't choose any answers that have you making sudden starts or stops or driving faster than the flow of traffic in bad weather.

Ride Before You Write

Before you sit down to take the civil service exam, you should ride the bus and watch how the driver handles driving situations. Watch the driver and see if you can distinguish between good driving strategies and bad ones. The situations you see during your research rides may pop up again on the exam.

Tips for Answering Safe Driving Questions

- Know the rules of the road—get a driver's license manual.
- Always choose the answer that keeps your bus and its passengers safest.
- Bring the questions to life—visualize the situations.
- Don't make the questions harder than they are.
- Ride the bus. Make it yours in your mind.

C·H·A·P·T·E·R

READING BULLETINS, SCHEDULES & ROUTE MAPS

7

CHAPTER SUMMARY

The Bus Operator written exam includes questions on reading and interpreting various kinds of materials bus operators actually have to work with, such as job bulletins and announcements, route schedules, and maps. This chapter shows you how these questions work and how to answer them.

Bus operators, like people in almost any career, need good reading skills to do well on the job. As a bus operator, you have to be able to read and understand your training materials as well as bulletins that announce changes in procedures once you're on the job. You'll need to know how to use the various forms that are part of your job and to read work schedules and bus schedules. And, naturally, you have to be able to read a bus route map. That's why reading questions are included on the bus operator exam: your employer needs to know that you have the reading skills you need to do the job.

Some of the reading questions on the bus operator exam will be similar to reading comprehension questions you may have encountered before on standardized tests, in which you read a paragraph and then answer questions about it. In other cases, what you'll be reading is a table or a map, but the basic skill is still the same: interpreting what you see on the page and answering questions about it. This chapter will show you how to deal with questions based on bulletins, schedules, and route maps.

STRATEGIES FOR READING QUESTIONS

The various kinds of materials you might be asked questions on will be dealt with in detail below, but there are some basic test-taking strategies that work for all kinds of materials.

Read the Questions First

Most people find that skimming over the questions before looking at the paragraph (or table or map) helps them look for the answers when they actually read the material. That way they don't get bogged down in other details when they actually turn to the paragraph. You don't have to use this strategy if it doesn't work for you, but try reading the questions first as you work through the sample exam material in this chapter to see if it does.

Read Carefully But Don't Read In

Every reading question on the exam is based *only* on the accompanying material. The answer is right there in front of you, and all you have to do is find it. *Don't add anything to what you see in the reading material.* You might think that the procedure outlined in the bulletin could be accomplished more efficiently. Your uncle the bus operator might have told you that bus operators never have to work more than six shifts in a row, but the work schedule in front of you has some operators working seven shifts. You might happen to know that the bus route shown on the map doesn't go to 79th Street any more. If you know or think you know any of those things, *forget them.* On reading questions, the examiners don't want to know how much you already know; they want to know how well you can *learn* by reading. Answer the question based *only* on the material in front of you.

Use Your Test Booklet

Unless you're specifically told not to mark in the test booklet, use your pencil on the paragraph or map. Underline important ideas in the paragraph, and draw a circle around any sentence that seems to summarize the whole paragraph. Put a star beside your starting point on the map and an X beside the ending point, and then use your pencil to trace your route. Even if you're not allowed to mark in the test itself, you can jot notes to yourself on a piece of scratch paper or trace your route holding your pencil just above the paper.

Read All the Answer Choices

Never, ever, light on the first answer that jumps out at you. That answer may well have been put there to jump out at you, while a better, more complete answer lurks somewhere in the other choices. Read *all* the answer choices, and use the process of elimination to help you come up with the *best* answer. There may be two or more answer choices that are close but not quite as close as the *best* answer. Here's another way that marking your test booklet helps; you can X out any answer choices you eliminate as definitely wrong, so you don't have to go back to them again, and put a check next to the good answers so you'll remember which one you thought might be the right answer when you come back to it.

Try these strategies as you work through the sample questions that follow on bulletins, schedules, and route maps.

READING BULLETINS

Questions based on job bulletins are a lot like the reading comprehension questions on other standardized exams. You read a paragraph and then answer questions that might ask you about details from the paragraph or its main idea. You may also be asked what a word in the passage means, or you could be asked to apply what you have read to a hypothetical situation, which is exactly what a bus operator has to do in real life.

Here's a sample bulletin, followed by questions about it. Skim the questions, and then read the passage and answer the questions. Then read through the answer explanations, which show you how to use the process of elimination to come up with the *best* answer.

SAMPLE BULLETIN AND QUESTIONS

Bus operators should try to discourage customers from eating and drinking on the bus. Such activities, though not actually illegal, make for a dirty bus as people leave their crumbs and containers in the seats and aisles. If they observe customers eating or drinking, bus operators should use the public address system to announce: "Please do not eat or drink on the bus." However, unless customers are consuming alcoholic beverages, operators should not ask customers who do not comply with this request to leave the bus, nor should they refuse entry to customers who are carrying food or beverages. Carrying open containers of alcoholic beverages on a bus is illegal. If customers refuse to close their containers of alcoholic beverages or leave the bus on request, operators should call the Command Center for instructions.

1. The passage states that if a bus operator sees people eating on the bus, the operator should
   a. ask them to leave the bus
   b. ignore them, since eating on the bus is legal
   c. make an announcement on the public address system
   d. call the Command Center

2. Which of the following best expresses the main idea of the passage?
   a. Bus operators should attempt to persuade customers not to eat or drink on the bus.
   b. Eating and drinking on the bus is legal but drinking alcohol is not.
   c. The public address system is the best means for discouraging eating and drinking on the bus.
   d. Bus operators should not eat or drink on the bus.

3. As it is used in the passage, the word "consuming" most nearly means
   a. wasting
   b. utilizing
   c. depleting
   d. taking in

4. Bus Operator Harrison sees that a customer who is about to board her bus is carrying a six-pack containing five beer cans and has one can open in his hand. What should Operator Harrison do?
   a. refuse to allow the man on the bus until he gets rid of all six beers
   b. refuse to allow the man on the bus until he gets rid of the open beer can
   c. ask the man not to drink his beer while he is on the bus and allow him on the bus if he agrees
   d. call the Command Center for assistance

ANSWERS AND STRATEGIES

Each of the questions above asks for a different kind of information and requires a different kind of thinking.

Fact or Detail Questions

1. c. Bus operators should use the public address system to ask people to stop eating on the bus.

Question 1 asks you to find the answer choice that restates a specific piece of information in the passage; in other words, it asks for a fact or detail from the passage. There are three steps to answering this kind of question:

1. Read the question carefully.

2. Go back to the passage and find the answer, *even if you think you remember it.*

3. Go through all the answer choices, using the process of elimination to find the answer that restates the fact from the passage.

Here's how you would use this process on question 1. You read the question and find that it asks what you should do if someone is eating on your bus. You go to the passage and find the answer in the third sentence: "bus operators should use the public address system to announce: 'Please do not eat or drink on the bus.'" Then you look at the answer choices. Choice **a**, "ask them to leave the bus," is what you would do if they were consuming alcoholic beverages and refused to close the container, not if they're just eating. So that's wrong. Choice **b**, "ignore them, since eating on the bus is legal," does contain a correct fact from the passage—eating on the bus *is* legal. But the advice to ignore the eating is wrong; you're supposed to make an announcement. And that's exactly what you find in choice **c**, "make an announcement on the public address system." Bingo; there's your answer. But you go on to choice **d** just in case it's even better. You quickly find out it's not, because calling the Command Center is what you would do if someone were drinking alcohol and refused to close their container or leave the bus. So you stick with choice **c**, the best choice.

Probably the majority of questions on bulletins will ask you for specific facts or details. That's good news because they're usually the easiest kind of question. Just make sure you read both the question and the passage carefully, and you shouldn't have any trouble.

Main Idea Questions

2. a. The passage is mainly about bus operators' obligations in regard to eating and drinking on the bus.

Question 2 asks you for the main idea of the paragraph. These questions can be a little trickier than fact questions, because some of the answer choices may well be contained in the passage but not be the main idea—they may, in other words, be facts from the passage. What you're looking for is a statement that could serve as an umbrella, or a net, for all the different facts in the passage. If you're lucky, there will be such a statement right in the paragraph, often in the first or last sentence of the paragraph. And it turns out with this passage, you do have such a sentence, the very first one: "Bus operators should try to discourage customers from eating and drinking on the bus." That's what the paragraph as a whole is about, and the rest of the sentences give more detail about that main idea. So when the question asks which is the main idea, you can simply look for a sentence that says the same thing in different words. And when you look at the answer choices, option **a**, "Bus operators should attempt to persuade customers not to eat or drink on the bus" leaps right out at you.

But you're a smart test-taker, so you mark choice **a** but check the other choices to be sure. When you look at choices **b** and **c**, you find that they are both ideas that are contained in the paragraph, but they are details. Yes, eating and drink on the bus is legal while drinking alcohol is not, but that's not an idea that encompasses all the other ideas in the paragraph as well, so it's not the *main* idea. Neither is the idea that the public address system is a good way to discourage eating and drinking on the bus. So you eliminate choices **b** and **c**. And it's easy to eliminate choice **d**, "Bus operators should not eat or drink on the bus," because that idea is never even mentioned in the paragraph, though it's certainly a logical conclusion based on the fact that *no one* should eat or drink on the bus. So your first choice, **a**, was the right one, and it's the one you should mark on your answer sheet.

Vocabulary Questions

3. d. In this paragraph, the word *consuming* most nearly means *taking in.*

Question 3 asks you about the meaning of a word as it is used in the passage. There are just two rules for answering vocabulary questions like this:

- **Do** try substituting each answer choice for the given word in the sentence where it appears.
- **Don't** assume that you know what the word means and neglect going back to the sentence where the word appears. Many words have more than one meaning, and the question asks what the word means *as it is used in the passage.*

The hardest part of answering vocabulary questions can be simply finding the sentence where the word is used. So go looking for the word *consuming,* and you'll find it in the fourth sentence: "However, unless customers are *consuming* alcoholic beverages, operators should not ask customers who do not comply with this request to leave the bus. . . ."

Now that you've found the sentence, you just take each of the answer choices and see if it fits in place of *consuming* in this sentence. You don't simply choose the option that means what you already know *consuming* means, because *all* of the answer choices are possible meanings of the word. So you try **a**, "wasting," but that makes nonsense of the sentence: "unless customers are *wasting* alcoholic beverages" is just silly. Choice **b**, "utilizing," makes more sense: "unless customers are *utilizing* alcoholic beverages." That's a possibility; people do *utilize*, or *use*, alcohol beverages. So you mark **b** as a possibility but try the others as well. Choice **c**, "depleting," makes about as much sense as *wasting* did, so you throw it out. But then choice **d**, "taking in," seems to fit really well in the sentence: "unless customers are *taking in* alcoholic beverages." *Taking in* is exactly what you do when you are drinking something. So you discard choice **b**, which was close but not as close, and mark choice **d** on your answer sheet.

Application Questions

4. b. Open cans of beer are illegal on the bus, though closed containers of alcohol are allowed.

Question 4 asks you to take information in the paragraph and apply it to a hypothetical situation. This kind of question can be a little more difficult, because the answer isn't right there in the passage; the paragraph never says what a bus operator should do if someone who wants to board the bus is carrying an open beer can. In fact, it never comes right out and says what a bus operator should do if someone who is already on the bus is drinking alcohol. But the answer is *implied* in the paragraph. The paragraph says that people who are eating or drinking should not be asked to leave the bus or not be allowed to board the bus *unless they are drinking alcoholic beverages*—which means that they *should* be asked to leave or refused entry if they *are* drinking alcohol. The paragraph also implies that bus operators should ask passengers either to close their containers of alcoholic beverages or leave the bus if they are drinking on board the bus.

So what does this mean a bus operator should do if a passenger tries to board the bus with five closed cans and one open can? It means the operator should insist that the open can not be allowed on board with the man. It does *not* mean that the operator should not allow the man to carry the five closed cans with him; nowhere in the paragraph does it suggest that people can't carry alcoholic beverages that are in closed containers.

Armed with this reasoning, you turn to the answer choices. Choice **a** is the one you just rejected; the man can carry his closed beer cans as long as he doesn't have the open one. Choice **b** looks right; the man shouldn't be allowed on the bus until he loses the open beer. But you check out the other choices to make sure. Choice **c**, letting the man get on if he promises not to drink his beer, looks plausible at first, but check the paragraph again. It clearly says, "Carrying open containers of alcoholic beverages on a bus is illegal." Whether or not the man drinks from the open container is irrelevant. So you reject that option and go on to **d**, which suggests calling the Command Center. The paragraph says you should call the Command Center if someone on the bus refuses your request to close a container or leave the bus. This man isn't even on the bus yet, and the bus operator hasn't yet asked him to get rid of his beer, so calling the Command Center would be premature. You're left with choice **b**, the best option for this situation.

Another kind of application question might ask you to apply information from one part of the passage to another part. For instance, instead of being given a hypothetical situation, you might have been asked straight out what the passage implies about letting people on the bus with closed containers of alcohol.

You've already been through the reasoning that would give you the answer: only open containers of alcohol are prohibited, so it's all right to let people on the bus with closed containers.

All this explanation and all these question types make the task of answering questions about bulletins look more complicated that it really is. It's really just a matter of reading carefully: read the question, read the paragraph, and read the answer choices, and you'll do fine.

READING SCHEDULES

Reading schedules is a lot like reading bulletins. You skim the questions and then turn to the schedule itself. The schedule might show when different bus operators are scheduled to work or when a bus is scheduled to reach various stops. Or it might, like the schedule that follows, show headway times—the amount of time between buses on a particular route at given times of the day. In addition to reading the schedule itself, you should also pay careful attention to any explanatory material that accompanies it. You will hardly ever have to answer main idea or vocabulary questions in dealing with schedules; most of the questions will ask you about details of the schedule or ask you to apply the schedule to a specific situation. Since schedules deal with time, be prepared to do some simple addition and subtraction.

SAMPLE SCHEDULE AND QUESTIONS

Using this schedule, try your hand at the sample questions that follow it, and then read the answer explanations, which will show you some strategies for dealing with schedule questions.

HEADWAY TIMES IN MINUTES

Time of Day	M–F	Sat	Sun
6:00 a.m.–7:30 a.m.	15	30	45
7:30 a.m.–9:30 a.m.	6	15	25
9:30 a.m.–2:00 p.m.	15	20	30
2:00 p.m.–4:00 p.m.	10	20	35
4:00 p.m.–7:00 p.m.	8	15	40
7:00 p.m.–11:30 p.m.	30	45	60
11:30 p.m.–6:00 a.m.	60	60	NS

Note: NS indicates no service. Sunday schedule is in effect on all holidays except Martin Luther King Day, Presidents' Day, and Columbus Day, when the Saturday schedule is in effect.

5. On Columbus Day at 8:30 a.m., a customer watches a bus pull away from his stop just as he rounds the corner. About how long will he have to wait for another bus?
   a. 6 minutes
   b. 15 minutes
   c. 20 minutes
   d. 30 minutes

6. As a bus operator, you have been instructed to lay over until you are back on schedule if you catch up with your leader, that is, the bus ahead of you. On a Thursday afternoon at 3:46 p.m., you see your leader a block ahead of you as it pulls up to the 92nd Street stop. How long should you lay over at 92nd Street?
   a. 4 minutes
   b. 6 minutes
   c. 8 minutes
   d. 10 minutes

7. Ms. Harrison usually takes the bus that comes to her stop at 2:48 p.m. on Sundays, but one Sunday she misses her bus. What time should she expect to catch the next bus?
   a. 3:18 p.m.
   b. 3:23 p.m.
   c. 3:28 p.m.
   d. 3:35 p.m.

ANSWERS AND STRATEGIES

5. **b.** You need the information from the Note at the bottom of the schedule to answer this question. The Saturday schedule is in effect on Columbus Day, so you should look at the Saturday column on the schedule. The customer sees his bus at 8:30 a.m., so you need to find the row on the schedule that corresponds to that time, which is the 7:30–9:30 a.m. row. Follow that row across to the Saturday column, and you see that the customer will have to wait 15 minutes for his next bus.

6. **d.** Once again, you simply have to find the right column and row. Thursday is a weekday, so you want the second column of the schedule. Your time of 3:46 p.m. falls into the 2:00–4:00 p.m. row. Follow that row to the Monday-through-Friday column to find out that there should be 10 minutes between buses. This means that you should lay over for 10 minutes.

7. **b.** Find the Sunday column and the 2:00–4:00 p.m. row to see that there will be a 35-minute wait until the next bus. But you're not finished, because the question asks not how long Ms. Harrison will have to wait but *what time* she will be able to catch a bus. So you'll have to add the 35 minutes to the time Ms. Harrison's usual bus comes, 2:48 p.m. Add 35 and 48 to get 83. Now obviously Ms. Harrison can't catch a bus at 2:83 p.m. Subtract 60 minutes

from 83 minutes to get 23 minutes, and then add 1 hour to 2 p.m. to get 3 p.m. So the next bus should come at 3:23 p.m.

Questions on schedules are not that difficult. As with other kinds of reading questions, you have to read the question itself carefully to find out exactly what it's asking, particularly what row of the schedule it's sending you to. Use your pencil to help you follow a particular row across to the proper column. And if you have to do some math, make sure you check your addition before you choose an answer.

READING MAPS

Reading maps is different from reading bulletins or schedules in that you have to be able to find your place on a two-dimensional representation of three-dimensional space. However, you should still read the question carefully to make sure that you know what it's asking you to do, and you should use your pencil to help you keep track of where you are on the map. Pay particular attention to the legend or key, if there is one. The legend is usually a box in one corner of the map that tells you what the symbols mean. Note, too, which direction is north on the map, if that is indicated.

There are several different kinds of questions you could be asked about a map. The most common asks you which route or combination of routes goes from one given point to another. You might also be asked questions about terminals, transfer points, or the location of various points of interest along a route.

SAMPLE MAP AND QUESTIONS

One thing you'll have to be able to do is to read a bus map grid. A map like the one on the facing page will come with directions something like this:

Questions 8–10 are based on the accompanying portion of a bus route map showing part of the upper (northern) portion of Manhattan. This map has spaces and numbers along the top and bottom, and spaces and letters along the sides. If the lines on the spaces and numbers and the lines on the spaces and letters were extended, they would form blocks, or quadrants. For example, the Schomberg Center is in quadrant F4. Grant's Tomb is in quadrant G2.

Note: This map is copyrighted by the New York City Transit Authority and is used with permission.

Some questions will require you to find a given landmark or street corner using the quadrant system. This actually makes it easier to find the given location, since you don't have to scan the entire map but only about one square inch, the part that falls within the given quadrant. Use your answer sheet or pencil to help you move across from where the letters and numbers are marked to the portion of the map you need.

Use the map on the facing page to answer the following questions. Then read the answer explanations to see what strategies you can use to answer these questions.

8. Which bus route should a passenger take to get from Columbia University (quadrant G–H3) to the corner of Fort Washington Avenue and West 168th Street (quadrant D2)?
   a. 104
   b. 4
   c. 60
   d. 11

©New York City Transit Authority. Reprinted with permission.

9. You are driving the route 116 bus westbound. A passenger boards at East 116th Street and 1st Avenue (quadrant G6) and asks you to announce where she should get off to transfer to the number 10 bus. Where should you make this announcement?
   a. Madison Avenue and East 116th Street
   b. Frederick Douglass Boulevard and Central Park North
   c. Adam Clayton Powell Jr. Boulevard and Martin Luther King Boulevard (West 125th Street)
   d. Frederick Douglass Boulevard and West 116th Street

10. Which bus route should a passenger take to get from the east side of upper Manhattan to the Hunts Point Food Center?
    a. Bx6
    b. Bx19
    c. Bx33
    d. Bx15

ANSWERS AND STRATEGIES

8. b. The 4 bus runs from Columbia University to the corner of Fort Washington Avenue and West 168th Street.

   First, find the beginning point, Columbia University. Look across from the border of letters G and H—since both letters are indicated, the university must lie on the borderline. Keep your finger on that spot and run another finger up from number 3. Look near where your two fingers cross and you should find Columbia University. You see that the 4, 104, 60, and 11 buses run past Columbia University. (You also notice that all of those bus routes are among the answer choices, so you know that you have to be careful to find the right route to get to the ending point.)

   Now find the ending point, Fort Washington Avenue and West 168th Street. Again, use the letter and number grid to find it. When you locate it, you see that only one bus route goes to that corner, the 4. Luckily, the 4 is also one of the routes that goes past Columbia University. Just for safety's sake, trace the route from the university to the given corner. Sure enough, the number 4 bus goes directly from Columbia University to the corner of Fort Washington and West 168th.

9. d. The number 10 bus runs up Frederick Douglass Boulevard.

   Find the given bus route, the 116. It runs from its terminal on Pleasant Avenue to 116th Street and then straight across. So all you have to do is to find the place where the 116 bus on 116th Street meets the 10 bus—and you've already eliminated choices b and c, because they indicate corners that the 116 bus never even crosses. Trace the 116 bus's route across 116th Street. You should quickly find that the 10 bus runs up Frederick Douglass Boulevard. So that's where you should make your announcement.

10. a. The Bx6 bus goes to Hunts Point.

    This time you don't really have to read routes. The routes of the Bronx buses no longer appear on this map once they leave Manhattan. So all you have to do is read the notes about the destinations of the buses. Those notes appear on the left side of the map, east of the Harlem River—where the Bronx would be if it appeared on this map. Only one note indicates a destination of Hunts Point Food Center, and that note appears next to the Macombs Dam Bridge in quadrant E4. The Bx6 is the bus you want.

    You're probably already used to reading maps, and you may even be familiar with a quadrant system for finding your way around. The questions about route maps will not be that difficult; you just have to be sure to read both the question and the map carefully. The practice exams in this book will give you opportunities to practice your map reading and gain confidence in your ability to perform this important task.

If, after you take the practice exam in Chapter 9, you still feel you need some extra help with your reading skill, turn to Chapter 10, "More Help with Reading."

How to Answer Reading Questions

Here are some tips on answering reading questions:

- Read the question carefully.
- Find the answer in the bulletin, schedule, or map.
- Read all the answer choices.
- Use the process of elimination to find the *best* answer.
- Don't "read in." Answer the question based *only* on what you see in the bulletin, schedule, or map.

C·H·A·P·T·E·R 8

GOOD JUDGMENT AND COMMON SENSE

CHAPTER SUMMARY

This chapter shows you how to deal with exam questions that test your judgment and common sense. Reading carefully and learning to think like a bus operator are the keys to doing well on these questions.

Y ou may assume that what Department of Buses officials want most is to hire men and women with top-notch driving skills for bus operator positions. That's certainly true, but the most sought-after candidates for bus operator positions are individuals with common sense and good judgment. These two qualities are what get satisfied bus passengers from Point A to Point B and put a smile on a supervisor's face.

Multiple-choice civil service exams are the quickest, most cost-effective way for the MTA to find applicants with common sense and good judgment. These exams feature judgment questions that reveal whether you can make a sound decision—pick the right multiple-choice answer—based on the information given to you. To come to the right conclusion, you will need your common sense, good judgment, and good reading skills. (A little good luck never hurts either, so feel free to stick that four-leaf clover in your pocket.)

Judgment questions usually fall into three categories: judgment based on routine or emergency situations, judgment based on public relations, and application of rules and procedures. This chapter will look at each category, take apart an example of each type of judgment question, and then identify the best approach to answering the question. There are also tips on what is most likely to trip up the unwary test-taker.

JUDGMENT IN ROUTINE OR EMERGENCY SITUATIONS

Situational judgment questions ask you to climb inside the mind of a bus operator and make decisions from this viewpoint. It isn't necessary for you to know MTA policies or technical information about operating a bus. The test itself will give you the information you need to answer the question.

Some exams load you right into the hot seat with language such as "You are driving in heavy rain when..." while other exams use a more subtle approach: "Bus Operator Jones pulls in to a stop where a man in a wheelchair is waiting." Although the approach is different, both test makers are asking you to look at their questions from the same viewpoint—a bus operator's view.

The structure of the questions is pretty simple. You'll be given a situation, and then you'll be asked to choose how you would handle the situation if you were the bus operator. The nice part is that you don't have to come up with your own plan. You get to choose the best answer from four multiple-choice options listed below the question. Eye-bulging panic, of course, will make all of the options appear to be the right one, but keep in mind that there is only *one* best answer.

Here's an example:

1. Bus Operator Jane Breda is pulling into a crowded bus stop during rush hour traffic. She notices that the bus is pulling hard to the right,

and after she stops she sees that her right front tire is almost flat. What is the most appropriate action for her to take?

a. tell boarding passengers to hurry so that she can get underway again before the tire goes completely flat
b. put on the Out of Service sign and change the tire
c. continue to the terminal of the route, driving slowly and carefully
d. tell the passengers that the bus is now out of service and call Command Center for assistance

Now would be a good time to pull out the common sense and good judgment skills. Put yourself in the driver's seat with Breda and look at this situation. The question tells you two things: it's rush hour, and Breda has just discovered a problem that may jeopardize the safety of her passengers as well as the condition of the bus. Keep this in mind as you read the four options.

Option a is not a good choice, because getting passengers on board quickly is not going to keep the tire from going flat. Option b is not a good choice, either, not only because putting on the Out of Service sign doesn't address the needs of passengers already on the bus, but because Breda can hardly change the tire by herself without special equipment—especially not with passengers on board. Option c is not a good choice because if Breda were to ignore the flat tire and continue the run she would be jeopardizing the safety of her passengers and of other vehicles on the road. That leaves option d as the wisest choice. Taking a bus out of service at this point may be irritating to customers waiting for a ride, but it's better to make customers wait a few minutes for another bus than it would be to strand them in traffic with a flat tire.

Along with using common sense and good judgment, you are using another tool to answer this question—the process of elimination. As you read each option, you make a decision about whether you want to eliminate this possibility or keep it. Sometimes even if you don't know for sure where the right answer is, you can find it by pitching out all the wrong ones.

The temptation with situational judgment questions is to project your thoughts and feelings into the scenario. You may catch yourself chewing on your pencil thinking, "Well, I'd make a sign that says 'Flat Tire.' That's what I would do." That may be how this situation would play out in real life, but that's not one of your options, so this kind of thinking merely complicates the question.

Another temptation is to read more into the situation than is there. You may think, "Maybe the flat tire is really obvious to passengers. . . ." Use the information you *see on the page*, not the information that *could* be there, to make your decision.

THROUGH THEIR EYES

It's easy to say "think like a bus operator" if you know how bus operators think. The ideal way to learn is to ride buses and watch what drivers handle in real, day-to-day settings. Do what you can to look at the world through their eyes.

After you see for yourself what bus operators do, then arm yourself with the next few paragraphs.

Safety First

If your momma always told you "safety first" when you went out to play as a child, then you are well-trained for *this* job. The safety and well-being of everyone aboard your bus is Priority Number One—yes, even including the passenger who sneers at you every day when he tosses his money in the farebox.

The safety issue pops up in judgment questions fairly often. As you read the questions during the test, keep the "Safety First" motto in the forefront of your mind. If you think this way, the right answer may suddenly stand out as if it were in bold print. Ask yourself, "How does this situation affect the safety of my passengers?" If you asked yourself this question when you answered the sample question above, then you probably eliminated all the wrong choices without a second thought, keeping only the one that kept the bus passengers safe. Any answer that places anyone in danger is not going to be the one you want.

Medical Emergencies

Along with safety issues, some of the questions on the test may deal with medical emergency situations. Consider the following example:

2. Bus Operator Margaret Hess is pulling into a crowded bus stop. A passenger who is walking toward the rear door trips and hits his head on one of the seats as he falls. He is unconscious on the floor of the bus when Hess checks on him. What action should she take?
   a. don't move the passenger, and call the Command Center for medical assistance
   b. pick the passenger up, put him in an empty seat, and wait for him to wake up
   c. pour cold water on the passenger to wake him up
   d. elevate the passenger's feet and wait for him to wake up

You may be thinking to yourself that this is not a fair question because you wouldn't be able to pick out the right answer unless you knew all about first aid. Well, that's the very reason this question is an easy question. The only option that mentions calling for help is option **a,** and your common sense should tell you that you will need to call for help under these conditions. If you also happen to know a little first aid, you may have realized that you shouldn't move the passenger because you could make any possible neck or back injuries worse.

That's why option **b** is not a good choice: You should never move someone when you do not know the extent of the injuries. Option **c** is not a good choice because, while pouring water on an unconscious victim may look good on the movie screen, it's not something you'd want to do in the real world: the victim could choke. Option **d** is not a good choice because elevating the passenger's feet involves moving him. It's best to leave the passenger where he is until help arrives, unless you can tell, of course, that the way he is positioned creates a life-threatening situation (for instance, he can't breathe). Getting help should be your first priority, and that's why **a** is the best choice.

Most people have been exposed to basic first aid principles at school or work or even through television. Just in case they've slipped your mind, here are a few short, easy-to-learn rules that may make answering emergency medical situation questions much easier.

- Before you do anything else, call for help.
- Don't move an injured person unless fire or some other life-threatening situation endangers the victim.
- If you have been trained, begin cardiopulmonary resuscitation (CPR) if the injured person is not breathing.

- If an injured person is bleeding, apply direct pressure to the wound with your hand or a clean cloth. Keep the pressure on until help arrives.
- Don't give an injured person anything to drink, not even if the person asks for water.
- To keep shock from setting in, keep the injured person covered with a coat or blanket until help arrives.
- If live electrical wires are involved, do not touch the injured person or the vehicle the victim is in. Tell the victim not to move until help arrives.

Physical Contact

In a medical emergency, a certain amount of physical contact with the victim may be necessary. Touching passengers is not always a good idea, however. Whenever you see an option in a multiple-choice question that suggests you come into physical contact with a passenger, you'll want to look at that option closely, and most times you should reject it. Touching a customer who does not consent to that contact—for instance, during a disagreement or when the situation requires you to ask the customer to get off your bus—can open you up to a lawsuit and/or minor criminal charges. Common sense strongly recommends that you keep your hands to yourself—especially in our lawsuit-happy society. So, if one of the options in a question suggests that you touch a customer (other than in a situation such as helping a disabled person who has asked for help to board your bus), keep the liability issue in mind when picking your answer.

JUDGMENT IN PUBLIC RELATIONS

Some questions may deal not so much with routine or emergency situations as with your relationships with customers. You'll be asked to choose the answers that show you have the ability to use good judgment in a situation that will have an impact on how customers view both you and bus service in general. For example, suppose you see the following question:

3. You see an elderly woman hurrying toward your bus with an arm full of groceries. As the last passenger boards the bus and you are ready to pull away from the curb, you see that the woman has dropped her groceries about ten yards from the bus and is picking them up from the pavement. What action should you take?
   a. ask one of your regular passengers to get off and wait for the next bus with the woman
   b. wait for the woman to get on board the bus
   c. pretend you didn't notice the woman and leave
   d. shout out the window that you don't have time to wait and then leave

Option a creates more of a problem than it solves. It doesn't make sense to ask someone to get off the bus to wait with this woman, and most people would refuse anyway. Option c is not good public relations. You *did* see the woman hurrying toward your bus, and chances are a lot of passengers did too. Neither they nor the woman would think it was very professional of you to leave. Option d is just as unprofessional. Your best choice is to wait the few extra seconds it will take to allow this woman to reach your bus.

Simply put, this kind of question will test how you relate to the public. Can you make choices that will demonstrate that you can get along with others and treat people with respect? This is what the test maker *and* your potential employer want to know.

APPLICATION OF RULES AND PROCEDURES

Another kind of test question asks you to read rules, laws, policies, or procedures and then apply those guidelines to a hypothetical situation. You may still be able to use your good judgment and common sense in these questions, but even more important is your ability to read carefully and accurately.

These kinds of questions ask you to do something bus operators do every day: take their knowledge of transit policies and procedures and use that knowledge to decide what to do in a given situation. The questions don't expect you to know the rules or procedures; they're right there as part of the test question. And that's why your reading skills really come into play.

In application of procedures questions, you'll be given information about procedures and then asked to apply these procedures to a hypothetical situation. You might have to decide which step in a set of procedures is the next step to be taken in the situation, or you might have to decide whether a hypothetical bus operator followed the procedures properly in the situation given. In either case, you're being tested on your ability to follow directions, including your reading comprehension skills.

The question is usually preceded by a brief passage telling you about the procedure; for example:

When a bus operator discovers property that has been left on board a bus by a customer, the bus operator should follow these procedures:

1. Fill out a Found Property Slip stating what the object is, where it was found, and who found it.

2. Place the property in a safe area near the driver's seat until the end of the shift.

3. Turn in the property to the Lost and Found department.

4. Turn one copy of the Found Property Slip into Lost and Found and keep the other for personal files.

4. Bus Operator Hortensio Enrico is halfway through his shift when a boy approaches him holding a watch. He tells Enrico that the man who got off the bus two stops back left the watch on the seat. Enrico takes the watch, fills out a Found Property slip, and slips the watch and the slip into his bag near his seat. At the end of the day, he turns in a copy of the Found Property slip, keeping a copy for himself, and goes home. Enrico's actions were
   a. improper, because he didn't write down the watch owner's name
   b. proper, because he filled out the required paperwork
   c. improper, because he failed to turn in the watch to the Lost and Found department
   d. proper, because he kept the watch in his bag after the boy gave it to him

What the test maker wants you to do is study how Enrico handled the found property case and see if he followed his department's rules on handling found property.

Each option actually has two parts that require you to make two decisions. You have to decide if the bus operator acted properly or improperly, and then you have to decide if the reason stated in the option is correct or incorrect. In this case, option **c** is correct on both counts because Enrico did not act properly, according to the procedures for turning in found property. He should have turned the watch in at the end of his shift (Step 3).

These questions can be tricky if you read too fast or read only part of the answer choices. Take your time and make sure both parts of the answer are correct. For example, in option **b**, the second part of the answer is correct. That action, filling out the required paperwork, is what Enrico is supposed to do according to Step 1. However, if you look at the first part of the answer it says Enrico acted correctly in this situation because he filled out the Found Property Slip. This is not the *best* answer because Enrico did *not* act properly since he failed to turn in the found property at the end of his shift. Remember, there's only one *best* answer.

Tips for Answering Application Questions

- Read what's there, not what might have been there.
- Read through all the options before you choose an answer.
- Find the spot in the rule or procedure that supports your answer.

IMPROVING YOUR JUDGMENT SKILLS

You have more options than you may realize when it comes to honing your judgment skills—not only for the exam, but also for your career as a bus operator. There are some surprisingly simple exercises you can do in your everyday life that will get you ready.

WHAT IF . . .

Exam preparation is not *all* work. There's a game you can play in your mind that will help you prepare for the test. It's called "What If." You've played before, but you may not have been aware of it. "What if I won the lottery tomorrow? If I did, I'd empty my desk drawers on top of my supervisor's desk and run screaming out of the building." Sound familiar?

Some professional baseball players watch slow-motion videos of a batter with perfect form in the hope that by memorizing and studying his moves, they will be able to improve their own performance. And research shows that this works: In times of stress, people are more likely to carry out a task if they've practiced it—mentally or physically.

You can use the same idea in preparing to think like a bus operator. Take the time to go for a little bus ride. When you get on board, watch what's going on in the bus. Say to yourself, "*What* would I do *if* I were driving the bus and the man boarding the bus right now couldn't speak English and wanted to know how to pay the fare?" Then decide how you'd handle it. The situation you dream up, and the solution, may be one you see on the test, or it might be what happens to you when you are driving your own route some day.

If you've thought about a situation and arrived at a conclusion about what you would do under the circumstances, you've given your brain a plan of action for when the situation actually arises. Practice. At the very least it may add a whole new dimension to your bus-riding experience.

SELF-CONFIDENCE CHECKS

Practice your self-confidence. Odd advice? Not really. Self-confidence is what makes most people able to make decisions with a minimum of confusion and self-doubt. You need self-confidence so that you will make the right decisions as a test taker. If you aren't confident about your judgment skills and your ability to decide what to do in a situation, then you are likely to torture yourself with every judgment question.

Believe it or not, it is possible to practice self-confidence. Many people practice the opposite of self-confidence by thinking and saying things like "I don't know if I can do that" or "What if I can't do that?"

Start listening to yourself to see if you talk like that. And then turn it around. Tell yourself and others, "The civil service test is coming up and I intend to ace it." And "I know I will make a good bus operator. I know that when I read the test questions I can rely on my own good judgment to help me. My common sense will point me in the right direction."

This isn't bragging. It's how you set yourself up for success. You'll start thinking of what you need to do to ace the test. You're practicing self-confidence right now by reading this book. You are getting the tools you need to do the job. Your self-confidence has no option but to shoot straight up—and your score along with it.

READ, READ, READ

Reading is as vital on judgment questions as it is on questions that call themselves reading questions. This isn't the kind of reading you do when you are skimming a novel or skipping through articles in a newspaper. It's the kind where you not only have to pay attention to what the writer is telling you, but you must make decisions based on the information you've received. There's a whole chapter in this book on reading. Check out the suggestions there, under Additional Resources, on ways to improve your reading skills.

C·H·A·P·T·E·R

MATH

9

CHAPTER SUMMARY

This chapter gives you some important tips for dealing with math questions on a civil service exam and reviews some of the most commonly tested concepts. If you've forgotten most of your high school math or have math anxiety, this chapter is for you.

Not all civil service exams test your math knowledge, but many do. Knowledge of basic arithmetic, as well as the more complex kinds of reasoning necessary for algebra and geometry problems, are important qualifications for almost any profession. You have to be able to add up dollar figures, evaluate budgets, compute percentages, and other such tasks, both in your job and in your personal life. Even if your exam doesn't include math, you'll find that the material in this chapter will be useful on the job.

The math portion of the test covers the subjects you probably studied in grade school and high school. While every test is different, most emphasize arithmetic skills and word problems.

MATH STRATEGIES

- **Don't work in your head!** Use your test book or scratch paper to take notes, draw pictures, and calculate. Although you might think that you can solve math questions more quickly in your head, that's a good way to make mistakes. Write out each step.
- **Read a math question in *chunks*** rather than straight through from beginning to end. As you read each *chunk*, stop to think about what it means and make notes or draw a picture to represent that *chunk*.
- **When you get to the actual question, circle it.** This will keep you more focused as you solve the problem.
- **Glance at the answer choices for clues.** If they're fractions, you probably should do your work in fractions; if they're decimals, you should probably work in decimals; etc.
- **Make a plan of attack** to help you solve the problem.
- **If a question stumps you, try one of the *backdoor* approaches** explained in the next section. These are particularly useful for solving word problems.
- **When you get your answer, reread the circled question to make sure you've answered it.** This helps avoid the careless mistake of answering the wrong question.
- **Check your work after you get an answer.** Test-takers get a false sense of security when they get an answer that matches one of the multiple-choice answers. Here are some good ways to check your work *if you have time*:
    - Ask yourself if your answer is reasonable, if it makes sense.
    - Plug your answer back into the problem to make sure the problem holds together.
    - Do the question a second time, but use a different method.
- **Approximate when appropriate.** For example:
    - $5.98 + $8.97 is a little less than $15. (Add: $6 + $9)
    - .9876 × 5.0342 is close to 5. (Multiply: 1 × 5)
- **Skip hard questions and come back to them later.** Mark them in your test book so you can find them quickly.

BACKDOOR APPROACHES FOR ANSWERING QUESTIONS THAT PUZZLE YOU

Remember those word problems you dreaded in high school? Many of them are actually easier to solve by backdoor approaches. The two techniques that follow are terrific ways to solve multiple-choice word problems that you don't know how to solve with a straightforward approach. The first technique, *nice numbers*, is useful when there are unknowns (like x) in the text of the word problem, making the problem too abstract for you. The second technique, *working backwards*, presents a quick way to substitute numeric answer choices back into the problem to see which one works.

Nice Numbers

1. When a question contains unknowns, like x, plug nice numbers in for the unknowns. A nice number is easy to calculate with and makes sense in the problem.

2. Read the question with the nice numbers in place. Then solve it.

3. If the answer choices are all numbers, the choice that matches your answer is the right one.

4. If the answer choices contain unknowns, substitute the same nice numbers into **all** the answer choices. The choice that matches your answer is the right one. If more than one answer matches, do the problem again with different nice numbers. You'll only have to check the answer choices that have already matched.

> **Example:** Judi went shopping with p dollars in her pocket. If the price of shirts was s shirts for d dollars, what is the maximum number of shirts Judi could buy with the money in her pocket?

    a. psd **b.** $\frac{ps}{d}$ **c.** $\frac{pd}{s}$ **d.** $\frac{ds}{p}$

To solve this problem, let's try these nice numbers: $p = \$100$, $s = 2$; $d = \$25$. Now reread it with the numbers in place:

> Judi went shopping with *$100* in her pocket. If the price of shirts was *2* shirts for *$25*, what is the maximum number of shirts Judi could buy with the money in her pocket?

Since 2 shirts cost $25, that means that 4 shirts cost $50, and 8 shirts cost $100. So our answer is *8*. Let's substitute the nice numbers into all 4 answers:

    a. $100 \times 2 \times 25 = 5000$ **b.** $\frac{100 \times 2}{25} = 8$ **c.** $\frac{100 \times 25}{2} = 1250$ **d.** $\frac{25 \times 2}{100} = \frac{1}{2}$

The answer is **b** because it is the only one that matches our answer of 8.

Working Backwards

You can frequently solve a word problem by plugging the answer choices back into the text of the problem to see which one fits all the facts stated in the problem. The process is faster than you think because you'll probably only have to substitute one or two answers to find the right one.

    This approach works only when:

- All of the answer choices are numbers.
- You're asked to find a simple number, not a sum, product, difference, or ratio.

    Here's what to do:

1. Look at all the answer choices and begin with the one in the middle of the range. For example, if the answers are 14, 8, 2, 20, and 25, begin by plugging 14 into the problem.

2. If your choice doesn't work, eliminate it. Determine if you need a bigger or smaller answer.

3. Plug in one of the remaining choices.

4. If none of the answers work, you may have made a careless error. Begin again or look for your mistake.

> **Example:** Juan ate $\frac{1}{3}$ of the jellybeans. Maria then ate $\frac{3}{4}$ of the remaining jellybeans, which left 10 jellybeans. How many jellybeans were there to begin with?

    a. 60   **b.** 80   **c.** 90   **d.** 120   **e.** 140

Starting with the middle answer, let's assume there were **90** jellybeans to begin with:

Since Juan ate $\frac{1}{3}$ of them, that means he ate 30 ($\frac{1}{3} \times 90 = 30$), leaving 60 of them ($90 - 30 = 60$). Maria then ate $\frac{3}{4}$ of the 60 jellybeans, or 45 of them ($\frac{3}{4} \times 60 = 45$). That leaves 15 jellybeans ($60 - 45 = 15$).

The problem states that there were **10** jellybeans left, and we wound up with **15** of them. That indicates that we started with too big a number. Thus, 90, 120, and 140 are all wrong! With only two choices left, let's use common sense to decide which one to try. The next lower answer is only a little smaller than 90 and may not be small enough. So, let's try **60**:

Since Juan ate $\frac{1}{3}$ of them, that means he ate 20 ($\frac{1}{3} \times 60 = 20$), leaving 40 of them ($60 - 20 = 40$). Maria then ate $\frac{3}{4}$ of the 40 jellybeans, or 30 of them ($\frac{3}{4} \times 40 = 30$). That leaves 10 jellybeans ($40 - 30 = 10$).

Because this result of **10** jellybeans left agrees with the problem, the right answer is **a.**

WORD PROBLEMS

Many of the math problems on tests are word problems. A word problem can include any kind of math, including simple arithmetic, fractions, decimals, percentages, even algebra and geometry.

The hardest part of any word problem is translating English into math. When you read a problem, you can frequently translate it *word for word* from English statements into mathematical statements. At other times, however, a key word in the word problem hints at the mathematical operation to be performed. Here are the translation rules:

EQUALS   key words: is, are, has

English	Math
Bob **is** 18 years old.	B = 18
There **are** 7 hats.	H = 7
Judi **has** 5 books.	J = 5

ADDITION   key words: sum; more, greater, or older than; total; altogether

English	Math
The **sum** of two numbers is 10.	X + Y = 10
Karen has $5 **more than** Sam.	K = 5 + S
The base is 3″ **greater than** the height.	B = 3 + H
Judi is 2 years **older than** Tony.	J = 2 + T
The **total** of three numbers is 25.	A + B + C = 25
How much do Joan and Tom have **altogether**?	J + T = ?

SUBTRACTION   key words: difference, less or younger than, remain, left over

English	Math
The **difference** between two numbers is 17.	X + Y = 17
Mike has 5 **less** cats **than** twice the number Jan has.	M = 2J − 5
Jay is 2 years **younger than** Brett.	J = B − 2
After Carol ate 3 apples, R apples **remained**.	R = A − 3

MULTIPLICATION   key words: of, product, times

English	Math
20% **of** Matthew's baseball caps	$.20 \times M$
Half **of** the boys	$\frac{1}{2} \times B$
The **product** of two numbers is 12	$A \times B = 12$

DIVISION   key word: per

English	Math
15 drops **per** teaspoon	$\frac{15 \text{ drops}}{\text{teaspoon}}$
22 miles **per** gallon	$\frac{22 \text{ miles}}{\text{gallon}}$

DISTANCE FORMULA: DISTANCE = RATE × TIME

The key words are movement words like: plane, train, boat, car, walk, run, climb, swim

- How far did the **plane** travel in 4 hours if it averaged 300 miles per hour?

    $D = 300 \times 4$

    $D = 1200$ miles

- Ben **walked** 20 miles in 4 hours. What was his average speed?

    $20 = r \times 4$

    5 miles per hour $= r$

SOLVING A WORD PROBLEM USING THE TRANSLATION TABLE

Remember the problem at the beginning of this chapter about the jellybeans?

Juan ate $\frac{1}{3}$ of the jellybeans. Maria then ate $\frac{3}{4}$ of the remaining jellybeans, which left 10 jellybeans. How many jellybeans were there to begin with?

      a. 60   b. 80   c. 90   d. 120   e. 140

We solved it by *working backwards*. Now let's solve it using our translation rules.

Assume Juan started with J jellybeans. Eating $\frac{1}{3}$ of them means eating $\frac{1}{3} \times J$ jellybeans. Maria ate a fraction of the **remaining** jellybeans, which means we must **subtract** to find out how many are left: $J - \frac{1}{3} \times J = \frac{2}{3} \times J$. Maria then ate $\frac{3}{4}$, leaving $\frac{1}{4}$ of the $\frac{2}{3} \times J$ jellybeans, or $\frac{1}{4} \times \frac{2}{3} \times J$ *jellybeans. Multiplying out* $\frac{1}{4} \times \frac{2}{3} \times J$ gives $\frac{1}{6}J$ as the number of jellybeans left. The problem states that there were **10 jellybeans left**, meaning that we set $\frac{1}{6} \times J$ equal to 10:

$$\frac{1}{6} \times J = 10$$

Solving this equation for J gives $J = 60$. Thus, the right answer is **a** (the same answer we got when we *worked backwards*). As you can see, both methods—working backwards and translating from English to math—work. You should use whichever method is more comfortable for you.

PRACTICE WORD PROBLEMS

You will find word problems using fractions, decimals, and percentages in those sections of this chapter. For now, practice using the translation table on problems that just require you to work with basic arithmetic. Answers are at the end of the chapter.

_____ **1.** Joan went shopping with $100 and returned home with only $18.42. How much money did she spend?

    a. $81.58   **b.** $72.68   **c.** $72.58   **d.** $71.68   **e.** $71.58

_____ **2.** Mark invited ten friends to a party. Each friend brought 3 guests. How many people came to the party, excluding Mark?

    a. 3   **b.** 10   **c.** 30   **d.** 40   **e.** 41

_____ **3.** The office secretary can type 80 words per minute on his word processor. How many minutes will it take him to type a report containing 760 words?

    a. 8   **b.** $8\frac{1}{2}$ **c.** 9   **d.** $9\frac{1}{2}$ **e.** 10

_____ **4.** Mr. Wallace is writing a budget request to upgrade his personal computer system. He wants to purchase 4 mb of RAM, which will cost $100, two new software programs at $350 each, a tape backup system for $249, and an additional tape for $25. What is the total amount Mr. Wallace should write on his budget request?

    a. $724   **b.** $974   **c.** $1049   **d.** $1064   **e.** $1074

FRACTION REVIEW

Problems involving fractions may be straightforward calculation questions, or they may be word problems. Typically, they ask you to add, subtract, multiply, divide, or compare fractions.

WORKING WITH FRACTIONS

A fraction is a part of something.

LearningExpress

20 Academy Street, P.O. Box 7100, Norwalk, CT 06852-9879

To provide you with the best test prep, basic skills, and
career materials, we would appreciate your help.
Please answer the following questions and return this postage paid piece.
Thank you for your time!

Name : _____

Address : _____

_____

Age : _____ Sex : ☐ Male ☐ Female

Highest Level of School Completed : ☐ High School ☐ College

1) I am currently :

    A student — Year/level: _____

    Employed — Job title: _____

    Other — Please explain: _____

2) Jobs/careers of interest to me are :

    1. _____

    2. _____

    3. _____

3) If you are a student, did your guidance/career counselor provide
you with job information/materials? _____

4) What newspapers and/or magazines do you subscribe to or
read regularly? _____

_____

5) Do you own a computer? _____

    If so, do you have Internet access? _____

    How often do you go on-line? _____

6) The last time you visited a bookstore, did you make a purchase?

_____

Have you purchased career-related materials from bookstores?

_____

7) Do you subscribe to cable TV? _____

    Which channels to you watch regularly (please give network
    letters rather than channel numbers)?

    _____

    _____

8) Which radio stations do you listen to regularly (please give call
    letters and city name)?

    _____

    _____

9) How did you hear about the book you just purchased from
    LearningExpress?

    An ad? _____

    If so, where? _____

    An order form in the back of another book? _____

    A recommendation? _____

    A bookstore? _____

    Other? _____

10) Title of the book this card came from:

    _____

LearningExpress books are also available in the test prep/study guide section of your local bookstore.

LEARNINGEXPRESS

The leading publisher of customized career and test preparation books!

LearningExpress is an affiliate of Random House, Inc.

Example: Let's say that a pizza was cut into 8 equal slices and you ate 3 of them. The fraction $\frac{3}{8}$ tells you what part of the pizza you ate. The pizza below shows this: 3 of the 8 pieces (the ones you ate) are shaded.

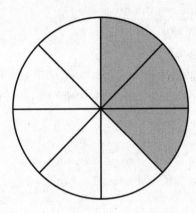

Three Kinds of Fractions

Proper fraction: The top number is less than the bottom number:

$\frac{1}{2}$; $\frac{2}{3}$; $\frac{4}{9}$; $\frac{8}{13}$

The value of a proper fraction is less than 1.

Improper fraction: The top number is greater than or equal to the bottom number:

$\frac{3}{2}$; $\frac{5}{3}$; $\frac{14}{9}$; $\frac{12}{12}$

The value of an improper fraction is 1 or more.

Mixed number: A fraction written to the right of a whole number:

$3\frac{1}{2}$; $4\frac{2}{3}$; $12\frac{3}{4}$; $24\frac{3}{4}$

The value of a mixed number is more than 1: it is the sum of the whole number plus the fraction.

Changing Improper Fractions into Mixed or Whole Numbers

It's easier to add and subtract fractions that are mixed numbers rather than improper fractions. To change an improper fraction, say $\frac{13}{2}$, into a mixed number, follow these steps:

1. Divide the bottom number (2) into the top number (13) to get the whole number portion (6) of the mixed number:

$$\begin{array}{r} 6 \\ 2\overline{)13} \\ \underline{12} \\ 1 \end{array}$$

2. Write the remainder of the division (1) over the old bottom number (2): $6\frac{1}{2}$

3. Check: Change the mixed number back into an improper fraction (see steps below).

Changing Mixed Numbers into Improper Fractions

It's easier multiply and divide fractions when you're working with improper fractions rather than mixed numbers. To change a mixed number, say $2\frac{3}{4}$, into an improper fraction, follow these steps:

1. Multiply the whole number (2) by the bottom number (4). $2 \times 4 = 8$
2. Add the result (8) to the top number (3). $8 + 3 = 11$
3. Put the total (11) over the bottom number (4). $\frac{11}{4}$
4. Check: Reverse the process by changing the improper fraction into a mixed
   number. If you get back the number you started with, your answer is right.

Reducing Fractions

Reducing a fraction means writing it in *lowest terms*, that is, with smaller numbers. For instance, 50¢ is $\frac{50}{100}$ of a dollar, or $\frac{1}{2}$ of a dollar. In fact, if you have 50¢ in your pocket, you say that you have half a dollar. Reducing a fraction does not change its value.

Follow these steps to reduce a fraction:

1. Find a whole number that divides *evenly* into both numbers that make up the fraction.
2. Divide that number into the top of the fraction, and replace the top of the fraction with the quotient (the answer you got when you divided).
3. Do the same thing to the bottom number.
4. Repeat the first 3 steps until you can't find a number that divides evenly into both numbers of the fraction.

For example, let's reduce $\frac{8}{24}$. We could do it in 2 steps: $\frac{8 \div 4}{24 \div 4} = \frac{2}{6}$; then $\frac{2 \div 2}{6 \div 2} = \frac{1}{3}$. Or we could do it in a single step: $\frac{8 \div 8}{24 \div 8} = \frac{1}{3}$.

Shortcut: When the top and bottom numbers both end in zeroes, cross out the same number of zeroes in both numbers to begin the reducing process. For example, $\frac{300}{4000}$ reduces to $\frac{3}{40}$ when you cross out 2 zeroes in both numbers.

Whenever you do arithmetic with fractions, reduce your answer. On a multiple-choice test, don't panic if your answer isn't listed. Try to reduce it and then compare it to the choices.

Reduce these fractions to lowest terms:

_____ **5.** $\frac{3}{12}$

_____ **6.** $\frac{14}{35}$

_____ **7.** $\frac{27}{72}$

Raising Fractions to Higher Terms

Before you can add and subtract fractions, you have to know how to raise a fraction to higher terms. This is actually the opposite of reducing a fraction.

Follow these steps to raise $\frac{2}{3}$ to 24ths:

1. Divide the old bottom number (3) into the new one (24): $3\overline{)24} = 8$
2. Multiply the answer (8) by the old top number (2): $2 \times 8 = 16$
3. Put the answer (16) over the new bottom number (24): $\frac{16}{24}$
4. Check: Reduce the new fraction to see if you get back the original one: $\frac{16 \div 8}{24 \div 8} = \frac{2}{3}$

Raise these fractions to higher terms:

_____ **8.** $\frac{5}{12} = \frac{}{24}$

_____ **9.** $\frac{2}{9} = \frac{}{27}$

_____ **10.** $\frac{2}{5} = \frac{}{500}$

ADDING FRACTIONS

If the fractions have the same bottom numbers, just add the top numbers together and write the total over the bottom number.

Examples: $\frac{2}{9} + \frac{4}{9} = \frac{2+4}{9} = \frac{6}{9}$ Reduce the sum: $\frac{2}{3}$

$\frac{5}{8} + \frac{7}{8} = \frac{12}{8}$ Change the sum to a mixed number: $1\frac{4}{8}$; then reduce: $1\frac{1}{2}$

There are a few extra steps to add mixed numbers with the same bottom numbers, say $2\frac{3}{5} + 1\frac{4}{5}$:

1. Add the fractions: $\frac{3}{5} + \frac{4}{5} = \frac{7}{5}$
2. Change the improper fraction into a mixed number: $\frac{7}{5} = 1\frac{2}{5}$
3. Add the whole numbers: $2 + 1 = 3$
4. Add the results of steps 2 and 3: $1\frac{2}{5} + 3 = 4\frac{2}{5}$

Finding the Least Common Denominator

If the fractions you want to add don't have the same bottom number, you'll have to raise some or all of the fractions to higher terms so that they all have the same bottom number, called the **common denominator.** All of the original bottom numbers divide evenly into the common denominator. If it is the smallest number that they all divide evenly into, it is called the **least common denominator (LCD).**

Here are a few tips for finding the LCD, the smallest number that all the bottom numbers evenly divide into:

- See if all the bottom numbers divide evenly into the biggest bottom number.
- Check out the multiplication table of the largest bottom number until you find a number that all the other bottom numbers evenly divide into.

- When all else fails, multiply all the bottom numbers together.

  Example: $\frac{2}{3} + \frac{4}{5}$

1. Find the LCD. Multiply the bottom numbers: $3 \times 5 = 15$

2. Raise each fraction to 15ths:

$$\frac{2}{3} = \frac{10}{15}$$
$$+ \frac{4}{5} = \frac{12}{15}$$
$$\overline{\quad\quad \frac{22}{15}}$$

3. Add as usual:

Try these addition problems:

_____**11.** $\frac{3}{4} + \frac{1}{6}$

_____**12.** $\frac{7}{8} + \frac{2}{3} + \frac{3}{4}$

_____**13.** $4\frac{1}{3} + 2\frac{3}{4} + \frac{1}{6}$

SUBTRACTING FRACTIONS

If the fractions have the same bottom numbers, just subtract the top numbers and write the difference over the bottom number.

  Example: $\frac{4}{9} - \frac{3}{9} = \frac{4-3}{9} = \frac{1}{9}$

  If the fractions you want to subtract don't have the same bottom number, you'll have to raise some or all of the fractions to higher terms so that they all have the same bottom number, or LCD. If you forgot how to find the LCD, just read the section on adding fractions with different bottom numbers.

  Example: $\frac{5}{6} - \frac{3}{4}$

1. Raise each fraction to 12ths because 12 is the LCD, the smallest number that 6 and 4 both divide into evenly:

$$\frac{5}{6} = \frac{10}{12}$$
$$- \frac{3}{4} = \frac{9}{12}$$
$$\overline{\quad\quad \frac{1}{12}}$$

2. Subtract as usual:

  Subtracting mixed numbers with the same bottom number is similar to adding mixed numbers.

  Example: $4\frac{3}{5} - 1\frac{2}{5}$

1. Subtract the fractions: $\frac{3}{5} - \frac{2}{5} = \frac{1}{5}$

2. Subtract the whole numbers: $4 - 1 = 3$

3. Add the results of steps 1 and 2: $\frac{1}{5} + 3 = 3\frac{1}{5}$

  Sometimes there is an extra "borrowing" step when you subtract mixed numbers with the same bottom numbers, say $7\frac{3}{5} - 2\frac{4}{5}$:

1. You can't subtract the fractions the way they are because $\frac{4}{5}$ is bigger than $\frac{3}{5}$.

So you borrow 1 from the 7, making it 6, and change that 1 to $\frac{5}{5}$ because

5 is the bottom number: $\qquad 7\frac{3}{5} = 6\frac{5}{5} + \frac{3}{5}$

2. Add the numbers from step 1: $\qquad 6\frac{5}{5} + \frac{3}{5} = 6\frac{8}{5}$

3. Now you have a different version of the original problem: $\qquad 6\frac{8}{5} - 2\frac{4}{5}$

4. Subtract the fractional parts of the two mixed numbers: $\qquad \frac{8}{5} - \frac{4}{5} = \frac{4}{5}$

5. Subtract the whole number parts of the two mixed numbers: $\qquad 6 - 2 = 4$

6. Add the results of the last 2 steps together: $\qquad 4 + \frac{4}{5} = 4\frac{4}{5}$

Try these subtraction problems:

_____**14.** $\frac{4}{5} - \frac{2}{3}$

_____**15.** $\frac{7}{8} - \frac{1}{4} - \frac{1}{2}$

_____**16.** $4\frac{1}{3} - 2\frac{3}{4}$

Now let's put what you've learned about adding and subtracting fractions to work in some real-life problems.

_____**17.** Patrolman Peterson drove $3\frac{1}{2}$ miles to the police station. Then he drove $4\frac{3}{4}$ miles to his first assignment. When he left there, he drove 2 miles to his next assignment. Then he drove $3\frac{2}{3}$ miles back to the police station for a meeting. Finally, he drove $3\frac{1}{2}$ miles home. How many miles did he travel in total?

  a. $17\frac{5}{12}$ **b.** $16\frac{5}{12}$ **c.** $15\frac{7}{12}$ **d.** $15\frac{5}{12}$ **e.** $13\frac{11}{12}$

_____**18.** Before leaving the fire station, Firefighter Sorensen noted that the mileage gauge on Engine 2 registered $4{,}357\frac{4}{10}$ miles. When he arrived at the scene of the fire, the mileage gauge then registered $4{,}400\frac{1}{10}$ miles. How many miles did he drive from the station to the fire scene?

  a. $42\frac{3}{10}$ **b.** $42\frac{7}{10}$ **c.** $43\frac{7}{10}$ **d.** $47\frac{2}{10}$ **e.** $57\frac{3}{10}$

MULTIPLYING FRACTIONS

Multiplying fractions is actually easier than adding them. All you do is multiply the top numbers and then multiply the bottom numbers.

  Examples: $\frac{2}{3} \times \frac{5}{7} = \frac{2 \times 5}{3 \times 7} = \frac{10}{21}$ $\frac{1}{2} \times \frac{3}{5} \times \frac{7}{4} = \frac{1 \times 3 \times 7}{2 \times 5 \times 4} = \frac{21}{40}$

Sometimes you can *cancel* before multiplying. Cancelling is a shortcut that makes the multiplication go faster because you're multiplying with smaller numbers. It's very similar to reducing: if there is a number that divides evenly into a top number and bottom number, do that division before multiplying. If you forget to cancel, you'll still get the right answer, but you'll have to reduce it.

Example: $\frac{5}{6} \times \frac{9}{20}$

1. Cancel the 6 and the 9 by dividing 3 into both of them: $6 \div 3 = 2$ and $9 \div 3 = 3$. Cross out the 6 and the 9.

$$\frac{5}{\overset{}{\underset{2}{6}}} \times \frac{9}{20}^{3}$$

2. Cancel the 5 and the 20 by dividing 5 into both of them: $5 \div 5 = 1$ and $20 \div 5 = 4$. Cross out the 5 and the 20.

$$\frac{^{1}5}{\underset{2}{6}} \times \frac{9}{20}^{3}_{4}$$

3. Multiply across the new top numbers and the new bottom numbers:

$$\frac{1 \times 3}{2 \times 4} = \frac{3}{8}$$

Try these multiplication problems:

_____**19.** $\frac{1}{5} \times \frac{2}{3}$

_____**20.** $\frac{2}{3} \times \frac{4}{7} \times \frac{3}{5}$

_____**21.** $\frac{3}{4} \times \frac{8}{9}$

To multiply a fraction by a whole number, first rewrite the whole number as a fraction with a bottom number of 1:

Example: $5 \times \frac{2}{3} = \frac{5}{1} \times \frac{2}{3} = \frac{10}{3}$ (Optional: convert $\frac{10}{3}$ to a mixed number: $3\frac{1}{3}$)

To multiply with mixed numbers, it's easier to change them to improper fractions before multiplying.

Example: $4\frac{2}{3} \times 5\frac{1}{2}$

1. Convert $4\frac{2}{3}$ to an improper fraction:

$$4\frac{2}{3} = \frac{4 \times 3 + 2}{3} = \frac{14}{3}$$

2. Convert $5\frac{1}{2}$ to an improper fraction:

$$5\frac{1}{2} = \frac{5 \times 2 + 1}{2} = \frac{11}{2}$$

3. Cancel and multiply the fractions:

$$\frac{\overset{7}{14}}{3} \times \frac{11}{\underset{1}{2}} = \frac{77}{3}$$

4. Optional: convert the improper fraction to a mixed number:

$$\frac{77}{3} = 25\frac{2}{3}$$

Now try these multiplication problems with mixed numbers and whole numbers:

_____**22.** $4\frac{1}{3} \times \frac{2}{5}$

_____**23.** $2\frac{1}{2} \times 6$

_____**24.** $3\frac{3}{4} \times 4\frac{2}{5}$

Here are a few more real-life problems to test your skills:

_____ **25.** After driving $\frac{2}{3}$ of the 15 miles to work, Mr. Stone stopped to make a phone call. How many miles had he driven when he made his call?

a. 5   b. $7\frac{1}{2}$ c. 10   d. 12   e. $15\frac{2}{3}$

_____ **26.** If Henry worked $\frac{3}{4}$ of a 40-hour week, how many hours did he work?

a. $7\frac{1}{2}$ b. 10   c. 20   d. 25   e. 30

_____ **27.** Technician Chin makes \$14.00 an hour. When she works more than 8 hours a day, she gets overtime pay of $1\frac{1}{2}$ times her regular hourly wage for the extra hours. How much did she earn for working 11 hours in one day?

a. \$77   b. \$154   c. \$175   d. \$210   e. \$231

DIVIDING FRACTIONS

To divide one fraction by a second fraction, invert the second fraction (that is, flip the top and bottom numbers) and then multiply. That's all there is to it!

    Example: $\frac{1}{2} \div \frac{3}{5}$

1. Invert the second fraction ($\frac{3}{5}$): $\frac{5}{3}$

2. Change the division sign ($\div$) to a multiplication sign ($\times$)

3. Multiply the first fraction by the new second fraction: $\frac{1}{2} \times \frac{5}{3} = \frac{1 \times 5}{2 \times 3} = \frac{5}{6}$

    To divide a fraction by a whole number, first change the whole number to a fraction by putting it over 1. Then follow the division steps above.

    Example: $\frac{3}{5} \div 2 = \frac{3}{5} \div \frac{2}{1} = \frac{3}{5} \times \frac{1}{2} = \frac{3 \times 1}{5 \times 2} = \frac{3}{10}$

When the division problem has a mixed number, convert it to an improper fraction and then divide as usual.

    Example: $2\frac{3}{4} \div \frac{1}{6}$

1. Convert $2\frac{3}{4}$ to an improper fraction: $2\frac{3}{4} = \frac{2 \times 4 + 3}{4} = \frac{11}{4}$

2. Divide $\frac{11}{4}$ by $\frac{1}{6}$: $\frac{11}{4} \div \frac{1}{6} = \frac{11}{4} \times \frac{6}{1}$

3. Flip $\frac{1}{6}$ to $\frac{6}{1}$, change $\div$ to $\times$, cancel and multiply: $\frac{11}{\underset{2}{4}} \times \frac{\overset{3}{6}}{1} = \frac{11 \times 3}{2 \times 1} = \frac{33}{2}$

Here are a few division problems to try:

_____ **28.** $\frac{1}{3} \div \frac{2}{3}$

_____ **29.** $2\frac{3}{4} \div \frac{1}{2}$

_____**30.** $\frac{3}{5} \div 3$

_____**31.** $3\frac{3}{4} \div 2\frac{1}{3}$

Let's wrap this up with some real-life problems.

_____**32.** If four friends evenly split $6\frac{1}{2}$ pounds of candy, how many pounds of candy does each friend get?
   a. $\frac{8}{13}$ **b.** $1\frac{5}{8}$ **c.** $1\frac{1}{2}$ **d.** $1\frac{5}{13}$ **e.** 4

_____**33.** How many $2\frac{1}{2}$-pound chunks of cheese can be cut from a single 20-pound piece of cheese?
   a. 2   **b.** 4   **c.** 6   **d.** 8   **e.** 10

_____**34.** Ms. Goldbaum earned $36.75 for working $3\frac{1}{2}$ hours. What was her hourly wage?
   a. $10.00   **b.** $10.50   **c.** $10.75   **d.** $12.00   **e.** $12.25

Decimals

WHAT IS A DECIMAL?

A decimal is a special kind of fraction. You use decimals every day when you deal with money—$10.35 is a decimal that represents 10 dollars and 35 cents. The decimal point separates the dollars from the cents. Because there are 100 cents in one dollar, 1¢ is $\frac{1}{100}$ of a dollar, or $.01.

Each decimal digit to the right of the decimal point has a name:

Example: .1 = 1 tenth = $\frac{1}{10}$
       .02 = 2 hundredths = $\frac{2}{100}$
       .003 = 3 thousandths = $\frac{3}{1000}$
       .0004 = 4 ten-thousandths = $\frac{4}{10,000}$

When you add zeroes after the rightmost decimal place, you don't change the value of the decimal. For example, 6.17 is the same as all of these:

6.170

6.1700

6.17000000000000000

If there are digits on both sides of the decimal point (like 10.35), the number is called a mixed decimal. If there are digits only to the right of the decimal point (like .53), the number is called a decimal. A whole number (like 15) is understood to have a decimal point at its right (15.). Thus, 15 is the same as 15.0, 15.00, 15.000, and so on.

CHANGING FRACTIONS TO DECIMALS

To change a fraction to a decimal, divide the bottom number into the top number after you put a decimal point and a few zeroes on the right of the top number. When you divide, bring the decimal point up into your answer.

Example: Change $\frac{3}{4}$ to a decimal.

1. Add a decimal point and 2 zeroes to the top number (3): 3.00

2. Divide the bottom number (4) into 3.00:

Bring the decimal point up into the answer:

$$\begin{array}{r} .75 \\ 4\overline{)3.00} \\ \underline{2\,8} \\ 20 \\ \underline{20} \\ 0 \end{array}$$

3. The quotient (result of the division) is the answer: .75

Some fractions may require you to add many decimal zeroes in order for the division to come out evenly. In fact, when you convert a fraction like $\frac{2}{3}$ to a decimal, you can keep adding decimal zeroes to the top number forever because the division will never come out evenly! As you divide 3 into 2, you'll keep getting 6's:

$$2 \div 3 = .6666666666 \text{ etc}$$

This is called a *repeating decimal* and it can be written as $.66\overline{6}$ or as $.66\frac{2}{3}$. You can approximate it as .67, .667, .6667, and so on.

CHANGING DECIMALS TO FRACTIONS

To change a decimal to a fraction, write the digits of the decimal as the top number of a fraction and write the decimal's name as the bottom number of the fraction. Then reduce the fraction, if possible.

Example: .018

1. Write 18 as the top of the fraction: $\frac{18}{}$

2. Three places to the right of the decimal means *thousandths,* so write 1000 as the bottom number: $\frac{18}{1000}$

3. Reduce by dividing 2 into the top and bottom numbers: $\frac{18 \div 2}{1000 \div 2} = \frac{9}{500}$

Change these decimals or mixed decimals to fractions:

_____**35.** .005

_____**36.** 3.48

_____**37.** 123.456

COMPARING DECIMALS

Because decimals are easier to compare when they have the same number of digits after the decimal point, tack zeroes onto the end of the shorter decimals. Then all you have to do is compare the numbers as if the decimal points weren't there:

Example: Compare .08 and .1

1. Tack one zero at the end of .1: .10
2. To compare .10 to .08, just compare 10 to 8.
3. Since 10 is larger than 8, .1 is larger than .08.

ADDING AND SUBTRACTING DECIMALS

To add or subtract decimals, line them up so their decimal points are even. You may want to tack on zeroes at the end of shorter decimals so you can keep all your digits lined up evenly. Remember, if a number doesn't have a decimal point, then put one at the right end of the number.

Example: 1.23 + 57 + .038

1. Line up the numbers like this:

$$\begin{array}{r} 1.230 \\ 57.000 \\ + .038 \\ \hline \end{array}$$

2. Add:

$$58.268$$

Example: 1.23 − .038

1. Line up the numbers like this:

$$\begin{array}{r} 1.230 \\ - .038 \\ \hline \end{array}$$

2. Subtract:

$$1.192$$

Try these addition and subtraction problems:

_____**38.** .905 + .02 + 3.075

_____**39.** .005 + 8 + .3

_____**40.** 3.48 − 2.573

_____**41.** 123.456 − 122

_____ **42.** Officer Peterson drove 3.7 miles to the state park. He then walked 1.6 miles around the park to make sure everything was all right. He got back into the car, drove 2.75 miles to check on a broken traffic light and then drove 2 miles back to the police station. How many miles did he drive in total?

a. 8.05   b. 8.45   c. 8.8   d. 10   e. 10.05

_____ **43.** The average number of emergency room visits at City Hospital fell from 486.4 per week to 402.5 per week. By how many emergency room visits per week did the average fall?

a. 73.9   b. 83   c. 83.1   d. 83.9   e. 84.9

MULTIPLYING DECIMALS

To multiply decimals, ignore the decimal points and just multiply the numbers. Then count the total number of decimal digits (the digits to the *right* of the decimal point) in the numbers you're multiplying. Count off that number of digits in your answer beginning at the right side and put the decimal point to the *left* of those digits.

Example: 215.7×2.4

1. Multiply 2157 times 24:

$$\begin{array}{r} 2157 \\ \times\ \ 24 \\ \hline 8628 \\ 4314\ \ \\ \hline 51768 \end{array}$$

2. Because there are a total of 2 decimal digits in 215.7 and 2.4, count off 2 places from the right in 51768, placing the decimal point to the *left* of the last 2 digits:

517.68

If your answer doesn't have enough digits, tack zeroes on to the left of the answer.

Example: $.03 \times .006$

1. Multiply 3 times 6: $3 \times 6 = 18$

2. You need 5 decimal digits in your answer, so tack on 3 zeroes: 00018

3. Put the decimal point at the front of the number (which is 5 digits in from the right):   .00018

You can practice multiplying decimals with these:

_____ **44.** $.05 \times .6$

_____ **45.** $.053 \times 6.4$

_____ **46.** $38.1 \times .0184$

_____**47.** Joe earns $14.50 per hour. Last week he worked 37.5 hours. How much money did he earn that week?

    a. $518.00   **b.** $518.50   **c.** $525.00   **d.** $536.50   **e.** $543.75

_____**48.** Nuts cost $3.50 per pound. Approximately how much will 4.25 pounds of nuts cost?

    a. $12.25   **b.** $12.50   **c.** $12.88   **d.** $14.50   **e.** $14.88

DIVIDING DECIMALS

To divide a decimal by a whole number, set up the division ($8\overline{).256}$) and immediately bring the decimal point straight up into the answer ($8\overline{).256}$). Then divide as you would normally divide whole numbers:

Example:

$$
\begin{array}{r}
.032 \\
8\overline{).256} \\
\underline{0} \\
25 \\
\underline{24} \\
16 \\
\underline{16} \\
0
\end{array}
$$

To divide any number by a decimal, there is an extra step to perform before you can divide. Move the decimal point to the very right of the number you're dividing by, counting the number of places you're moving it. Then move the decimal point the same number of places to the right in the number you're dividing into. In other words, first change the problem to one in which you're dividing by a whole number.

Example: $.06\overline{)1.218}$

1. Because there are 2 decimal digits in .06, move the decimal point 2 places to the right in both numbers and move the decimal point straight up into the answer:

    $.06.\overline{)1.21.8}$

2. Divide using the new numbers:

$$
\begin{array}{r}
20.3 \\
6\overline{)121.8} \\
\underline{12} \\
01 \\
\underline{00} \\
18 \\
\underline{18} \\
0
\end{array}
$$

Under certain conditions, you have to tack on zeroes to the right of the last decimal digit in number you're dividing into:

- If there aren't enough digits for you to move the decimal point to the right, or
- If the answer doesn't come out evenly when you do the division, or
- If you're dividing a whole number by a decimal. Then you'll have to tack on the decimal point as well as some zeroes.

Try your skills on these division problems:

_____ **49.** $7\overline{)9.8}$

_____ **50.** $.0004\overline{).0512}$

_____ **51.** $.05\overline{)28.6}$

_____ **52.** $.14\overline{)196}$

_____ **53.** If James Worthington drove his truck 92.4 miles in 2.1 hours, what was his average speed in miles per hour?

    a. 41   b. 44   c. 90.3   d. 94.5   e. 194.04

_____ **54.** Mary Sanders walked a total of 18.6 miles in 4 days. On average, how many miles did she walk each day?

    a. 4.15   b. 4.60   c. 4.65   d. 22.60   e. 74.40

PERCENTS

WHAT IS A PERCENT?

A percent is a special kind of fraction or part of something. The bottom number (the *denominator*) is always 100. For example, 17% is the same as $\frac{17}{100}$. Literally, the word *percent* means *per 100 parts*. The root *cent* means 100: a *century* is 100 years, there are 100 *cents* in a dollar, etc. Thus, 17% means 17 parts out of 100. Because fractions can also be expressed as decimals, 17% is also equivalent to .17, which is 17 hundredths.

    You come into contact with percents every day. Sales tax, interest, and discounts are just a few common examples.

    If you're shaky on fractions, you may want to review the fraction section before reading further.

CHANGING A DECIMAL TO A PERCENT AND VICE VERSA

To change a decimal to a percent, move the decimal point two places to the **right** and tack on a percent sign (%) at the end. If the decimal point moves to the very right of the number, you don't have to write the decimal point. If there aren't enough places to move the decimal point, add zeroes on the **right** before moving the decimal point.

    To change a percent to a decimal, drop off the percent sign and move the decimal point two places to the **left**. If there aren't enough places to move the decimal point, add zeroes on the **left** before moving the decimal point.

Try changing these decimals to percents:

_____**55.** .45

_____**56.** .008

_____**57.** $.16\frac{2}{3}$

Now change these percents to decimals:

_____**58.** 12%

_____**59.** $87\frac{1}{2}\%$

_____**60.** 250%

CHANGING A FRACTION TO A PERCENT AND VICE VERSA

To change a fraction to a percent, there are two techniques. Each is illustrated by changing the fraction $\frac{1}{4}$ to a percent:

Technique 1: Multiply the fraction by 100%.
Multiply $\frac{1}{4}$ by 100%:

$$\frac{1}{\underset{1}{4}} \times \frac{\overset{25}{\cancel{100\%}}}{1} = 25\%$$

Technique 2: Divide the fraction's bottom number into the top number; then move the decimal point two places to the **right** and tack on a percent sign (%).
Divide 4 into 1 and move the decimal point 2 places to the right:

$$4\overline{)1.00}^{\;.25} \qquad .25 = 25\%$$

To change a percent to a fraction, remove the percent sign and write the number over 100. Then reduce if possible.

Example: Change 4% to a fraction

1. Remove the % and write the fraction 4 over 100: $\frac{4}{100}$

2. Reduce: $\frac{4 \div 4}{100 \div 4} = \frac{1}{25}$

Here's a more complicated example: Change $16\frac{2}{3}\%$ to a fraction

1. Remove the % and write the fraction $16\frac{2}{3}$ over 100: $\frac{16\frac{2}{3}}{100}$

2. Since a fraction means "top number divided by bottom number," rewrite the fraction as a division problem: $16\frac{2}{3} \div 100$

3. Change the mixed number ($16\frac{2}{3}$) to an improper fraction ($\frac{50}{3}$): $\frac{50}{3} \div \frac{100}{1}$

4. Flip the second fraction ($\frac{100}{1}$) and multiply: $\frac{\overset{1}{\cancel{50}}}{3} \times \frac{1}{\underset{2}{\cancel{100}}} = \frac{1}{6}$

Try changing these fractions to percents:

_____ **61.** $\frac{1}{8}$

_____ **62.** $\frac{13}{25}$

_____ **63.** $\frac{7}{12}$

Now change these percents to fractions:

_____ **64.** 95%

_____ **65.** $37\frac{1}{2}$%

_____ **66.** 125%

Sometimes it is more convenient to work with a percentage as a fraction or a decimal. Rather than have to *calculate* the equivalent fraction or decimal, consider memorizing the equivalence table below. Not only will this increase your efficiency on the math test, but it will also be practical for real life situations.

CONVERSION TABLE

Decimal	%	Fraction
.25	25%	$\frac{1}{4}$
.50	50%	$\frac{1}{2}$
.75	75%	$\frac{3}{4}$
.10	10%	$\frac{1}{10}$
.20	20%	$\frac{1}{5}$
.40	40%	$\frac{2}{5}$
.60	60%	$\frac{3}{5}$
.80	80%	$\frac{4}{5}$
$.33\overline{3}$	$33\frac{1}{3}$%	$\frac{1}{3}$
$.66\overline{6}$	$66\frac{2}{3}$%	$\frac{2}{3}$

PERCENT WORD PROBLEMS

Word problems involving percents come in three main varieties:

- Find a percent of a whole.

     Example: What is 30% of 40?

- Find what percent one number is of another number.

     Example: 12 is what percent of 40?

- Find the whole when the percent of it is given.

     Example: 12 is 30% of what number?

While each variety has its own approach, there is a single shortcut formula you can use to solve each of these:

$$\frac{is}{of} = \frac{\%}{100}$$

The *is* is the number that usually follows or is just before the word *is* in the question.

The *of* is the number that usually follows the word *of* in the question.

The % is the number that in front of the % or **percent** in the question.

Or you may think of the shortcut formula as:

$$\frac{part}{whole} = \frac{\%}{100}$$

To solve each of the three varieties, we're going to use the fact that the **cross-products** are equal. The cross-products are the products of the numbers diagonally across from each other. Remembering that *product* means *multiply*, here's how to create the cross-products for the percent shortcut:

$$\frac{part}{whole} = \frac{\%}{100}$$
$$part \times 100 = whole \times \%$$

Here's how to use the shortcut with cross-products:

- Find a percent of a whole.

    What is 30% of 40?

    30 is the % and 40 is the *of* number:

    Cross-multiply and solve for *is*:

    $$\frac{is}{40} = \frac{30}{100}$$
    $$is \times 100 = 40 \times 30$$
    $$is \times 100 = 1200$$
    $$\mathbf{12} \times 100 = 1200$$

    Thus, **12** *is* 30% of 40.

- Find what percent one number is of another number.

    12 is what percent of 40?

    12 is the *is* number and 40 is the *of* number:

    Cross-multiply and solve for %:

    $$\frac{12}{40} = \frac{\%}{100}$$
    $$12 \times 100 = 40 \times \%$$
    $$1200 = 40 \times \%$$
    $$1200 = 40 \times \mathbf{30}$$

    Thus, 12 is **30%** of 40.

- Find the whole when the percent of it is given.

    12 is 30% of what number?

    12 is the *is* number and 30 is the %:

    Cross-multiply and solve for the *of* number:

$$\frac{12}{of} = \frac{30}{100}$$
$$12 \times 100 = of \times 30$$
$$1200 = of \times 30$$
$$1200 = \mathbf{40} \times 30$$

Thus 12 is 30% *of* **40**.

You can use the same technique to find the percent increase or decrease. The *is* number is the actual increase or decrease, and the *of* number is the original amount.

Example: If a merchant puts his $20 hats on sale for $15, by what percent does he decrease the selling price?

1. Calculate the decrease, the *is* number: $20 − $15 = $5

2. The *of* number is the original amount, $20

3. Set up the equation and solve for *of* by cross-multiplying:

$$\frac{5}{20} = \frac{\%}{100}$$
$$5 \times 100 = 20 \times \%$$
$$500 = 20 \times \%$$
$$500 = 20 \times 25$$

4. Thus, the selling price is decreased by **25%**.

If the merchant later raises the price of the hats from $15 back to $20, don't be fooled into thinking that the percent increase is also 25%! It's actually more, because the increase amount of $5 is now based on a lower original price of only $15:

$$\frac{5}{15} = \frac{\%}{100}$$
$$5 \times 100 = 15 \times \%$$
$$500 = 15 \times \%$$
$$500 = 15 \times 33\tfrac{1}{3}$$

Thus, the selling price is increased by **33%**.

Find a percent of a whole:

_____**67.** 1% of 25

_____**68.** 18.2% of 50

_____**69.** $37\tfrac{1}{2}$% of 100

_____**70.** 125% of 60

Find what percent one number is of another number.

_____**71.** 10 is what % of 20?

_____**72.** 4 is what % of 12?

_____**73.** 12 is what % of 4?

Find the whole when the percent of it is given.

_____**74.** 15% of what number is 15?

_____**75.** $37\frac{1}{2}$% of what number is 3?

_____**76.** 200% of what number is 20?

Now try your percent skills on some real life problems.

_____**77.** Last Monday, 20% of the 140-member nursing staff was absent. How many nurses were absent that day?
   a. 14   **b.** 20   **c.** 28   **d.** 112   **e.** 126

_____**78.** 40% of Vero's postal service employees are women. If there are 80 women in Vero's postal service, how many men are employed there?
   a. 32   **b.** 112   **c.** 120   **d.** 160   **e.** 200

_____**79.** Of the 840 crimes committed last month, 42 involved petty theft. What percent of the crimes involved petty theft?
   a. .5%   **b.** 2%   **c.** 5%   **d.** 20%   **e.** 50%

_____**80.** Sam's Shoe Store put all of its merchandise on sale for 20% off. If Jason saved $10 by purchasing one pair of shoes during the sale, what was the original price of the shoes before the sale?
   a. $12   **b.** $20   **c.** $40   **d.** $50   **e.** $70

ANSWERS TO MATH PROBLEMS

WORD PROBLEMS

1. a
2. d
3. d
4. e

FRACTIONS

5. $\frac{1}{4}$
6. $\frac{2}{5}$
7. $\frac{3}{8}$
8. 10
9. 6
10. 200
11. $\frac{11}{12}$
12. $\frac{55}{24}$ or $2\frac{7}{24}$
13. $7\frac{1}{4}$
14. $\frac{2}{15}$
15. $\frac{1}{8}$
16. $\frac{19}{12}$ or $1\frac{7}{12}$
17. a
18. b
19. $\frac{2}{15}$
20. $\frac{8}{35}$
21. $\frac{2}{3}$
22. $\frac{26}{15}$ or $1\frac{11}{15}$
23. 15
24. $\frac{33}{2}$ or $16\frac{1}{2}$
25. c
26. e
27. c
28. $\frac{1}{2}$
29. $5\frac{1}{2}$
30. $\frac{1}{5}$
31. $\frac{45}{28}$ or $1\frac{17}{28}$
32. b
33. d
34. b

DECIMALS

35. $\frac{5}{1000}$ or $\frac{1}{200}$
36. $3\frac{12}{25}$
37. $123\frac{456}{1000}$ or $123\frac{57}{125}$
38. 4
39. 8.305
40. .907
41. 1.456
42. b
43. d
44. .03
45. .3392
46. .70104
47. e
48. e
49. 1.4
50. 128
51. 572
52. 1400
53. b
54. c

PERCENTS

55. 45%
56. .8%
57. 16.67% or $16\frac{2}{3}$%
58. .12
59. .875
60. 2.5
61. 12.5% or $12\frac{1}{2}$%
62. 52%
63. 58.33% or $58\frac{1}{3}$%
64. $\frac{19}{20}$
65. $\frac{3}{8}$
66. $\frac{5}{4}$ or $1\frac{1}{4}$
67. $\frac{1}{4}$ or .25
68. 9.1
69. $37\frac{1}{2}$ or 37.5
70. 75
71. 50%
72. $33\frac{1}{3}$%
73. 300%
74. 100
75. 8
76. 10
77. c
78. c
79. c
80. d

C·H·A·P·T·E·R 10

BUS OPERATOR PRACTICE EXAM 2

CHAPTER SUMMARY

This is the second of three practice exams in this book based on the most commonly tested areas on bus operator written exams nationwide. After working through the instructional material in the previous chapters, use this test to see how much your score has improved since you took the first exam.

The exam that follows is based on exams previously given nationwide for the position of bus operator. Though the actual exam may differ somewhat from the exam you're about to take, you should find that most of the same skills are tested on the real exam as on this one. This test includes 70 multiple-choice questions on reading schedules, bulletins, and route maps; rules of the road and safe driving; judgment and the ability to follow procedures in routine and emergency situations; courtesy to passengers; and mathematics.

For this exam, simulate the actual test-taking experience as much as possible. Find a quiet place to work where you won't be interrupted. Tear out the answer sheet on the next page and find some number 2 pencils to fill in the circles with. Set a timer or stopwatch, and give yourself two hours for the entire exam.

After the exam, use the answer key that follows it to see how you did and to find out why the correct answers are correct. The answer key is followed by a section on how to score your exam.

1.	ⓐ	ⓑ	ⓒ	ⓓ
2.	ⓐ	ⓑ	ⓒ	ⓓ
3.	ⓐ	ⓑ	ⓒ	ⓓ
4.	ⓐ	ⓑ	ⓒ	ⓓ
5.	ⓐ	ⓑ	ⓒ	ⓓ
6.	ⓐ	ⓑ	ⓒ	ⓓ
7.	ⓐ	ⓑ	ⓒ	ⓓ
8.	ⓐ	ⓑ	ⓒ	ⓓ
9.	ⓐ	ⓑ	ⓒ	ⓓ
10.	ⓐ	ⓑ	ⓒ	ⓓ
11.	ⓐ	ⓑ	ⓒ	ⓓ
12.	ⓐ	ⓑ	ⓒ	ⓓ
13.	ⓐ	ⓑ	ⓒ	ⓓ
14.	ⓐ	ⓑ	ⓒ	ⓓ
15.	ⓐ	ⓑ	ⓒ	ⓓ
16.	ⓐ	ⓑ	ⓒ	ⓓ
17.	ⓐ	ⓑ	ⓒ	ⓓ
18.	ⓐ	ⓑ	ⓒ	ⓓ
19.	ⓐ	ⓑ	ⓒ	ⓓ
20.	ⓐ	ⓑ	ⓒ	ⓓ
21.	ⓐ	ⓑ	ⓒ	ⓓ
22.	ⓐ	ⓑ	ⓒ	ⓓ
23.	ⓐ	ⓑ	ⓒ	ⓓ
24.	ⓐ	ⓑ	ⓒ	ⓓ

25.	ⓐ	ⓑ	ⓒ	ⓓ
26.	ⓐ	ⓑ	ⓒ	ⓓ
27.	ⓐ	ⓑ	ⓒ	ⓓ
28.	ⓐ	ⓑ	ⓒ	ⓓ
29.	ⓐ	ⓑ	ⓒ	ⓓ
30.	ⓐ	ⓑ	ⓒ	ⓓ
31.	ⓐ	ⓑ	ⓒ	ⓓ
32.	ⓐ	ⓑ	ⓒ	ⓓ
33.	ⓐ	ⓑ	ⓒ	ⓓ
34.	ⓐ	ⓑ	ⓒ	ⓓ
35.	ⓐ	ⓑ	ⓒ	ⓓ
36.	ⓐ	ⓑ	ⓒ	ⓓ
37.	ⓐ	ⓑ	ⓒ	ⓓ
38.	ⓐ	ⓑ	ⓒ	ⓓ
39.	ⓐ	ⓑ	ⓒ	ⓓ
40.	ⓐ	ⓑ	ⓒ	ⓓ
41.	ⓐ	ⓑ	ⓒ	ⓓ
42.	ⓐ	ⓑ	ⓒ	ⓓ
43.	ⓐ	ⓑ	ⓒ	ⓓ
44.	ⓐ	ⓑ	ⓒ	ⓓ
45.	ⓐ	ⓑ	ⓒ	ⓓ
46.	ⓐ	ⓑ	ⓒ	ⓓ
47.	ⓐ	ⓑ	ⓒ	ⓓ
48.	ⓐ	ⓑ	ⓒ	ⓓ

49.	ⓐ	ⓑ	ⓒ	ⓓ
50.	ⓐ	ⓑ	ⓒ	ⓓ
51.	ⓐ	ⓑ	ⓒ	ⓓ
52.	ⓐ	ⓑ	ⓒ	ⓓ
53.	ⓐ	ⓑ	ⓒ	ⓓ
54.	ⓐ	ⓑ	ⓒ	ⓓ
55.	ⓐ	ⓑ	ⓒ	ⓓ
56.	ⓐ	ⓑ	ⓒ	ⓓ
57.	ⓐ	ⓑ	ⓒ	ⓓ
58.	ⓐ	ⓑ	ⓒ	ⓓ
59.	ⓐ	ⓑ	ⓒ	ⓓ
60.	ⓐ	ⓑ	ⓒ	ⓓ
61.	ⓐ	ⓑ	ⓒ	ⓓ
62.	ⓐ	ⓑ	ⓒ	ⓓ
63.	ⓐ	ⓑ	ⓒ	ⓓ
64.	ⓐ	ⓑ	ⓒ	ⓓ
65.	ⓐ	ⓑ	ⓒ	ⓓ
66.	ⓐ	ⓑ	ⓒ	ⓓ
67.	ⓐ	ⓑ	ⓒ	ⓓ
68.	ⓐ	ⓑ	ⓒ	ⓓ
69.	ⓐ	ⓑ	ⓒ	ⓓ
70.	ⓐ	ⓑ	ⓒ	ⓓ

BUS OPERATOR PRACTICE EXAM 2

1. At a crowded bus stop a five-year-old boy boards the bus. He is crying and tells you he is lost. He says that his mother and brother got on a bus that is just ahead of your bus. Which of the following actions is the most appropriate one for you to take?
   a. ask the boy to get off the bus and explain to him that he can find a police officer to help him
   b. ask a passenger to get off the bus and stay with the boy until help arrives
   c. call the Command Center, ask them to contact the bus ahead of yours to find out if the boy's mother is on board, and then await instructions
   d. tell the boy to sit down, that you'll help him find his mother after you've completed this run

2. A green arrow on a traffic light means
   a. you can go in the direction of the arrow without stopping
   b. no one else in the intersection can go except those who have the green arrow
   c. you should come to a complete stop and then go when it is safe to do so
   d. the light is about to turn red

3. You are in traffic behind a school bus, and you see railroad tracks are just ahead. What should you be ready for the school bus driver to do?
   a. pull over to allow traffic to pass
   b. stop at the railroad crossing even if a train is not visible
   c. slow down, but keep going across the tracks if a train is not visible
   d. slow down and put on the hazard lights

4. Manny works Monday through Friday each week. His bus fare to and from work is $1.10 each way. How much does Manny spend on bus fare each week?
   a. $10.10
   b. $11.00
   c. $11.10
   d. $11.20

Questions 5 through 7 are based on the schedule shown below.

ROUTE # 72 SCHEDULE					
Lv Elm & Oak Sts	Arr Linn & Maple Sts	Arr Pine & Ash Sts	Arr Willow & Apple Sts	Arr Pear & Beech Sts	Arr Fir & Linder Sts
6:30 a.m.	6:35 a.m.	6:42 a.m.	6:44 a.m.	6:50 a.m.	6:52 a.m.
7:00	7:05	7:12	7:14	7:20	7:22
7:30	7:35	7:42	7:44	7:50	7:52
8:00	8:05	8:12	8:14	8:20	8:22
8:30	8:35	8:42	8:44	8:50	8:52
9:30	9:35	9:42	9:44	9:50	9:52
10:30	10:35	10:42	10:44	10:50	10:52
11:30	11:35	11:42	11:44	11:50	11:52
12:30	12:35	12:42	12:44	12:50	12:52

5. A passenger boards the bus at Linn and Maple Streets at 8:35. What time will the passenger arrive at Pear and Beech Streets?
   a. 8:44
   b. 8:50
   c. 8:52
   d. 9:30

6. The 10:30 bus is delayed in leaving Elm and Oak Streets by 3 minutes. As the route progresses, the driver is unable to make up any time. What time will the bus arrive at Fir and Linder Streets?
   a. 10:52
   b. 10:53
   c. 10:54
   d. 10:55

7. A passenger wishes to take the bus from Willow and Apple Streets to Fir and Linder Streets, arriving at Fir and Linder no later than 9:30 a.m. What time should the passenger catch the bus at Willow and Apple?
   a. 8:44
   b. 8:50
   c. 8:42
   d. 8:35

8. In a hard day-time rainstorm when visibility is poor, which of the situations below is most dangerous?
   a. tailgating the vehicle in front of you
   b. driving with your headlights on
   c. making a right turn at a red light
   d. making a complete stop at a stop sign

9. You are driving along a two-way road and see a car up ahead that is being parallel parked. When you get close, the car is half-in and half-out of the parking space. What action should you take?
   a. honk your horn to let that driver know that his car is in the way
   b. swing into the opposite lane of traffic to go around the car
   c. stop far enough away to give the car enough room to finish parking
   d. maintain your speed and assume the car will get out of the way in plenty of time

10. You are driving north on Main Street, a one-way street. At the intersection, you turn onto a one-way west-bound street known as La Rue Street. What kind of turn did you make?
    a. right turn
    b. left turn
    c. U-turn
    d. illegal turn

11. The fares collected for one bus on Route G47 on Monday are as follows:
    Run 1—$419.50
    Run 2—$537.00
    Run 3—$390.10
    Run 4—$425.50

    What is the total amount collected?
    a. $1,661.10
    b. $1,762.20
    c. $1,772.10
    d. $1,881.00

12. You've been scheduled to drive a bus from one terminal depot to another without taking on any passengers. Which of the following is the appropriate action for you to take?
    a. leave the destination sign blank so customers at bus stops along the route can see that your bus is not in service
    b. do not speed, but drive as quickly as possible past all bus stops so that customers won't think the bus is in service
    c. stop and pick up customers, but only at very crowded bus stops
    d. make sure the destination sign on the bus reads "Not in Service" before you begin your drive to the other terminal depot

13. Late one night, as you are loading passengers at a bus stop, a young male passenger who has been on board for a while approaches you. He tells you that he has pain shooting down his left arm and feels as if a vice grip is tightening around his chest. Then he passes out and falls in the aisle. What action should you take?
    a. call the Command Center to report a medical emergency and hold the bus where it is until an ambulance arrives
    b. call the police since the man is so young and therefore probably drunk or high
    c. discharge your passengers, giving them transfers if they want them, and then drive the man to the nearest hospital
    d. have a passenger help you put the man in one of the vacant seats, and then call an ambulance

14. You're on a four-lane roadway in heavy traffic. The vehicle next to you pulls in front of you abruptly because your lane appears to be moving faster. What action should you take?

   a. maintain your current speed, and then brake at the last second so that the driver will think the maneuver almost caused an accident

   b. honk your horn to warn the driver that the maneuver was dangerous

   c. drive as closely as possible behind the driver so that no other cars will try the same maneuver

   d. slow down enough to put a safe distance between you and this driver

15. You are in heavy traffic and a man in a car behind you is irate because he is behind your bus. He is tailgating you, honking, and cursing out the window. What action should you take?

   a. tap your brakes to warn this driver to quit following so closely

   b. drive more slowly to compensate for the driver's erratic behavior

   c. continue your route without letting his driving influence your driving

   d. pull over and let him get in front of your bus

16. To keep passengers in your bus from falling or having other accidents when the bus begins to move forward, which of the following actions should you choose?

   a. accelerate slowly and smoothly

   b. accelerate quickly to reach normal driving speed as soon as possible

   c. alternate between accelerating and braking until you blend into traffic

   d. warn the passengers to hang on and then accelerate quickly into traffic

17. Eric's walking speed is $2\frac{1}{2}$ miles per hour. If it takes Eric 6 minutes to walk from his home to the bus stop, how far is the bus stop from his home?

   a. $\frac{1}{8}$ mile

   b. $\frac{1}{4}$ mile

   c. $\frac{1}{2}$ mile

   d. 1 mile

Answer questions 18 through 22 on the basis of the incident description below and the Incident Report Form that follows.

On January 4, 1996, Operator Jody Schmidt was driving bus number 42 on route number 17. She had been on duty since 2:00 p.m. and was scheduled to go off duty at 10:00 p.m. At approximately 7:22 p.m., she stopped the bus at the corner of Gable and Lombard Streets in response to a passenger ringing the bell requesting a stop. When she opened the front door of the bus, a man ran toward the bus from about one-quarter block away. Meanwhile, the passenger, a woman approximately forty years old, rose from her seat and approached the door. Just as the woman started to exit the bus, the man reached the door and attempted to enter the bus; however, he was unable to do so because he collided with the passenger. The woman fell into a sitting position, hitting her head on the fare box and sustaining a small cut. The man stumbled backwards and complained that he hurt his ankle.

Police Officer Melinda Luz, badge number #7291, from precinct 14, arrived and summoned paramedics and an ambulance. While the paramedics attended to the injured passengers, another passenger on the bus approached the driver and began complaining about the delay. Schmidt attempted to calm the passenger, explaining that the delay was unavoidable and that the next bus would be along in 12 minutes. The man became extremely upset and lunged at Schmidt. He was then taken into custody by the police. He told police his name was James Gallagher. Meanwhile, the paramedics had bandaged the woman passenger's head and she refused further treatment. She also refused to give her name to Schmidt and then exited the bus. The injured man, who told the driver his name was Alvin Rickman, was transported by the paramedics to the hospital.

18. Which of the following should Operator Schmidt enter in space 6?
   a. on bus #42
   b. January 4, 1996
   c. at the corner of Gable Street and Lombard Street
   d. on Route #17

19. Which of the following should Operator Schmidt enter in spaces 10 and 11?
   a. "James Gallagher" and "Alvin Rickman"
   b. "Alvin Rickman" and "Officer #7291"
   c. "Alvin Rickman" and "Operator Schmidt"

   d. "James Gallagher" and "woman, refused to give name"

20. Which of the following should Operator Schmidt enter in space 20?
   a. on the bus
   b. by ambulance
   c. by taxi
   d. in the police car

21. Which of the following should Operator Schmidt enter in space 25?
   a. 14
   b. 42
   c. 17
   d. 72

22. Which of the following should Operator Schmidt enter in space 2?
   a. 2:00 p.m.
   b. 10:00 p.m.
   c. 7:22 p.m.
   d. January 4, 1996

Incident Report Form To Be Completed By The Bus Driver

Date of Incident **1** Time of Incident **2** Route number **3**
Bus number **4** Driver **5** Location of Incident **6**
Did the incident occur while the bus was moving? **7**
Did the incident involve other vehicles? **8**
Did the incident involve bus passengers? **9** If yes, list their names: **10**, **11**, **12**
Did the incident involve other citizens who were not passengers? **13** If yes, list their names: **14**, **15**, **16**
Were there any injuries as a result of the incident? **17** Was anyone treated by medical personnel (doctors, nurses, paramedics)? **18** Was anyone taken to a hospital or other medical facility? **19** Method of transport? **20** Was the bus operator injured? **21**
Was a police officer present? **22** Officer's badge number? **23** Were there any arrests as a result of the incident? **24** To which precinct were arrestees taken? **25**
Please describe the incident: **26**

Answer questions 23 through 25 based on the following information.

Loud noises on buses not only irritate passengers but also create unsafe situations. They are prohibited by law and by agency policy. Therefore, bus operators are expected to follow the procedures outlined below:

1. In the event a passenger creates a disturbance by playing excessively loud music or creating loud noises in some other manner, the bus operator will first politely ask the passenger to turn off the music or stop making the loud noise.

2. If the passenger refuses to comply with the bus operator's request, the bus operator will tell the passenger that he or she is in violation of the law and bus policy and will have to leave the bus if he or she will not comply.

3. If the passenger does not comply, the bus operator will pull into the next bus stop and tell the passenger to get off the bus.

4. If the passenger refuses, the bus operator will radio the Command Center and ask for police assistance to remove the passenger.

5. If at any point the situation escalates so that the bus operator thinks the confrontation may become physical, the bus operator is encouraged to activate the silent alarm on the console.

6. If police assistance is requested, the bus operator will stay at the location from which the call to the Command Center was placed or the silent alarm used. The bus operator will wait there until the police arrive. Passengers are allowed off the bus at this point, but no passengers are allowed on until the situation is resolved.

23. Bus Operator Letha Wilkins picks up a man carrying a large radio with the volume turned up completely. The passenger turns the music off when Wilkins politely asks him to do so and walks to the back of the bus. When Wilkins pulls away from the bus stop the passenger turns the radio back on. Wilkins tells him to turn the music down or she'll put him off at the next stop. He responds by saying that he paid his money and he isn't leaving. He shouts that he will punch her if she doesn't quit bugging him about his music. Wilkins hits her silent alarm and continues to drive. Wilkins's actions were entirely
    a. proper, because the passenger indicated that he would physically harm the bus operator
    b. improper, because the passenger turned the music down the first time the bus operator asked him
    c. proper, because the bus operator began with a polite request that the passenger turn the music down
    d. improper, because the bus operator should have stayed at the location where she hit her silent alarm

24. Bus Operator Frank Gianelli stops to load passengers at a crowded bus stop. He picks up 15 passengers and waits until they move to the back of the bus. One of the passengers stays up front and shouts to a friend who is standing at the rear of the bus. She is shouting so loudly that the other passengers can't hear Gianelli when he calls out the next stop. Gianelli explains to the woman that she is talking too loudly. The woman lowers her voice but mumbles an insult about the bus operator's appearance, which causes a brief spurt of laughter

throughout the bus. Gianelli ignores this and drives on. Gianelli's actions were

a. proper, because he started with the least confrontational approach and behaved reasonably thereafter

b. proper, because public relations might have been damaged if he spent any more time on something as minor as loud talking

c. improper, because a verbal insult can escalate to violence, and he should have ordered the woman to leave the bus

d. improper, because the laughter of the other passengers showed that they were not irritated by the woman, and he should have ignored her loud talking

25. At the Ninth Street bus stop, three passengers try to board Bus Operator Edwina Simpson's bus. She has allowed several passengers to get off her bus, but she will not allow these three passengers on board. Simpson is waiting for the police to remove a passenger from the bus who is blasting music on his radio and threatening to punch Simpson if she tries to make him leave the bus. One of the waiting passengers explains she is a friend of the man causing the disruption and can quiet him down if she is allowed on the bus. Simpson refuses. Simpson's actions were

a. improper, because she should have allowed all three passengers on board so that the bus could leave immediately after the police handled the situation

b. proper, because the fact that the passenger who wishes to board knows the man does not in any way alter the rules

c. improper, because Simpson should have given the second passenger a chance to calm the troublemaker and thus avoid escalation of the problem

d. proper, because Simpson started with the most polite and least confrontational approach to the situation

26. A small boy on board your bus has been playing with a knife his mother didn't know he had. He cuts himself on the arm and is bleeding profusely. What action should you take?

a. drive on, looking for a police officer to help with the emergency

b. stop the bus and find some ice to apply to the wound

c. have the mother apply pressure directly to the wound, and then call the Command Center for help

d. give the mother a Band-Aid from the first aid kit, stop while she puts it on, and then continue on your route

Answer questions 27 and 28 on the basis of the following passage.

Bus operators driving buses that are equipped with wheelchair lifts are required to become familiar with the wheelchair tie-down system installed in these buses. After a wheelchair passenger enters the bus, the driver will fold up one of the front, sideways seats, and the passenger will position his or her wheelchair at the tie-downs. One strap of the tie-down should be attached to each corner of the wheelchair frame. Straps should not be attached to the wheelchair pedals as they may come loose. The passenger should also set the brakes on the wheelchair. Finally, the seat belt should be inserted under the arms of the wheelchair and fastened across the passenger's lap. Most wheelchair passengers are familiar with the tie-down system, but it is the bus operator's responsibility to make sure the wheelchair is secured properly.

27. While Operator Jenkins is attaching the tie-down to a passenger's wheelchair, the passenger reaches for the seat belt, passes it over the arms of her wheelchair, and buckles it. Operator Jenkins should
    a. make sure the tie-down is attached tightly
    b. unbuckle the seat belt, pass it under the arms of the chair, and refasten it
    c. not say anything, so as not to embarrass the passenger
    d. ask the passenger if the seat belt is snug enough

28. Operator Teller has read the above instructions but has never actually secured a wheelchair. Wheelchair passenger Finch enters Teller's bus. Teller folds up the seat and tells Finch, "I've never done this." Finch says, "Don't worry, I ride all the time. I'll do it." What should Operator Teller do?
    a. attach the tie-down based on the directions he read and ask Finch for help when necessary
    b. return to the driver's seat and let Finch secure the wheelchair
    c. ask if any of the other passenger know how the tie-downs work
    d. tell Finch he will not be able to ride today because Teller does not know how the tie-downs work

29. A customer on board your bus is irate because he thinks you gave him the wrong information about the route your bus follows. He demands to be let off at the next stop with a refund. Though bus drivers no longer handle money,

the passenger wants his fare back in cash right now. You are almost certain you did give him the correct information. Which of the following actions is the best one for you to take?
    a. explain to the man that you are not allowed to handle refunds, give him a refund form along with instructions on how to use it, and let him off at the next stop
    b. in order to improve public relations, take money from your own pocket for the refund, give it to the man, and then ask the bus company to reimburse you
    c. call the Command Center, explain the situation, and ask permission to give the man back his money
    d. since you are sure you gave the man correct information, tell him so and explain to him that he is not due a refund

Answer questions 30 and 31 on the basis of the following passage.

May is National Reading Month. In conjunction with the Public Library, the City is offering half fare rides to anyone carrying a library card. In order to receive the half-price fare, each passenger must show the driver his or her current library card and deposit one-half the fare in the collection box. Drivers will record these fares in the "special fares" section on the trip sheets for each route.

30. John and Mary Burton get on the bus driven by Operator Hudson at the corner of Sherman Avenue and West 123rd Street. John shows Hudson his library card and deposits half fare in the collection box. Mary deposits half fare in the collection box. The couple move toward their seats. What should Operator Hudson do?

a. proceed to the next stop

b. inform Mary that she must exit the bus

c. assume Mary has a library card, too

d. tell Mary that if she does not have a library card, she will have to pay full fare

31. The passage implies that

a. many bus passengers like to read

b. many transit employees have library cards

c. bus drivers regularly deal with special fares

d. several bus routes service the Public Library

32. A passenger signals that she wants to get off at the next stop. In order to pull into the stop in a way that will keep passengers safe inside the bus, what action should you take?

a. gradually slow down and then stop abruptly at the curb

b. gradually slow down and smoothly apply the brakes to glide the bus to a stop

c. whip in to the bus stop and quickly apply the brakes

d. tell everyone to hold on for the stop and then apply the brakes

33. You are traveling along your route at the legal speed limit. You have a green light at the next intersection, but the light turns yellow as you enter the intersection. What should you do?

a. warn your passengers, and then apply your brakes

b. slow down and move slowly through the intersection

c. proceed through the intersection without altering your speed

d. speed up to get through the intersection as quickly as possible

34. You are just about to pull into a bus stop when a taxi pulls in front of you, clipping the front end of your bus. The taxi driver pulls over and gets out to inspect the damage, which looks minor to you from where you sit. Which of the following is the most appropriate action for you to take?

a. tell the taxi driver that you'll meet with him later since the damage is minor, take down his cab number, and complete your run

b. pull into the bus stop, have a passenger get out to check the damage, and then decide what action to take

c. pull into the bus stop, make sure all passengers are okay, and let them know that the bus will be out of service until the problem has been taken care of

d. stop the bus where it is, exchange information with the taxi driver before he has a chance to leave, and then continue on your route

35. A car traveling in front of your bus is stopping and starting erratically in traffic. The driver is hanging out of the window yelling for people to get out of the way. How should you handle this situation?

a. speed up to get past this driver as quickly as possible

b. stay close so the driver will see that the behavior is interfering with bus traffic

c. honk your horn to warn this driver that you are close behind

d. slow down and give yourself enough room to stop if necessary

36. If one inch equals 2.54 centimeters, how many inches are there in 20.32 centimeters?
   a. 7.2
   b. 8
   c. 9
   d. 10.2

37. During the month of May, $\frac{1}{6}$ of the buses in District A were in the garage for routine maintenance. In addition, $\frac{1}{8}$ of the buses were in for other repairs. If a total of 28 buses were in for maintenance and repairs, how many buses did District A have altogether?
   a. 80
   b. 84
   c. 91
   d. 96

Answer questions 38 through 43 on the basis of the accompanying portion of a bus route map. This map has spaces and numbers along the bottom edge, and spaces and letters along the right edge. If the lines on the spaces and numbers and the lines on the spaces and letters were extended, they would form blocks, or quadrants. For example, the Jewish Museum is in quadrant I5. Gracie Mansion is in quadrant I7.

38. Which bus route goes from the Museum of the City of New York (quadrant I5) to the corner of Columbus Avenue and West 96th Street (quadrant I3)?
   a. 106
   b. 96
   c. 4
   d. 18

39. Which bus route goes from the Cathedral of St. John the Divine (quadrant H3) to the American Museum of Natural History (quadrant J 3-4)?
   a. 4
   b. 18
   c. 11
   d. 104

40. Which bus route goes from the Metropolitan Museum of Art (quadrant J5) to the Cathedral of St. John the Divine (quadrant H3)?
   a. 1
   b. 2
   c. 3
   d. 4

41. Which bus route goes from the corner of 1st Avenue and East 91st Street (quadrant I6) to John Jay Park (quadrant J7)?
   a. 86
   b. 31
   c. 15
   d. 79

42. Which is the best bus route to take from the Children's Museum of Manhattan (quadrant J3) to the corner of Lexington Avenue and East 86th Street (quadrant J5)?
   a. 104
   b. 79
   c. 86
   d. 7

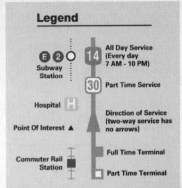

Legend

Ⓔ ❷ ○ Subway Station

Hospital Ⓗ

Point Of Interest ▲

Commuter Rail Station

⟨14⟩ All Day Service (Every day 7 AM - 10 PM)

⟨30⟩ Part Time Service

Direction of Service (two-way service has no arrows)

Full Time Terminal

□ Part Time Terminal

43. Which bus route goes from the corner of Duke Ellington Boulevard and Columbus Avenue (quadrant H3) to the American Museum of Natural History (quadrant J3)?
   a. both 7 and 11
   b. 7 only
   c. 11 only
   d. 104

44. You've been assigned to a position known as "shifter," and your job is to move buses around the yard for cleaning and maintenance. You have been asked to go get a particular bus that needs repair. When you find this bus, you see that you can't back it out of its parking place without someone directing you from outside. No one is around to help. Which of the following is the best action for you to take?
   a. leave the bus and go to find someone to assist you
   b. honk the horn until someone comes to see what you need
   c. back up the bus carefully and slowly, getting out every few seconds to see if everything is okay at the rear of the bus
   d. pick another bus that looks as if it needs cleaning and maintenance, and take that bus instead

45. You are making what is known as a "short trip," a route that ends before the usual terminal station. You want to make sure that you let your passengers know that your bus may not be going as far as they may want. Which of the following is the best action for you to take?
   a. pay attention to your driving, and depend on the passengers to be responsible for reading the destination sign

   b. tell passengers as they come aboard, and make frequent announcements letting them know how close you are getting to the final stop
   c. assign one passenger near the front of the bus to tell the other passengers as they board
   d. post a sign saying "This bus is making a Short Run"

Answer questions 46 and 47 based on the following information.

No smoking is allowed aboard buses. Anyone failing to comply with the policy will be asked to leave the bus.

46. Bus Operator Ricardo Kipfer is driving along his route when he notices that a passenger standing near the front doors of the bus is about to light a cigarette. Kipfer reminds the passenger that no smoking is allowed on the bus. The passenger puts the cigarette in his pocket and turns away from Kipfer. Kipfer allows the passenger to stay aboard the bus. Kipfer's actions were
   a. proper, because cigarette smoking is unhealthy, both for the smoker and for others around him
   b. improper, because the passenger will probably try to smoke again after the bus starts moving, and he should have been asked to leave
   c. improper, because tobacco is not allowed on buses, and the man should have been asked to leave
   d. proper, because the passenger complied with the policy by not smoking the cigarette

47. Bus Operator Liam Sieland has reboarded the bus after taking a short comfort stop. He has a half-finished cigarette in his left hand. Knowing he is about to get behind schedule, he starts up the bus, pulls away from the curb, and continues on his route, holding the cigarette out the open window. Sieland's actions were

a. proper, because holding the cigarette out of the window keeps the smoke from bothering the passengers

b. improper, because the rules clearly indicate that he should finish or put out the cigarette before boarding the bus

c. proper, because although he is allowed to stop for breaks, he is not allowed to get behind schedule

d. improper, because bus operators are not allowed to smoke at comfort stops

48. You have picked up passengers at a bus stop and are ready to pull into traffic. After turning on your left turn signal to indicate that you will be pulling into traffic, you should

a. pull out into traffic immediately because other drivers should give the bus right-of-way

b. hold your left hand out of the window and try to stop traffic so that you can pull out

c. honk your horn to warn other drivers and then pull out

d. wait until it is safe before pulling out into traffic

49. When approaching a banked curve in your bus, you should

a. reduce the speed of the bus before entering the curve

b. apply the brakes gently all the way through the curve

c. speed up to allow centrifugal force to carry you through the curve

d. come to a complete stop before entering the curve

50. A passenger boarding your bus is carrying a skateboard. He pays his fare, puts the board down, and starts to skate down the aisle. What action should you take?

a. tap the brakes as you pull away from the curb so he'll stop skateboarding

b. ask him to pay an additional fare for having the skateboard on the bus

c. pay no attention to this harmless activity and continue on your route

d. ask him not to use the skateboard while he's on the bus

51. As you approach a crowded bus stop, you make the following announcement to the passengers already on board: "Please use the rear doors if you need to exit at this stop." When you stop the bus and open both the front and rear doors, two passengers stand up and start to walk out the front doors. Which of the following is the most appropriate action for you to take?

a. ignore those passengers and continue with the boarding process when they are out of the way

b. stop the two passengers before they can get off the bus, chastise them, and tell them exit using the rear doors

c. close the doors before the two passengers can get off the bus, and ask them to use the rear doors

d. let the two passengers get off in the front, but tell them that in the future they may not be allowed on your bus if they cannot follow the rules

52. After all of your passengers have exited the bus at its terminal stop, you discover that someone left an expensive umbrella on a seat. You're not certain, but you think it belongs to one of your regular riders. You notice that someone's name is engraved on the handle. Which of the following actions is most appropriate for you to take?

a. take the umbrella with you on your next shift so that if the passenger asks about it you'll be able to return it to her

b. turn the umbrella in to the Lost and Found department

c. leave the umbrella on the bus seat so that the owner can find it when she rides the bus again

d. keep the umbrella, since the owner should be more careful with her property

53. One of your regular customers gets on your bus one day and tells you that the bench in the bus shelter needs repair. You know that the city's transportation division, not the bus company, is responsible for the upkeep of the bus shelters. Which of the following responses is the best one for you to use with this customer?

a. tell the customer that the city has responsibility for bus shelter conditions and that he should call the transportation division about the problem

b. tell the customer to avoid sitting on the bench until it is repaired

c. thank the customer and say that you will notify the proper authorities about the problem

d. tell the customer that there's nothing you can do about this particular problem but that you apologize for the difficult conditions in the shelter

54. Several students are standing at an intersection that is controlled by a stop sign for your lane of traffic. There are no crosswalks marked for pedestrians. As you come to a stop behind the stop line, a student starts to cross the street in front of your bus. What action should you take?

a. proceed quickly in order to keep the student from crossing

b. wait for the student to cross in front of your bus and then proceed

c. honk your horn and point at the student to make her get back on the curb

d. back up a few feet to be sure you are clear of the unmarked crosswalk

55. You are legally in an intersection with a green light and are waiting for the last oncoming car to clear so that you can make your left turn. The light turns red just as you begin your turn. What should you do?

a. stop immediately and wait for a green light

b. back up until you are out of the middle of the intersection

c. wait for police assistance to back up safely

d. complete your turn smoothly and safely

Answer questions 56 and 57 on the basis of the following chart.

Wednesday, September 17

	Bus # 52	Bus # 53	Bus # 54	Bus # 55	Bus # 56
300 Gallons					
250 Gallons					■
200 Gallons			■	■	■
150 Gallons	■		■	■	■
100 Gallons	■	■	■	■	■

56. According to the chart, which bus used the least fuel on Wednesday, September 17?
   a. Bus # 52
   b. Bus # 54
   c. Bus # 55
   d. Bus # 53

57. Assuming that the bus with the longest route also uses the most fuel, according to the chart, which bus has the longest route?
   a. Bus # 56
   b. Bus # 54
   c. Bus # 52
   d. Bus # 53

Answer questions 58 and 59 on the basis of the memo below.

Beginning next month, City Transit will institute the Stop Here Program, which will be in effect every night from 10:00 p.m. until 4:00 a.m. The program will allow drivers to stop the bus wherever a passenger wishes, so long as the place is safe. This will reduce the amount of walking that passengers will have to do after dark. Passengers may request a stop anywhere along the bus route by pulling the bell cord a block ahead; however, they may board the bus only at designated stops. For the first two months of the program, when a passenger attempts to flag down a bus anywhere but at a designated stop, the bus driver should proceed to the next stop and wait for the passenger to board the bus. Then the driver should give the passenger a brochure that explains the Stop Here Program.

58. Operator Gray is driving the Route 98 bus beginning at 9:00 p.m. After driving for an hour and a half, Operator Gray notices a person who is near but not at a bus stop waving for the bus to stop. Operator Gray should
   a. stop for the passenger this time and explain the Stop Here Program
   b. stop for the passenger and give the passenger a Stop Here brochure
   c. proceed to the bus stop and wait for the person to walk to the stop and get on the bus
   d. proceed to the bus stop, stop the normal amount of time, and leave, whether the person has gotten on the bus or not

59. According to the memo, the main reason for instituting the Stop Here Program is most likely
   a. to save time on the night bus routes
   b. to increase night ridership
   c. to make it easier for bus operators to stay on schedule at night
   d. to make it safer for passengers when they get off the bus

60. The traffic light at the intersection you are approaching is flashing red for all directions. What should you do?
   a. treat this intersection as if it had four-way stop signs
   b. stop and back up the bus
   c. go through the intersection without stopping as buses have the right-of-way
   d. make a right turn at the intersection to avoid waiting for traffic on your left

61. Children who are 44 inches or below in height are allowed to ride the bus free. A passenger with a child gets on board your bus one afternoon and says his son should ride free because he is only 49 inches tall. Other passengers with small children are already on board your bus. Which is the most appropriate action for you to take?

a. let the boy ride free this one time, but tell the father he will have to pay for his son to ride in the future

b. explain to the father that, in fairness to other passengers who have children and who paid the fare, he will be required to do the same

c. drop money from your own pocket into the fare box to settle the situation and to help with public relations

d. ask the other passengers with children on board how they feel about letting this man's son ride free, and then go with the consensus

62. A firefighter wearing full firefighting gear is not required to pay a fare in order to ride a bus. One evening a firefighter in gear gets aboard, and the woman who boards after the firefighter complains because she has to pay but the firefighter does not. Which of the following is the best response for you to make in this situation?

a. explain to her that you are merely following the rules, and refer her to the fire department for further clarification

b. ask the firefighter to explain to the woman why the bus company allows firefighters to ride free

c. ignore the woman, but if she really starts to make a scene ask her to get off the bus

d. explain the policy regarding emergency services personnel, and tell her that if she wishes to file a formal complaint you will give her the proper phone number

Answer questions 63 and 64 on the basis of the following passage.

The supervisors have received numerous complaints over the last several weeks about buses on several routes running hot. Drivers are reminded that each route has several check points at which drivers should check the time. If the bus is ahead of schedule, drivers should delay at the check point until it is the proper time to leave. If traffic makes it unsafe for a driver to delay at a particular check point, the driver should proceed at a reasonable speed to the next stop. The driver should hold there until the bus is back on schedule.

63. Based on the passage, which of the following describes a bus that is "running hot?"

a. The engine of the bus is over-heating.

b. The bus is running ahead of schedule.

c. The air conditioning on the bus is not working.

d. There is no more room on the bus for passengers.

64. Based only on the information in the passage, which of the following is true?

a. Every bus stop is also a check point.

b. It is important to keep customer complaints to a minimum by running on time.

c. Some drivers may tend to rush their routes so they can leave work early.

d. Each bus route has several points at which drivers should check the time.

65. You are doing your pre-trip inspection just before taking your bus out for the first run of the day. You notice that the hazard lights aren't functioning correctly, but you see that you'll start your run late if you have to check out another bus. Which is the most appropriate action for you to take?

    a. go ahead and take the bus out on the run as hazard lights are seldom needed

    b. take the bus, and call the broken lights in as a breakdown situation once your run is underway

    c. contact your supervisor, explain the problem, and take another bus

    d. take this bus, explain to the passengers as they get on that there is a problem with the lights, and let them decide if they want to wait for the next bus

66. You are stopped in heavy traffic on a four-lane roadway. You are in the lane nearest to the center stripe. A car headed in the opposite direction comes to a stop, and you see that the driver wants to turn into the driveway on your right. However, you are aware that she cannot see if anyone is coming in the lane of traffic to your right. What action should you take?

    a. stay where you are and do not interfere with the driver's decision whether or not to turn

    b. back up until the driver can see the lane on the other side of you

    c. pull up so that the driver cannot turn until you are out of the way

    d. look to see if the lane to your right is clear and, if it is, signal to the other driver to make the turn

67. The streets are icy and you are running behind schedule. Which of the following is your safest driving strategy?

    a. drive faster between stops to make up for lost time

    b. keep the bus rolling slightly while loading passengers to keep good traction on the road

    c. drive more slowly than usual and allow room for slow, steady braking

    d. stop every 50 feet to throw sand on the roadway so that your bus will have better traction

68. The wheelchair lift breaks down while you are on a run. At the next stop a customer in a wheelchair asks you to activate the lift so that he can get on board the bus. When you tell him that the lift does not work, the customer becomes irate and accuses you of lying about the lift so that you don't have to help him on board. Which of the following actions is most appropriate for you to take?

    a. ask a passenger to help you pick up the man's wheelchair manually and get him aboard the bus

    b. explain that a bus will be along soon with a functioning wheelchair lift, and offer him the Customer Relations Center number if he wants to make a complaint

    c. apologize to the customer, continue boarding other passengers, and continue on your route, since there's nothing you can do at this point

    d. call a taxi for the customer, and offer to split the fare with him in order to enhance public relations

69. As you pull away from a bus stop, a late customer runs up and bangs on the front doors for you to stop. You decide to let him in. What action should you take?

    a. open the doors and slow down enough for him to jump aboard

    b. quickly apply the brakes where you are and let him on board

    c. pull out into the lane of traffic and stop long enough for him to get on board

    d. come to a complete stop out of the way of traffic and then let him on board

70. You are at a stop sign and are attempting to make a left turn. You look to your left and see that it's clear. However, as you look to the right, a passenger inside the bus steps forward into your line of view. What should you do?

    a. pull into the intersection while asking the passenger to step back out of the way

    b. open the front doors so that you can see around the passenger while rolling forward

    c. have the passenger move so you can see both left and right, and then make the turn if it's safe to do so

    d. make a right turn instead of a left since you know no one is coming from that direction

ANSWERS

1. **c.** The safety of the boy is most important under these circumstances, and the Command Center is in the best position to help you reunite him with his mother. It would be inappropriate, and might be dangerous, to turn him over to another passenger, as in choice **b.**

2. **a.** The green arrow means traffic may flow in the direction in which it is pointing. You do not have to stop or yield to other traffic.

3. **b.** School buses have to stop completely at railroad crossings, whether or not a train is visible.

4. **b.** This is a multiplication problem. Manny spends $1.10 each way and makes 10 trips each week. 1.10 times 10 is 11.00.

5. **b.** According to the schedule, the bus will arrive at Pear and Beech Streets at 8:50.

6. **d.** The bus will arrive at Fir and Linder Streets three minutes late, or 10:55.

7. **a.** The passenger would need to take the bus that leaves Willow and Apple Streets at 8:44.

8. **a.** It's never wise to follow another vehicle closely, but in low visibility conditions it's especially important to keep your distance from other vehicles.

9. **c.** This car still has right-of-way in this lane of traffic so you are required to wait until the car is safely out of the way. Honking the horn, as in choice **a**, is inappropriate, as the other car is performing a legal maneuver. The other two choices are likely to be dangerous.

10. **b.** If you are going north, you have to turn left to go west.

11. **c.** This is a simple addition problem. Add the four numbers together to arrive at the answer, which is $1772.10.

12. **d.** It is good for public relations to let people know when a bus is not in service, and the best way is to display a destination sign to that effect. If the bus is marked "Not in Service," then no passengers are to be picked up.

13. **a.** The passenger is exhibiting the warning signs of a heart attack, which can happen at any age. Even if you don't recognize the warning signs of a particular illness, you should contact the Command Center for any type of medical emergency. To assume the man is drunk, as in choice **b**, would be reckless.

14. **d.** You should be driving defensively at all times and must be ready to compensate for bad drivers. It would be dangerous to try to teach this driver a lesson.

15. **c.** You are responsible for the safety and well-being of your passengers. Under these circumstances, your best option is to drive normally.

16. **a.** Smooth, even acceleration will keep the ride safe for passengers.

17. **b.** This is a multiplication of fractions problem. Six minutes is $\frac{6}{60}$ of an hour, which is reduced to $\frac{1}{10}$; $2\frac{1}{2} = \frac{5}{2}$. Next, multiply. $\frac{1}{10} \times \frac{5}{2} = \frac{1}{4}$.

18. **c.** The incident occurred at the corner of Gable and Lombard.

19. **d.** The passengers involved in the incident were James Gallagher and a woman who refused to give her name. (Choice **a** may at first seem plausible; however, according to the sixth sentence of the passage, Alvin Rickman did not actually board the bus.)

20. **b.** The injured person was transported to the hospital by ambulance.

21. a. Since Alvin Rickman was arrested by an officer from precinct 14, Rickman was taken to that precinct when he was taken into custody.

22. c. The incident occurred at 7:22 p.m.

23. d. Wilkins failed to follow step 6 in the loud noise procedure, which is to remain where she hit the silent alarm.

24. a. Gianelli began with the first step in the loud noise procedure and got the woman's cooperation. Thus, none of the other steps became necessary. The subsequent laughter by the other passengers was too brief to be a problem.

25. b. Simpson acted properly by following step 6 of the loud noise procedure. It would not be safe to involve other passengers in the problem, even the one who said she knew the man (choices **a** and **c**). Choice **d** is wrong because there is no mention of how Simpson started to deal with the problem.

26. c. You should contact the Command Center for instructions whenever you have an injury aboard your bus. In this situation, allowing the mother to handle the injured child is best and applying pressure directly to a wound is a sound first aid strategy.

27. b. The passage states that the seat belt should pass under the arms of the wheelchair and that it is up to the bus operator to make sure the chair is secure.

28. a. Teller should secure the tie-down based on what he remembers of the directions, asking Finch for help when necessary.

29. a. Giving the man a refund form is the best way to handle this situation, although you may be tempted to give the passenger money from your own pocket, as in choice **b**, just so you won't have to listen to him any longer. Since bus operators no longer handle money, asking the Command Center if you can refund his money and be reimbursed, as in choice **c**, is not an option. Choice **d** would simply antagonize the man further.

30. d. According to the third sentence of the passage, each passenger must show the driver a library card in order to receive half fare.

31. c. According to the last sentence of the passage, the trip sheet has a "special fare" section, implying that drivers regularly deal with special fares.

32. b. A smooth, gentle stop will keep passengers from losing their balance.

33. c. You are legally in the intersection so you are not required to speed up or slow down in these circumstances. A yellow light means that you should exercise caution, but you need not come to a stop.

34. c. Your first obligation is always to the safety and well-being of your passengers. You need to make sure that your bus is still in safe operating condition before you continue your run. It would never be appropriate to involve a passenger in bus operation problems, as in choice **b**.

35. d. The safest choice for everyone at this point is to stay behind this driver. Leave enough room to allow for a quick stop without putting passengers at risk of injury.

36. b. You must divide 20.32 by 2.54. First, move each number over two decimal places: 2032 divided by 254 is 8.

37. d. First you must add the two fractions to determine what fraction of the total number of buses was in for maintenance and repair. The common denominator for $\frac{1}{6}$ and $\frac{1}{8}$ is 24, so $\frac{1}{6} + \frac{1}{8} = \frac{4}{24} + \frac{3}{24}$, or $\frac{7}{24}$. Next, divide 28 by $\frac{7}{24}$ for a total of 96.

38. a. Bus route 106 goes from the Museum of the City of New York to the corner of Columbus Avenue and West 96th Street.

39. c. Bus route 11 goes from the Cathedral of St. John the Divine to the American Museum of Natural History.

40. d. Bus route 4 goes from the Metropolitan Museum of Art to the Cathedral of St. John the Divine.

41. b. Bus route 31 goes from the corner of 1st Avenue and East 91st Street to John Jay Park.

42. c. Bus route 86 is the best route to take from the Children's Museum of Manhattan to the corner of Lexington Avenue and East 86th Street.

43. a. Both bus route 7 and bus route 11 go from the corner of Duke Ellington Boulevard and Columbus Avenue to the American Museum of Natural History.

44. a. You should find someone to assist you in moving the bus. Honking the horn until someone comes, as in choice **b**, would be inappropriate and inconsiderate. It would be poor judgment to risk an accident by moving the bus without assistance, as in choice **c**. It is more professional to take the bus you've been assigned to take than to pick another one on your own, as in choice **d**.

45. b. It is part of the bus operator's job to give customers enough information to let them know how to plan their ride. Some may need transfers and some may need to wait for another bus that can get them where they are going. A sign such as that in choice **d** may not be readily understood by the passengers.

46. d. The passenger complied, so Kipfer was right in letting him stay on the bus.

47. b. No smoking is allowed on the bus; the bus operator is not an exception to this rule.

48. d. The fact that you have your turn signal on does not mean that you can take the right-of-way from other vehicles. You are still obligated to make sure the lane is clear before you enter it.

49. a. You should slow down before entering a curve. The other options would show poor judgment.

50. d. Riding a skateboard on a bus is not safe. Simply asking the passenger not to use it while he's on the bus should be enough to handle the situation.

51. a. The passengers may simply be rebellious, but, on the other hand, they may have good reasons for not complying with your request. For instance, disabled persons often find it easier to exit through the front doors and a person's disability is not always readily apparent. In this case it is in the best interest of the other passengers, as well as being more efficient, to simply ignore this minor infraction of rules.

52. b. Once the passenger realizes that the umbrella is missing, she will most likely call Lost and Found, so turning it in is the most logical solution.

53. c. The customer's main interest is probably having a comfortable place to wait for the bus, and it's good public relations to help make sure that happens. It also takes less time to handle the problem by reporting it to the proper authorities than it does to try to explain to a customer why you aren't responsible, as in choice **a**. It would be insulting to tell the customer to avoid sitting on the bench, as in choice **b**.

54. b. Pedestrians have right-of-way under these circumstances, even if there is no formal painted set of lines for a crosswalk. In this case you stopped at the stop line, so there is no need for you to back up, as in choice **d**.

55. d. Once you have entered an intersection legally, you have the right to proceed with the turn in a safe manner. (This rationale does not apply to intersections blocked by heavy traffic since entering a blocked intersection is illegal.)

56. d. Bus # 53 used the least fuel.

57. a. Bus #56 used the most fuel and therefore has the longest route.

58. c. The passage states the driver should proceed to the stop and wait for the passenger.

59. d. The passage indicates that the goal of the program is to decrease the distance passengers have to walk. Since it is only in effect at night, it is probably out of concern for passenger safety.

60. a. Flashing red lights in all directions are a signal for drivers to treat the intersection as a four-way stop.

61. b. To be fair to other passengers who have paid the fare without question, your best option is to ask the father to pay a fare for his son. It is inappropriate to involve other passengers in bus operation problems, as in choice d.

62. d. You should always respond to passengers in a polite, professional manner.

63. b. The passage explains the procedure for bus drivers to follow when their bus gets ahead of schedule; therefore, "running hot" means running ahead of schedule.

64. d. The passage indicates that each route contains several check points at which drivers should check the time to see if they are running on schedule.

65. c. The safety of passengers is a bus operator's first concern. Taking a bus out on the street when a safety feature is not operating properly is dangerous.

66. a. If the other driver cannot see clearly, she is required by law to wait until traffic is clear enough to make the turn. It is unsafe for you back up or to direct traffic from the driver's seat as this may cause an accident.

67. c. It's always safe and sound strategy to drive slowly and smoothly in icy conditions. Choices a and b would show poor judgment. Choice d is impractical.

68. b. Your best option is to be honest with the customer and let him know in a professional manner what the options are. Choice c is rude and choice d is inappropriate and unprofessional. For another passenger to help, as in choice a, could cause injury.

69. d. You must stop out of the way of traffic in order to let the man board. Options a, b, and c would be very dangerous as well as illegal.

70. c. The safety of your passengers comes first, and pulling into traffic when you don't know if it is clear is not safe. Also, passengers should not be permitted to stand far enough forward in the bus to block the driver's view.

SCORING

In order to score your exam, begin by counting the total number of questions you got right out of the 70 questions on the test. Next, you have to convert that score into a percentage. Divide your correct answer score by 0.7 to get the total percentage of right answers. The table below will help you check your math by giving you percentage equivalents for several possible scores.

Number of questions right	Approximate percentage
70	100%
65	93%
60	86%
55	79%
50	71%
45	64%
40	57%
35	50%

You need a score of at least 70 percent to pass the bus operator exam. However, since your rank on the eligibility list may well be based, in whole or in part, on your score on the written exam, you should try for the highest score you can possibly reach. You have probably seen improvement between your first practice exam score and this one. If you didn't improve as much as you would like, here are some options:

- **If you scored below 60 percent,** you should do some serious thinking about whether you're really ready to take the bus operator exam. An adult education course in reading comprehension at a high school or community college would be a very good strategy. If you don't have time for a course,

you should at least try to get some private tutoring.

- **If your score is in the 60 to 70 percent range,** you need to work as hard as you can in the time you have left to boost your skills. Consider the LearningExpress book *Reading Comprehension in 20 Minutes a Day* (order information at the back of this book) or other books from your public library. Also, re-read Chapters 6–9 of this book, and make sure you take *all* of the advice there for improving your score. Enlist friends and family to help you by making up mock test questions and quizzing you on them.

- **If your score is between 70 and 90 percent,** you could still benefit from additional work to help improve your score. Go back to Chapters 6–9, and study your driver's manual carefully between now and test day.

- **If you scored above 90 percent,** congratulations! Your score should be high enough to make you an attractive candidate to the Department of Buses. Make sure you don't lose your edge; keep studying this book up to the day before the exam.

If you didn't score as well as you would like, try to analyze the reasons why. Did you run out of time before you could answer all the questions? Did you go back and change your answer from the right one to a wrong one? Did you get flustered and sit staring at a hard question for what seemed like hours? If you had any of these problems, go back and review the test-taking strategies in Chapter 4 to learn how to avoid them.

You should also look at how you did on each kind of question on the test. You may have done very well on reading comprehension questions and poorly on driving questions, or vice versa. If you can figure out where your strengths and weaknesses lie, you'll know where to concentrate your efforts in the time you have left before the exam. The table on this page identifies which questions on the practice exam fall into which categories and tells you which chapters to review if you had trouble with a particular type.

Before you take the third practice exam in Chapter 11, re-read with the chapters that cover the areas you had most trouble. After you work through those chapters, take the third practice exam in Chapter 11 and once again check your improvement.

BUS OPERATOR EXAM 2		
Question Type	**Question numbers**	**Chapter**
Rules of the road and safe driving	2, 3, 8–10, 14–16, 32–33, 35, 48, 49, 54, 55, 60, 66, 67, 70	6, "Safe Driving"
Reading bulletins, schedules, and route maps	5–7, 18–22, 27, 28, 30, 31, 38–43, 46–47, 56–59, 63, 64	7, "Reading Bulletins. Schedules, and Route Maps"
Judgment, application of procedures, and courtesy to passengers	1, 12, 13, 23–26, 29, 34, 44, 45, 50, 51–53, 61, 62, 65, 68, 69	8, "Good Judgment and Common Sense"
Math	4, 11, 17, 36, 37	9, "Mathematics"

C·H·A·P·T·E·R

BUS OPERATOR PRACTICE EXAM 3

CHAPTER SUMMARY

This is the third of three practice exams in this book. As explained previously, the exams are based on the most commonly tested areas on bus operator written exams across the country. You have now worked through the instructional material in the previous chapters and have taken the second practice exam. Use this third exam to see how much your score has improved since you took the second one.

The actual exam you take may be somewhat different from the ones in this book; however, you should find that most of the same skills are tested on the real exam as on these practice exams. This test, like the previous two, includes 70 multiple-choice questions on reading schedules, bulletins, and route maps; rules of the road and safe driving; judgment and the ability to follow procedures in routine and emergency situations; courtesy to passengers; and mathematics.

As you did when your took the second practice exam, try to come as close to the actual test-taking experience as possible. Work in a quiet place where you won't be disturbed. Tear out the answer sheet on the next page and fill in the circles with your number 2 pencils. Give yourself two hours for the entire exam, using a timer or stopwatch.

After the exam, again use the answer key that follows it to see how you did; the answer explanations in that section should be helpful. Following the answer key you will find a section on how to score your exam.

1.	ⓐ	ⓑ	ⓒ	ⓓ
2.	ⓐ	ⓑ	ⓒ	ⓓ
3.	ⓐ	ⓑ	ⓒ	ⓓ
4.	ⓐ	ⓑ	ⓒ	ⓓ
5.	ⓐ	ⓑ	ⓒ	ⓓ
6.	ⓐ	ⓑ	ⓒ	ⓓ
7.	ⓐ	ⓑ	ⓒ	ⓓ
8.	ⓐ	ⓑ	ⓒ	ⓓ
9.	ⓐ	ⓑ	ⓒ	ⓓ
10.	ⓐ	ⓑ	ⓒ	ⓓ
11.	ⓐ	ⓑ	ⓒ	ⓓ
12.	ⓐ	ⓑ	ⓒ	ⓓ
13.	ⓐ	ⓑ	ⓒ	ⓓ
14.	ⓐ	ⓑ	ⓒ	ⓓ
15.	ⓐ	ⓑ	ⓒ	ⓓ
16.	ⓐ	ⓑ	ⓒ	ⓓ
17.	ⓐ	ⓑ	ⓒ	ⓓ
18.	ⓐ	ⓑ	ⓒ	ⓓ
19.	ⓐ	ⓑ	ⓒ	ⓓ
20.	ⓐ	ⓑ	ⓒ	ⓓ
21.	ⓐ	ⓑ	ⓒ	ⓓ
22.	ⓐ	ⓑ	ⓒ	ⓓ
23.	ⓐ	ⓑ	ⓒ	ⓓ
24.	ⓐ	ⓑ	ⓒ	ⓓ
25.	ⓐ	ⓑ	ⓒ	ⓓ
26.	ⓐ	ⓑ	ⓒ	ⓓ
27.	ⓐ	ⓑ	ⓒ	ⓓ
28.	ⓐ	ⓑ	ⓒ	ⓓ
29.	ⓐ	ⓑ	ⓒ	ⓓ
30.	ⓐ	ⓑ	ⓒ	ⓓ
31.	ⓐ	ⓑ	ⓒ	ⓓ
32.	ⓐ	ⓑ	ⓒ	ⓓ
33.	ⓐ	ⓑ	ⓒ	ⓓ
34.	ⓐ	ⓑ	ⓒ	ⓓ
35.	ⓐ	ⓑ	ⓒ	ⓓ
36.	ⓐ	ⓑ	ⓒ	ⓓ
37.	ⓐ	ⓑ	ⓒ	ⓓ
38.	ⓐ	ⓑ	ⓒ	ⓓ
39.	ⓐ	ⓑ	ⓒ	ⓓ
40.	ⓐ	ⓑ	ⓒ	ⓓ
41.	ⓐ	ⓑ	ⓒ	ⓓ
42.	ⓐ	ⓑ	ⓒ	ⓓ
43.	ⓐ	ⓑ	ⓒ	ⓓ
44.	ⓐ	ⓑ	ⓒ	ⓓ
45.	ⓐ	ⓑ	ⓒ	ⓓ
46.	ⓐ	ⓑ	ⓒ	ⓓ
47.	ⓐ	ⓑ	ⓒ	ⓓ
48.	ⓐ	ⓑ	ⓒ	ⓓ
49.	ⓐ	ⓑ	ⓒ	ⓓ
50.	ⓐ	ⓑ	ⓒ	ⓓ
51.	ⓐ	ⓑ	ⓒ	ⓓ
52.	ⓐ	ⓑ	ⓒ	ⓓ
53.	ⓐ	ⓑ	ⓒ	ⓓ
54.	ⓐ	ⓑ	ⓒ	ⓓ
55.	ⓐ	ⓑ	ⓒ	ⓓ
56.	ⓐ	ⓑ	ⓒ	ⓓ
57.	ⓐ	ⓑ	ⓒ	ⓓ
58.	ⓐ	ⓑ	ⓒ	ⓓ
59.	ⓐ	ⓑ	ⓒ	ⓓ
60.	ⓐ	ⓑ	ⓒ	ⓓ
61.	ⓐ	ⓑ	ⓒ	ⓓ
62.	ⓐ	ⓑ	ⓒ	ⓓ
63.	ⓐ	ⓑ	ⓒ	ⓓ
64.	ⓐ	ⓑ	ⓒ	ⓓ
65.	ⓐ	ⓑ	ⓒ	ⓓ
66.	ⓐ	ⓑ	ⓒ	ⓓ
67.	ⓐ	ⓑ	ⓒ	ⓓ
68.	ⓐ	ⓑ	ⓒ	ⓓ
69.	ⓐ	ⓑ	ⓒ	ⓓ
70.	ⓐ	ⓑ	ⓒ	ⓓ

BUS OPERATOR PRACTICE EXAM 3

1. You are driving west on a two-lane, one-way street. Ahead you see construction cones blocking off your lane and forcing traffic into the far left lane. Which of the following actions is best for you to take?
   a. stop the bus and wait until the work crew moves the cones
   b. signal and move into the left lane when safe to do so
   c. drive so that the bus straddles the cones
   d. find a place to turn around so you can avoid the work area

2. Buses on Loop III run every 18 minutes. If one bus leaves Stop 6 at 1:55 p.m., when is the next bus due to arrive at Stop 6?
   a. 2:07
   b. 2:13
   c. 2:16
   d. 2:17

3. Two passengers standing in the rear of your bus start punching each other as you pull up to a bus stop. From your window you can see two police officers standing near the stop and talking. What action should you take?
   a. stop the bus and politely ask the fighters to stop fighting
   b. ask the other passengers to break up the fight
   c. brake quickly to get the two fighters' attention and tell them to cut it out
   d. stop at the bus stop and ask the officers for help

4. You pull up to an intersection to make a right turn. The signal light is red, and next to it is a sign that reads: "No Right on Red." What does this sign mean?
   a. right turns are not allowed at this intersection
   b. cars turning right have the right-of-way
   c. cars may turn right only when the light is green
   d. cars in the right-hand lane may not turn right

Answer questions 5–10 on the basis of the map on the next page.

5. Which is the best bus route to take from the Ocean Museum to the State Capitol?
   a. 42
   b. 33
   c. 37
   d. 59

6. Which bus route goes from the Star Theater to St. Agatha's?
   a. 59
   b. 15
   c. 17
   d. 37

7. Which is the best bus to take from the General Hospital to the Court House?
   a. 37
   b. 21
   c. 15
   d. 59

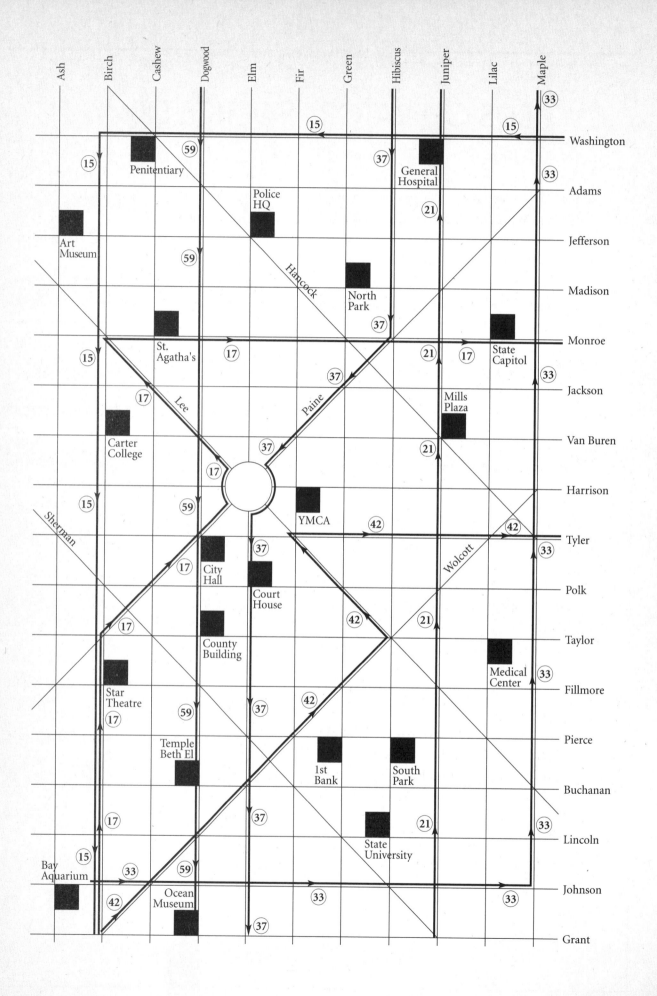

8. Which is the best bus to take from the Art Museum to the Bay Aquarium?
   a. 17
   b. 59
   c. 42
   d. 15

9. Which is the best bus route to take from City Hall to the State Capitol?
   a. 37
   b. 59
   c. 17
   d. 33

10. Which bus is the best one to take from St. Agatha's to Temple Beth El?
   a. 59
   b. 42
   c. 17
   d. 37

11. You are pulling away from a bus stop after boarding passengers. A man is running along the sidewalk cursing and waving a knife. He yells angrily at you to pull over because his wife is on that bus. What action should you take?
   a. stop and ask the man's wife if she wants to get off the bus and deal with her husband
   b. keep driving, but call the Command Center so police can be notified of a person threatening with a weapon
   c. stop and do what the man tells you to do, as you may endanger the people on the sidewalk if you do not
   d. simply ignore the man and drive on, as it would be inappropriate for you to become involved in a fight between a husband and wife

12. After loading several passengers on board your bus, you are ready to continue straight along Redfern Drive. The signal light at the intersection several feet in front of you has been yellow for several seconds. What is the safest action for you to take?
   a. proceed swiftly through the intersection, as this is only a "caution" light
   b. stop at this intersection and wait for the next yellow light
   c. honk your horn to warn other drivers, then proceed through the intersection
   d. stop at this intersection and wait for the next green light

Answer questions 13–15 on the basis of the chart below.

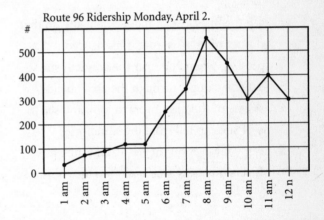

Route 96 Ridership Monday, April 2.

13. According to the chart, the greatest increase in ridership on April 2 on Route 96 occurred
   a. between 4 a.m. and 5 a.m.
   b. between 8 a.m. and 9 a.m.
   c. between 10 a.m. and 11 a.m.
   d. between 7 a.m. and 8 a.m.

14. According to the chart, the busiest hour in the morning on April 2 on Route 96 is
  a. 6 a.m.
  b. 7 a.m.
  c. 8 a.m.
  d. 9 a.m.

15. The morning hours with the least number of passengers on Route 96 on April 2 were
  a. 5 a.m. and 6 a.m.
  b. 1 a.m. and 2 a.m.
  c. 4 a.m. and 5 a.m.
  d. 6 a.m. and 7 a.m.

16. You are driving past a traffic accident and notice an ambulance and police car at the scene. You wonder what happened and whether additional help might be needed. What should you do?
  a. stop the bus close to the accident site, so that you can offer assistance if it's needed
  b. speed up when you near the accident site so that you can get through the area quickly
  c. ask one of the passengers to look and see if he or she can tell what the situation is
  d. keep your eyes on the road and watch for officers directing traffic around the collision site

17. A seventeen-year-old is trying to board your bus one afternoon with his seven-year-old brother. The youngest boy is waving a pellet gun around. What action should you take?
  a. tell them they cannot ride the bus with a pellet gun and refuse to allow them on board
  b. let the older brother on, but leave the seven-year-old with the pellet gun behind

  c. let the boys on, but ask one of the passengers to make sure the youngest one doesn't shoot the gun
  d. ask for the boys' home phone number and have the Command Center call the boys' parents to ask if it's okay for them to have the gun

18. A teenager wearing sunglasses and carrying a white cane is waiting at one of your bus stops, a large dog at his side. What should you do?
  a. apologize to the teenager, but let him know that animals are not allowed on the bus
  b. allow the teenager and the animal on board the bus only if the dog is a seeing eye dog
  c. call Command Center and request that they send a taxi for this teenager as animals are not allowed on the bus
  d. drive past the bus stop without stopping because animals are not allowed on the bus

19. While assisting a handicapped passenger aboard your bus you drop and break your glasses. You have only one more block to go before ending your route. You can see large objects, but otherwise things are a little blurry without glasses. What action should you take?
  a. drive more slowly than usual, as you have only one more block to go, and only large objects are likely to cause danger
  b. ask if anyone on board the bus has a commercial license; if so, ask that person to drive the bus to the next stop
  c. ask a passenger to stand next to you while you drive and help you watch traffic
  d. call Command Center, place your bus out of service, and ask passengers to wait for the next bus

20. It's after midnight and you are two stops away from completing your run and going home for the night. The light is red for your lane of traffic and you notice that you are the only vehicle at the intersection with no others in sight in any direction. What should you do?

    a. drive on through the intersection since it's late and no other cars are around

    b. wait for the green light and proceed

    c. turn right on the red light and go around the block

    d. honk your horn and proceed with caution through the intersection

21. You are driving your bus in a lane marked "Buses Only" during rush hour traffic. Suddenly you notice that a car is broken down in your lane. What should you do?

    a. stop behind the car and let the driver know that it was illegal for him or her to be in the bus lane in the first place

    b. stop the bus and get out to see if there is something you can do to help

    c. call the Command Center and notify them that a car has broken down in the bus lane, then proceed on your route

    d. push the car off the freeway for the other driver using the bumper of the bus

22. A passenger you know slightly, and whom you find very attractive, boards your bus at rush hour. This person smiles and winks at you. What should you do?

    a. reach out and pat this person's arm

    b. ask for this person's home phone number

    c. smile at the person and continue your route

    d. invite the person to stand in the stairwell and talk to you while you drive

23. You are driving north on the freeway. You take the next exit and then turn west onto Hackberry Drive. What kind of turn did you make?

    a. left turn

    b. right turn

    c. U-turn

    d. an illegal turn

24. You are boarding passengers at a crowded bus stop at the peak of rush hour traffic. A male passenger is waiting in line to get aboard the bus. He has a large tire with him and tries to drag it up the stairs as he boards the bus. What action should you take?

    a. tell the man to leave the tire in the bus shelter and you'll pick it up for him later when the bus is less crowded

    b. tell the man to place the tire into the front stairwell as soon as everyone is finished boarding and then let him on

    c. charge the man double the normal fare for having a large object with him, as it takes up at least as much room as a small child

    d. tell the man that you do not have room on the bus for both him and the tire and that he cannot board

25. Your throat was very sore this morning and by the time you got to work you realized your voice was completely gone. You don't feel ill and don't like to use sick leave. It's time to check out your bus and start your route. What should you do?

    a. go ahead and start your route as your voice will likely return

    b. tell your supervisor about your problem immediately

    c. drive for a few hours, take the bus back to the shed, and then go home sick

    d. take a pad and pen with you, so you can write messages to the passengers

26. You are driving south on Comal Street, a one-lane street. Ahead, you see that Comal merges with Anderson Lane, another one-lane, south-bound street. You have a yield sign. What should you do?

    a. maintain your normal speed and merge with Anderson Lane traffic

    b honk your horn to alert Anderson Lane traffic, then merge without waiting

    c. come to a complete stop, even if Anderson Lane has no traffic, then proceed

    d. slow down and give right-of-way to traffic already on Anderson Lane

27. You are running behind on your afternoon route. You hear a train whistle and suddenly realize that unless you skip the next bus stop you will have to wait for the train at the railroad crossing. You see one passenger waiting at this stop. What action should you take?

    a. skip this stop so that you can arrive at the railroad crossing before the train

    b. stop at the bus stop, pick up the passenger, and proceed along your route

    c. stop at the bus stop and hurry the passenger on so that perhaps you can get to the rail crossing before the train does

    d. stop at the bus stop, pick up the passenger, and wait at the bus stop until you see that the railroad crossing is clear

28. You are driving along a residential street with over 40 passengers on your bus. The wind is blowing hard and you see a cardboard box approximately the size of a loaf of bread bouncing down the middle of the street. As you near the box it bounces in front of your bus. What should you do?

    a. run over the box without swerving or putting on the brakes

    b. put on the brakes and turn the wheel sharply to the right to avoid the box

    c. stop the bus as quickly and smoothly as possible

    d. put on the brakes and turn the wheel sharply to the left to avoid the box

29. District C spends about $4,446.00 on diesel fuel each week. If the cost of diesel fuel to the district is about $1.17 per gallon, about how many gallons of diesel fuel does the district use in one week?

    a. 3,800.00

    b. 3,810.00

    c. 3,972.00

    d. 5,202.00

30. A teenager boards your bus during rush hour traffic and tells you that she is doing a research paper for school on mass transportation. She asks if you will give her some information on bus driving. What should you do?

   a. tell her it's unsafe to answer her questions on a moving bus and suggest she pick another topic to write about

   b. have her stand next to you, continue on your route, and answer as many of her questions as you can

   c. tell her to meet you at a coffee shop immediately after you get off work and you'll answer her questions

   d. give her a brochure with the Command Center's phone number on it and ask her to call them so that they can help with her project

31. Your bus is crowded and passengers are standing. You have just pulled away from the Lamar Street bus stop when a woman loses her balance, falls down, and cries out. What should you do?

   a. stop the bus until she has regains her composure, then ask her if she feels she's seriously hurt

   b. stop the bus, call Command Center, and request medical assistance for the woman, then put the bus will be out of service until the situation can be handled

   c. stop the bus, walk quickly to the woman and pick her up, then carry her off of the bus to wait for medical help

   d. call for medical help, but request that the woman wait in the bus shelter as she does not appear seriously hurt, then continue on your route

32. A police officer is directing traffic at the next intersection. The officer directs you to proceed through the intersection even though the signal light is red. What should you do?

   a. come to a complete stop first, then continue through the intersection

   b. proceed through the intersection as directed

   c. treat the intersection as if it were a four-way stop

   d. yield to other traffic, then proceed through the intersection

33. At the next bus stop you see several teenagers waiting to board the bus. Teenagers in this area have been known to belong to gangs and to make serious trouble. You know that another bus is only a minute or so behind your bus. What action should you take?

   a. stop and wait for the other bus to pull up, so you'll have help if there's trouble

   b. tell them you'll have to frisk them for weapons before you allow them on board

   c. stop, let them on board, and treat them the same as the other passengers

   d. let only the female teenagers on board because they are usually less rowdy

34. Which kind of turn is the safest one to make during rush hour traffic?

   a. a right turn from a one-way street onto another one-way street

   b. a left turn from a two-way street onto a one-way street

   c. a left turn from a two-way street onto another two-way street

   d. a U-turn on a two-way street

35. A drunk man is trying to board your bus at the Trinity Street bus stop. He is holding a half-empty wine bottle. He smiles, holds up a cork, and shows you that he is putting the cork into the bottle. He starts to climb up the stairs of the bus and trips. What should you do?

    a. tell the man that he cannot get on, because no alcohol is allowed on board the bus

    b. let the man on as long as he promises to keep the bottle corked while the bus is moving

    c. ask the man to leave the bottle with you for safekeeping until he's ready to get off the bus

    d. charge the man twice the normal fare so he will be discouraged from bringing alcohol on board again

36. You are driving north on a two-way street. A driver headed south on this street begins to drift across the center yellow double stripe into your lane. What is the best action for you to take?

    a. continue to drive straight, but honk your horn to warn the other driver

    b. start moving your bus to the left to avoid the drifting car

    c. start moving your bus to the right to avoid the drifting car

    d. speed up so as to pass this dangerous driver as quickly as possible

37. A young woman you know slightly boards your bus wearing a T-shirt that says, "Unions are for losers!" She's made hostile remarks about unions to you before, and you know she's aware that the bus drivers in your city are all union members. What should you do?

    a. let her board and, as you drive, calmly try to persuade her to your point of view

    b. allow her to board, but tell her you don't appreciate her anti-union attitudes

    c. tell her that the bus fare just went up and her bus pass won't cover it today

    d. treat her as you do all the other passengers and continue on your route

38. You are driving in a heavy downpour when your bus begins to slide sideways. What action should you take?

    a. slam on the brakes so as to stop as quickly as you can

    b. brake and turn the steering wheel in the opposite direction from where you want the bus to go

    c. do not use your brakes and turn the steering wheel in the direction you want the bus to go

    d. keep the steering wheel as straight as possible

39. "Countersteering" is turning the wheel of a vehicle quickly back in the opposite direction from where you just turned it. Under what circumstances would you want to use this kind of steering?

    a. after swerving around a ball that bounced in front of your bus

    b. when trying to make a left turn

    c. when trying to make a right turn

    d. when trying to make a U-turn

40. Kendra earns $12.50 an hour. When she works more than 8 hours in one day, she earns 1 1/2 times her regular hourly wage. If she earns $137.50 for one day's work, how many hours did she work that day?

    a. 8.5

    b. 9

    c. 10

    d. 11

41. In an emergency, if you are forced to drive off of a paved street onto an unpaved gravel shoulder, what is the best action for you to take?

a. quickly turn the steering wheel as hard as you can to the right

b. brake hard so that your bus will come quickly to a complete stop

c. turn the bus so it goes gently back and forth from paved to unpaved surface

d. avoid braking until your speed has slowed to 20 mph

42. You are driving down a very steep hill on a residential street. Which of the following is the best braking technique to use?

a. step on the brake until the bus stops, then release; repeat the process until you reach the bottom of the hill

b. brake firmly and continuously as your bus descends, until you reach the bottom of the hill

c. brake until you feel your bus slow down, then release; repeat the process until you reach the bottom of the hill

d. shift into a high gear, but keep the brakes pressed at least halfway to the floor as you proceed down the hill

Answer questions 43–46 on the basis of the information below.

At the beginning of each shift, every driver shall do the following:

1. Record the beginning mileage on the route sheet.
2. Note the fuel level on the route sheet.
3. Reset the passenger counter.

4. Check and adjust all inside and outside mirrors.
5. Adjust the driver's seat and fasten the seat belt. Drivers are required to wear seat belts at all times.

At the end of each shift, every driver shall:

1. Record the ending mileage on the route sheet.
2. Fill the fuel tank if below half.
3. Record the number from the passenger counter on the route sheet.
4. Remove all money from the fare box.
5. Walk through the bus checking for lost items and trash.
6. Remove all trash and personal belongings.

43. Operator Jamison is just beginning his shift. He has recorded the beginning mileage on the route sheet, reset the passenger counter, checked and adjusted all outside mirrors, and adjusted the driver's seat and fastened the seat belt. He now begins his run. Operator Jamison's actions are

a. proper, because he has performed all actions except adjusting all mirrors

b. improper, because he has not yet noted the fuel level or adjusted all mirrors

c. proper, because he has performed all actions except filling the fuel tank

d. improper, because he has not yet filled the fuel tank or recorded ending mileage

44. Operator Miller is just ending her shift. She has recorded the ending mileage on the route sheet, filled the fuel tank, removed all money from the fare box, walked through the bus checking for lost items and trash, and removed all trash and personal belongings. What does she still need to do before ending her shift?

a. note the fuel level on the route sheet

b. reset the passenger counter

c. record the number from the passenger counter on the route sheet

d. count the money in the fare box

45. Operator Stein has just ended his shift. He has recorded the ending mileage on the route sheet, filled the fuel tank, recorded the number from the passenger counter on the route sheet, walked through the bus checking for lost items and trash, and removed all trash and personal belongings. Before leaving, Stein needs to

a. remove all money from the fare box

b. reset the passenger counter

c. adjust all the mirrors

d. make sure all headlights and signal lights are working

46. Operator Hanson is just starting her shift. She has noted the fuel level on the route sheet, reset the passenger counter, checked and adjusted all inside and outside mirrors, and adjusted the driver's seat. What does she still need to do before beginning her route?

a. reset the passenger counter

b. remove the money from the fare box

c. walk through the bus checking for lost items and trash

d. record the beginning mileage on the route sheet

47. The City Bus Department operates 200 bus routes. Of these, 5.5% are express routes. How many express routes are there?

a. 11

b. 15

c. 22

d. 25

Answer questions 48–52 on the basis of the following bus schedule.

ROUTE 17								
State Center	Ridge & Pine	Ridge & Oak	Brown & First	Bryant Mall	Ocean & First	Rose Park	Rice Plaza	Hayes School
2:30	2:35	2:45	2:51	3:00	3:05	3:15	3:22	3:30
3:00	3:05	3:15	3:21	3:30	3:35	3:45	3:52	4:00
3:30	3:35	3:45	3:51	4:00	4:05	4:15	4:22	4:30
4:00	4:05	4:15	4:21	4:30	4:35	4:45	4:52	5:00
4:30	4:35	4:45	4:51	5:00	5:05	5:15	5:22	5:30
5:00	5:05	5:15	5:21	5:30	5:35	5:45	5:52	6:00
5:30	5:35	5:45	5:51	6:00	6:05	6:15	6:22	6:30

48. A passenger wishing to arrive at Bryant Mall no later than 3:20 should catch the bus at Ridge and Pine at
   a. 2:30
   b. 2:35
   c. 2:45
   d. 3:05

49. A passenger leaving Bryant Mall at 4:00 will arrive at Hayes School at
   a. 5:00
   b. 4:22
   c. 4:30
   d. 4:35

50. The bus scheduled to leave State Center at 2:30 is delayed 3 minutes and is unable to make up the time as the route progresses. What time will the bus arrive at Rice Plaza?
   a. 3:22
   b. 3:19
   c. 3:18
   d. 3:25

51. A passenger who wants to arrive at Rose Park by 4:30 should catch the bus at Ridge and Oak at
   a. 3:45
   b. 4:15
   c. 3:35
   d. 4:05

52. A bus leaving Brown and First at 5:21 will arrive at Ocean and First at
   a. 5:30
   b. 5:51
   c. 5:35
   d 6:05

53. A man boards your crowded bus one afternoon with a wrapped box in his hands. He's very nervous and is taking great care not to shake the box. He pays his fare, sets the box on a seat, and then walks to the rear doors of the bus. He gets off of your bus and starts running. What action should you take?
   a. get everyone, including yourself, off the bus immediately, and then call the Command Center to report the suspicious package
   b. stop the bus and cautiously examine the package to see if it really does appear dangerous
   c. stop the bus, throw your jacket over the package, and very carefully carry it off the bus
   d. drive the bus straight to the nearest police substation and ask for help from someone who has expertise in explosives

54. Around midnight you are on your last run. You have only two short blocks left to drive. Suddenly, your headlights go out and you can barely see the roadway in front of you. What should you do?
   a. slow down and carefully finish your run
   b. turn on your emergency flashers and finish your run using these lights to see
   c. place your bus out of service, and call the Command Center to ask for help
   d. request that a passenger to come forward to help you see, then proceed

55. A passenger in the rear of the bus begins screaming, "Stop the bus, stop the bus!" You pull to the curb and stop immediately. The passenger laughs and says he just wanted to see if you'd really pull over. What action should you take?
   a. be a good sport and laugh along with him, then continue on your route
   b. refuse to move the bus until he apologizes for his behavior
   c. tell him that his behavior can't be tolerated, and ask him to leave the bus
   d. warn him that if he repeats his irresponsible behavior you will radio the police

Answer questions 56–58 on the basis of the following memo.

Effective immediately City Transit is increasing its base fare. The base fare—for passengers traveling within one zone—will be $1.50. The charge for each additional zone will remain at $0.75. In addition, there will now be a $0.25 surcharge for transfers.

56. A passenger traveling a total of two zones on the same bus should pay a fare of
   a. $1.50
   b. $2.25
   c. $1.75
   d. $3.00

57. A passenger traveling a total of three zones on two buses should pay a fare of
   a. $3.25
   b. $3.00
   c. $2.50
   d. $3.75

58. A passenger traveling a total of four zones on the same bus should pay a fare of
   a. $4.00
   b. $3.50
   c. $3.75
   d. $4.25

59. Bus Operator Cassidy earns $28,200 a year. What is her salary each month?
   a. $2,305
   b. $2,350
   c. $2,400
   d. $2,405

60. A man boards your bus and sits down near the front. As you pull away from the curb he shouts to you that he needs to know how many stops there are before you reach 59th Street. You answer, but he keeps yelling the question so you are fairly sure he is hard of hearing. A passenger offers to talk to the man for you. What should you do?
   a. thank the passenger and let her pass on the information to the man
   b. tell her that you'll handle the situation and ask her not to interfere
   c. explain to both passengers that it's unsafe to talk to you while you're driving
   d. let the other passenger help but ask the man to leave the bus at the next stop

Answer questions 61–63 on the basis of the following memo.

City Transit buses have experienced more down time this year than in each of the last three years, at a cost of over $3 million. Any time a bus is down, not only is it not making money by collecting fares, it is usually costing money because repair work is being done. Of course, all buses must be down on occasion for routine maintenance.

In an effort to decrease bus down time, each bus will be stocked with a clipboard containing maintenance sheets. Each driver will fill out a maintenance sheet at the end of each shift, indicating any potential problems with the bus. This includes the bus engine, transmission, brakes, tires, lights, and mirrors and any other problems a driver may note. If the driver is unaware of any problems, the maintenance sheet must still be signed and turned in at the transit office.

61. According to the memo, "down time" is
   a. the time a bus sits at a bus stop
   b. the time a bus spends stuck in traffic
   c. the time a bus sits at red lights
   d. the time a bus spends being serviced or repaired

62. During the course of his shift, Operator Fox has not noticed any problems with the bus. At the end of his shift he should
   a. sign the maintenance sheet and turn it in at the transit office
   b. not turn in a maintenance sheet as there are no problems with the bus
   c. note on the maintenance sheet that this bus seems fine but the bus he drove yesterday made a grinding noise when the brakes were applied
   d. double-check everything on the bus to see if he can find something wrong

63. According to the memo, any time a bus is down
   a. it is being repaired
   b. it is not making money by collecting fares
   c. it is because of operator negligence
   d. it is because the bus has been in an accident

64. You are waiting to make a left turn at a green light. One car is coming toward you ready to pass through the intersection. This car's right turn signal comes on just as the car enters the intersection. What should you do?
   a. go ahead and start your left turn because the other driver is signaling, and you are both headed in the same direction
   b. proceed on through the intersection and make your left turn at the next intersection
   c. pull out in front of the other car quickly so as to be ahead of it after you make your turn
   d. wait until the car completes its turn because, in this case, the right turn signal may not necessarily mean the driver will actually turn

65. It's late afternoon and you're running behind on your route. A uniformed police officer boards your bus and instructs you not to move the bus until she tells you to. What action should you take?
   a. explain that you are running behind and wish to continue on your route
   b. call the Command Center and ask your supervisor to advise you what to do
   c. without comment, do what the officer asks you to do
   d. ask the officer to show you a warrant and tell her you can't comply otherwise

Answer questions 66–68 on the basis of the following bus schedule.

SUMMER HILL ROUTE					
Lv. Harbor & Main	Arr. Ash & Main	Arr. Milford Mall	Arr. Hayes & Ocean	Arr. James & Ocean	Arr. Summer Hill
6:17	6:22	6:27	6:40	6:46	6:52
6:47	6:52	6:57	7:10	7:16	7:22
7:17	7:22	7:27	7:40	7:46	7:52
7:47	7:52	7:57	8:10	8:16	8:22
8:17	8:22	8:27	8:40	8:46	8:52
8:47	8:52	8:57	9:10	9:16	9:22
9:17	9:22	9:27	9:40	9:46	9:52
9:47	9:52	9:57	10:10	10:16	10:22
10:17	10:22	10:27	10:40	10:46	10:52
10:47	10:52	10:57	11:10	11:16	11:52

66. A passenger wishing to arrive at Milford Mall for a 9:00 appointment should catch the bus at Harbor and Main at
   a. 8:17
   b. 8:47
   c. 8:52
   d. 8:22

67. A passenger boarding the Summer Hill bus at Ash and Main at 6:52 will arrive at Summer Hill at
   a. 7:16
   b. 7:10
   c. 6:57
   d. 7:22

68. A passenger who catches the bus at Milford Mall at 9:27 will arrive at James and Ocean at
   a. 9:40
   b. 9:46
   c. 9:52
   d. 9:57

69. A passenger, known to you to be very eccentric and a bit of a troublemaker, calls out that she thinks she is starting to have a seizure. What should you do?
   a. pull to the curb immediately and call Command Center for medical help
   b. keep driving because she's probably just repeating her usual odd behavior
   c. ask her to hold on for another block until you reach the next bus stop
   d. stop, tell her you're tired of her behavior, and ask her to get off of the bus

70. One of your passengers yells out to you that a man on rollerblades is holding onto the rear of the bus so that it will pull him along. What should you do?

a. tap the brakes gently to dislodge the rollerblader

b. weave side-to-side slightly to dislodge the rollerblader

c. keep driving in a normal fashion so the rollerblader will have to let go

d. pull to the curb slowly, stop the bus, and ask the rollerblader to let go

ANSWERS

1. **b.** The best action is to use your turn signal and change lanes when it's safe to do so. The work crew may not move the cones for hours. Straddling the cones would move the bus into the work area and would be unsafe. There's no need to turn around as there's a way to go past the work area safely.

2. **b.** Add 18 minutes to 1:55 to arrive at the answer, which is 2:13.

3. **d.** Asking the officers to help with this situation makes the most sense. Two men fighting on a bus can endanger the other passengers, and the situation is too intense to attempt to handle it yourself. You should not put other passengers in danger by asking them to break up the fight. Braking quickly might endanger the other passengers.

4. **c.** This sign means that cars cannot turn right unless the signal light is green.

5. **b.** According to the map, the 33 bus route is the best one to take from the Ocean Museum to the State Capitol.

6. **c.** According to the map, the 17 bus route goes from the Star Theater to St. Agatha's.

7. **a.** According to the map, the 37 bus route is the best one to take from General Hospital to the Court House.

8. **d.** According to the map, the 15 bus route is the best one to take from the Art Museum to the Bay Aquarium.

9. **c.** According to the map, the 17 bus route is the best one to take from City Hall to the State Capitol.

10. **a.** According to the map, the 59 bus route is the best one to take from St. Agatha's to Temple Beth El.

11. **b.** None of the other choices are good because they all involve placing you and your passengers in danger from this man who is brandishing a weapon. Your safest choice is to keep the bus moving and call in the situation so that police can handle the man.

12. **d.** Because the "caution" light has been on a while, your safest choice is to stop and wait for the next green light.

13. **d.** The chart shows that the largest increase is between 7 a.m. and 8 a.m.

14. **c.** The chart shows that the busiest hour is at 8 a.m.

15. **b.** The chart shows that the least busy morning hours are 1 a.m. and 2 a.m.

16. **d.** "Rubber-necking," even with the best of intentions, is dangerous; it's best near an accident to keep the flow of traffic as normal as possible. Your responsibility is to keep your eyes on the road and obey officers at the scene.

17. **a.** "Safety First" is still the rule. Under no circumstances would it be wise to allow a person on board with a weapon—even pellet guns can do serious damage. It would be irresponsible to allow the older brother on board and leave a seven-year-old boy unattended.

18. **b.** Since the passenger is blind, if the animal is a seeing eye dog then it and its owner should be allowed on the bus. Requesting that a taxi be called for a stranger would be inappropriate. Passing up the stop because a dog is standing by its owner is not the correct decision.

19. **d.** If your vision is even a little impaired, you should not continue to drive, nor should you let anyone who is not an employee of the bus company operate your bus. It's better to inconvenience passengers for a few moments than to place them in an unsafe situation.

20. b. Only in an extreme emergency should you ever consider violating a traffic law. You should wait until the light turns green and proceed normally.

21. c. Your safest option is to call the Command Center, which will allow officials to send help for this motorist. Stopping yourself, for any reason, will be dangerous.

22. c. No other behavior would be professional in this environment. It's never acceptable to touch a passenger under these conditions, even if it's only on the arm and even if you know the person slightly. In fact, you could be opening yourself or the company up to legal trouble. It is unsafe for anyone to stand in the stairwell while the bus is moving.

23. a. Heading west means you took a left turn. A right turn would head you in an easterly direction and a U-turn would mean you are now heading south. There's nothing in this question to indicate that turning west would be illegal.

24. d. It will not be safe to allow this man to bring such a large object on board a crowded bus nor would it be safe to store it in the stairwell. It's also never wise to tell a passenger that you will accept responsibility for his or her possessions, and by telling this man that you'll come back for his tire if he'll leave it at the bus shelter you are doing just that. It is not your place as the driver to determine the bus fares for the company, so you cannot charge anyone "double" to ride the bus.

25. b. If your voice is gone you cannot communicate with passengers or handle the day-to-day duties of a bus driver. You cannot even ask for help if you need it! You really can't be sure it'll return soon. Your best option is to work out this situation with your supervisor.

26. d. A yield sign means that you should give the right-of-way to other traffic. You are not required to stop unless you need to wait for an opening in traffic on Anderson Lane. It is always dangerous to force your way into traffic or to drive into traffic without looking.

27. b. You should run your route professionally and safely without worrying about whether or not waiting for a train will put you a little more behind the clock. Your passengers' safety and comfort are your main concern.

28. a. Coming to a complete stop or swerving around this obstacle might endanger your passengers. As the box is obviously empty, the safest maneuver is to simply run over it.

29. a. This is a division problem. 4446 divided by 1.17 is 3800.

30. d. It's not safe to carry on a running conversation while you're driving the bus, and it's inappropriate to suggest meeting this teenager after work, even with the best of intentions. Your safest and most courteous option is to refer her to the Command Center where she can be referred to the people who can give her the information she will need for her paper.

31. b. Once again, the safety of your passengers is your responsibility. You should not move an injured person, as there is no way that you—or even the woman herself—can tell whether the injury is serious or not. Getting medical help is your only safe option.

32. b. Go on through the intersection as directed. A police officer's directions always override the traffic control device at an intersection. The officer is probably there because the signal is malfunctioning.

33. c. Passing on your problems, real or imagined, to another bus driver would not be professional (and you can bet it wouldn't go unnoticed by your coworkers). You can't pass up passengers at bus stops just because a certain area has a poor reputation. And you should never touch a passenger without a *very* good reason; to frisk someone would be inappropriate and possibly illegal, since you are not a peace officer.

34. a. The safest turn is from a one-way onto another one-way street, because that means you would not have to cross in front of any other traffic.

35. a. Allowing an obviously intoxicated person on board a bus creates an unsafe situation for everyone. Your safest option is to tell him he cannot board.

36. c. Your safest choice is to start moving to the right. The other driver is very likely to realize what is happening and swerve back into his own lane. If you swerve to your left, you will move into his lane of traffic. If you speed up, you may have a head-on collision at a higher rate of speed than the one at which you were originally driving. Not moving and honking your horn instead will also place you in danger of having a head-on collision, as you can't assume the other driver will hear your horn.

37. d. As a professional driver, you must behave in a professional manner. Your personal beliefs can't be allowed to have any bearing on who rides, or doesn't ride, the bus, nor would it be safe to enter into a discussion with the woman while the bus is in motion. You must bite your tongue and treat her like everyone else.

38. c. To stop skidding, you should always turn the wheel in the direction you want your vehicle to head. You shouldn't use your brakes at any point during the skid. Keeping the steering wheel straight would only mean you would continue to skid sideways.

39. a. Countersteering is used after swerving when you are trying to avoid an obstacle or to get a vehicle under control during a skid. You would not use countersteering when making an ordinary turn.

40. c. This is a four-step problem. First, determine how much she earns in one 8-hour day: 8 times $12.50 is $100.00. Next, subtract $100.00 from $137.00 to find how much overtime she earned: $137.50 minus $100.00 is $37.50. Next, to find out how much her hourly overtime pay is, multiply 1.5 times 12.50, which is 18.75. To find out how many overtime hours she worked, divide: 37.50 divided by 18.75 is 2. Add these two hours to her regular 8 hours for a total of 10 hours.

41. d. If you are forced to drive off the road, your safest choice is to stay off the brakes and let the vehicle slow down by itself to a manageable speed of about 20 mph and then stop. Steering as hard as you can to the right might cause the vehicle to roll over. Swerving back and forth would most likely force the bus out of control.

42. c. A gentle brake-and-release technique will get the best results in this situation. Stepping on the brakes until the bus stops is unnecessary and will jolt the passengers. "Riding" the brakes may burn out the brake pads.

43. b. Jamison has not yet noted the fuel level, nor has he adjusted all mirrors; he's only adjusted the outside mirror.

44. c. According to step 3 of the procedure, Miller still needs to record the number from the passenger counter on the route sheet.

45. a. According to step 4 of the procedure, Stein needs to remove the money from the fare box.

46. d. According to step 1 of the procedure, Hanson needs to record the beginning mileage on the route sheet.

47. a. The easiest way to solve this problem is to convert 5.5% to a decimal: 0.055. Then multiply: 200 times 0.055 is 11.

48. b. According to the schedule, the passenger should catch the bus at Ridge and Pine at 2:35 to arrive at Bryant Mall at 3:00.

49. c. According to the schedule, the bus leaving Bryant Mall at 4:00 arrives at Hayes School at 4:30.

50. d. The bus is scheduled to arrive at Rice Plaza at 3:22. If it is 3 minutes late it will arrive at 3:25.

51. a. According to the schedule, the passenger should take the 3:45 bus to arrive at Rose Park at 4:15.

52. c. According to the schedule, the bus leaving Brown and First at 5:21 will arrive at Ocean and First at 5:35.

53. a. It's always better to be safe than sorry. That passenger's behavior is more than enough to alarm a cautious person, and it's entirely reasonable to suspect that the package might contain a bomb. You and the passengers should exit to safety as soon as possible. You should not attempt to deal with the package yourself in any way.

54. c. Your passenger's safety should always be your first concern. By driving with defective lights, even for two short blocks, you are placing your passengers and other drivers in jeopardy. It's better to inconvenience the passengers than to involve them in a collision.

55. c. Interfering with public transportation in this manner is irresponsible and can even be dangerous; it is against the law in most states. It's your responsibility to let this man and the other passengers know this.

56. b. The base fare for the first zone is $1.50, and the charge for the second zone is $0.75, for a total of $2.25.

57. a. The base fare for the first zone is $1.50. The charge for two more zones is $1.50 (0.75 times 2), and the surcharge for the transfer is $0.25 for a total of $3.25.

58. c. The base fare for the first zone is $1.50, and the charge for three more zones is $2.25 (0.75 times 3), for a total of $3.75.

59. b. This is a division problem. 28,200 divided by 12 (months) is 2350.

60. a. In this situation it would be great to get a little help from a passenger, and thanking her is appropriate. The man has done nothing that would warrant putting him off the bus.

61. d. The passage indicates that down time is time that a bus spends being repaired.

62. a. The passage indicates that Fox should sign the sheet and turn it in at the transit office, even if there is nothing to report.

63. b. According to the memo, a bus may be down for different reasons, but whenever it is down, it is not collecting fares.

64. d. A defensive driver doesn't assume other drivers will drive as they should. This driver's signal came on as the car entered the intersection, which means the signal may be accidental. Also, drivers have been known to change their minds about turning, as well as to keep going with signals flashing brightly. There's no reason not to turn, but your safest choice is to wait until the intersection is clear before doing so.

65. c. You will never make the wrong decision by following the orders of a police officer. Choosing any other option in this situation may put you and everyone else on the bus in jeopardy, especially since you don't know why the officer is asking you not to move the bus.

66. b. According to the schedule, the 8:47 bus arrives at Milford Mall at 8:57, which would be in time for a 9:00 appointment.

67. d. According to the schedule, the bus that leaves Ash and Main at 6:52 arrives at Summer Hill at 7:22.

68. b. According to the schedule, the bus that leaves Milford Mall at 9:27 arrives at James and Ocean at 9:46.

69. a. A passenger's safety should always be your first concern. Even if the woman is eccentric, there is no way you can judge whether or not she really is about to have a seizure. It's far better to err on the side of caution.

70. d. All the options but this one are dangerous. The safest choice is to stop and insist the rollerblader let go of the bus.

SCORING

Once again, in order to score your exam, start by counting the total number of questions you got right out of the 70 questions on the test. Next, convert that score into a percentage, and divide your correct answer score by 0.7 to get the total percentage of right answers. Use the table below to check your math; it will give you percentage equivalents for several possible scores.

Number of questions right	Approximate percentage
70	100%
65	93%
60	86%
55	79%
50	71%
45	64%
40	57%
35	50%

As previously stated, you will need a score of at least 70 percent to pass; however, you should strive for the best score you can achieve, since your rank on the eligibility list may well depend on it, in whole or in part. You have probably seen improvement between your second practice exam score and this one. If you didn't improve as much as you would like, follow the suggestions at the end of the second practice exam.

You should again examine how you did on each kind of question on the test, in order to spot where your strengths and weaknesses lie. That way you'll know which areas require special effort in the time you have left before the exam. The table on this page identifies which questions on the third practice exam fall into which categories and lets you know which chapters to review if you had trouble with a particular type.

Keep in mind that self-confidence is the key and that in using this book, you're making yourself better prepared than other people who may be taking the exam with you. You've taken practice exams, diagnosed where your strengths and weaknesses lie, and learned how to deal with the various kinds of questions on the test. So go into the exam with confidence, knowing that you've done your best to become prepared.

BUS OPERATOR EXAM 3

Question Type	Question numbers	Chapter
Rules of the road and safe driving	1, 4, 12, 16, 20, 21, 23, 26, 28, 32, 34, 36, 38, 39, 41, 42, 54, 64, 70	6, "Safe Driving"
Reading bulletins, schedules, and route maps	5–10, 13–15, 48–52, 56–58, 61–63, 66–68	7, "Reading Bulletins, Schedules, and Route Maps"
Judgment, application of procedures, and courtesy to passengers	3, 11, 17–19, 22, 24, 25, 27, 30, 31, 33, 35, 37, 43–46, 53, 55, 60, 65, 69	8, "Good Judgment and Common Sense"
Math	2, 29, 40, 47, 59	9, Mathematics

C·H·A·P·T·E·R

MORE HELP WITH READING

CHAPTER SUMMARY

Understanding what you read is vital to success on the Bus Operator exam. If you need extra work on your reading skills, this chapter is for you.

A s you probably noticed when you took the practice exams in this book, the New York City Bus Operator exam draws heavily on your reading skills. Some questions, of course, are specifically designed to test your reading ability. But even on questions about driving or customer relations, you have to be able to read well to answer correctly. These questions often describe a situation and ask what you should do—and you have to understand the situation completely in order to choose the right answer.

Good reading skills are important on the job and in your daily life as well. This chapter will help you improve your reading ability, focusing on three of the most important things you have to do when reading during the test or on the job:

- Understanding the basic facts
- Finding the main idea
- Making inferences or drawing conclusions

Accomplishing these tasks starts with active reading.

ACTIVE READING

Perhaps the most important thing you can do to build your reading skills is to become an *active reader*. Active readers generally do two things when they read:

1. They mark up the text.
2. They make specific observations about the text.

MARKING UP THE TEXT

Marking the text actively engages you with the words and ideas you are reading. Marking up the text includes three specific strategies:

- Underlining key words and ideas
- Circling and defining any unfamiliar words or phrases
- Recording your reactions and questions in the margins

When you **underline key words and ideas,** you highlight the most important parts of the text you are reading. You also make it easier to summarize and remember the key points.

Circling unfamiliar vocabulary words is important, too, because a key word or phrase could change the meaning of an entire passage. As an active reader, make sure you look up unknown words immediately. If no dictionary is available, try to determine the meaning of the word as best you can from the surrounding sentences (the *context*).

Finally, **recording your reactions and questions in the margins** turns you from a passive receiver of information into an active learner. You will be much more likely to profit from the ideas and information you read about if you create a "conversation" with the writer in this way.

Of course, if this or any other book you read comes from the library, it's only polite to avoid marking in the book itself. Other readers may have other reactions to record. If the book you're reading belongs to someone else, mark key points on a piece of paper instead.

MAKING OBSERVATIONS

Good readers know that writers use many different strategies to express their ideas. Even if you know very little about writing strategies, you can make useful observations about what you read that will help you better understand the author's ideas. You can notice, for example, the author's choice of words; the structure of sentences and paragraphs; any repetition of words or ideas; important details about people, places, and things; and so on.

This step—making observations—is essential because our observations are what lead us to logical *inferences* about what we read. Inferences are conclusions based on reason, fact, or evidence. When we misunderstand what we read, it is often because we haven't looked closely enough at the text, and so we base our inferences on our own ideas, not on what's actually written in the text. We end up forcing our own ideas on the author rather than listening to what the author has to say and *then* forming our own ideas about it.

FINDING THE FACTS

Imagine, for a moment, that you are a detective. You have just been called to the scene of a crime; a house has been robbed. What's the first thing you should do when you arrive?

　　a. see what's on the TV
　　b. check what's in the fridge
　　c. get the basic facts of the case

The answer, of course, is **c**, get the basic facts of the case: the who, what, when, where, how, and why.

As a reader faced with a text, you go through a similar process. The first thing you should do is establish the facts. What does this piece of writing tell you? What happens? To whom? When, where, how, and why? If you can answer these basic questions, you're on your way to really comprehending what you read.

Let's start with a definition. A **fact** is:

- Something that we know for certain to have happened
- Something that we know for certain to be true
- Something that we know for certain to exist

Much of what you read, especially today in this "Information Age," is designed to provide you with facts. You may read, for example, about a new office procedure that you must follow; about how the new computer system works; about what happened at the staff meeting. If you're taking a standardized test to help you get a job, you'll probably have to answer reading comprehension questions that ask you about the facts in a passage you read. It is very important, therefore, for you to be able to read through these materials and understand the information they convey. What facts are you expected to know? What are you to learn or be aware of? What happened? What is true? What exists?

Fact-Finding Practice 1

Jump right into the task of finding facts. The brief passage below is similar to something you might see in a newspaper. Read the passage carefully, and then answer the questions that follow. Remember, careful reading is active reading, so mark up the text as you go. Underline key words and ideas; circle and define any unfamiliar words or phrases; record your reactions and questions in the margins.

On Tuesday, August 30, Mr. Blank, a prominent local citizen, arrived home from work to find his apartment had been robbed. The thieves somehow managed to slip past building security at 131 West Elm Street with nearly all of Mr. Blank's belongings. In fact, the thieves left behind nothing but a stack of old *Home Decorator* magazines and a can of pork and beans. The robbery was reported by Mr. Blank's neighbor, who found Mr. Blank unconscious in his doorway. Apparently Mr. Blank was so shocked by the robbery that he fainted. His neighbor immediately called an ambulance and then the police. Mr. Blank is now staying with relatives and is offering a reward of $25,000 for any information leading to the arrest of the thieves.

1. What happened to Mr. Blank?

2. When did it happen?

3. Where did it happen?

4. How did Mr. Blank react?

5. Who called the police?

6. What was left in the apartment?

Remember, good reading is active reading. Did you mark up the passage? If so, it may have looked something like this:

standing out; widely & popularly known

when *who*

On Tuesday, August 30, Mr. Blank, a (prominent) local citizen, arrived home from work to find his apartment had been robbed. The thieves somehow managed to slip past building security at 131 West Elm Street with nearly all of Mr. Blank's belongings. In fact, the thieves left behind nothing but a stack of old *Home Decorator* magazines and a can of pork and beans. The robbery was reported by Mr. Blank's neighbor, who found Mr. Blank unconscious in his doorway. Apparently Mr. Blank was so shocked by the robbery that he fainted. His neighbor immediately called an ambulance and then the police. Mr. Blank is now staying with relatives and is offering a reward of $25,000 for any information leading to the arrest of the thieves.

} What happened — robbery

— where

how did they manage this?

interesting detail.

who else was involved

Wow!

lots of $!

You'll notice that the answers to the questions have all been underlined, because these are the key words and ideas in this passage. But here are the answers in a more conventional form:

1. What happened to Mr. Blank? *His apartment was robbed.*

2. When did it happen? *Sometime while Mr. Blank was at work on Tuesday, August 30.*

3. Where did it happen? *131 West Elm Street.*

4. How did Mr. Blank react? *He fainted.*

5. Who called the police? *Mr. Blank's neighbor.*

6. What was left in the apartment? *Some old Home Decorator magazines and a can of pork and beans.*

Notice that these questions went beyond the basic who, what, when, and where to include some of the details, like what was left in the apartment. This is because details in reading comprehension, as well as in detective work, can be very important clues that may help answer the remaining questions: who did it, how, and why.

Fact-Finding Practice 2

Here's another passage, this time something a little more like what you might see at work. Read the passage carefully and answer the questions that follow:

> To: All New Employees
> From: Human Resources
>
> In order for your first paycheck to be processed, we must have a number of documents completed and in our files. Once these documents are in our hands, you will be entered into our payroll system. These documents include: a completed company application; a W-4 form; an I-9 form; a Confidentiality Agreement, if applicable; an emergency contact sheet; and a copy of your resume. You should be sure all of these documents are filled out within your first week of work. In addition, we will need the following documents from you for your file to be complete: two letters of recommendation from previous employers, a high school and college transcript, and an insurance coverage application. We request that you complete your file within your first month of employment.

7. What papers must new employees have on file? List them below.

8. In your list above, circle the items that employees must have on file in order to get paid.

9. When should these circled items be completed?

10. When must the rest of the file be completed?

11. True or False: Everyone must sign a Confidentiality Agreement.

Before you look at the answers, look at the next page to see how you might have marked up the passage to highlight the important information:

To: All New Employees
From: Human Resources

In order for your first paycheck to be processed, we must have a number of documents completed and in our files. Once these documents are in our hands, you will be entered into our payroll system. These documents include: [a completed company application; a W-4 form; an I-9 form; a Confidentiality Agreement, if applicable; an emergency contact sheet; and a copy of your resume.] You should be sure all of these documents are filled out within your first week of work. In addition, we will need the following documents from you for your file to be complete: [two letters of recommendation from previous employers, a high school and college transcript, and an insurance coverage application.] We request that you complete your file within your first month of employment.

Important deadline!

Official copy of a student's educational record

Documents I need in order to get paid

Documents I need to complete file

Deadline for completing file

With a marked-up text like this, it's very easy to find the answers.

7. What papers must new employees have on file?
Company application
W-4 form
I-9 form
Confidentiality Agreement (if applicable)
Emergency contact sheet
Resume
Two letters of recommendation
High school and college transcripts
Insurance coverage application

8. In the list above, the items that employees must have on file in order to get paid are circled.

9. When should these circled items be completed? *Within the employee's first week of work.*

10. When must the rest of the file be completed? *Within the employee's first month of work.*

11. True or False: Everyone must sign a Confidentiality Agreement. *False; only those for whom it is "applicable."*

Fact-Finding Practice 3

Now look at one more short passage. Again, read carefully and then answer the questions that follow:

> Today's postal service is more efficient and reliable than ever before. Mail that used to take months to move by horse and by foot now moves around the country in days or hours by truck, train, and plane. First class mail usually moves from New York City to Los Angeles in three days or less. If your letter or package is urgent, the U.S. Postal Service offers Priority Mail and Express Mail services. Priority Mail is guaranteed to go anywhere in the U.S. in two days or less. Express Mail will get your package there overnight.

12. Who or what is this passage about?

13. How was mail transported in the past?

14. How is mail transported now?

15. How long does first class mail take?

16. How long does Priority Mail take?

17. How long does Express Mail take?

Once again, here's how you might have marked up this passage:

> then →
> now →
>
> *Are there other services?*
>
> Today's postal service is more efficient and reliable than ever before. Mail that used to take <u>months</u> to move by <u>horse</u> and by <u>foot</u> now moves around the *What a long time!* country in days or hours by <u>truck, train, and plane</u>. <u>First class mail</u> usually moves from New York City to Los Angeles in three days or less. If your letter or package is urgent, the U.S. Postal Service offers <u>Priority Mail</u> and <u>Express Mail</u> services. Priority Mail is guaranteed to go anywhere in the U.S. in two days or less. Express Mail will get your package there overnight.
>
> *3 services listed—*
> *First class—3days*
> *Priority—2 days*
> *Express—Overnight*
> *Fastest*

You can see how marking up a text helps make it easier to understand the information a passage conveys.

12. Who or what is this passage about? *The U.S. Postal Service.*

13. How was mail transported in the past? *By horse and foot.*

14. How is mail transported now? *By truck, train, and plane.*

15. How long does first class mail take? *Three days or less.*

16. How long does Priority Mail take? *Two days or less.*

17. How long does Express Mail take? *Overnight.*

Active reading is the first essential step to comprehension. Why? Because active reading forces you to really *see* what you're reading, to look closely at what's there. Like a detective who arrives at the scene of a crime, if you look carefully and ask the right questions (who, what, when, where, how, and why), you're on your way to really comprehending what you read.

FINDING THE MAIN IDEA

When the previous section talked about establishing the facts—the who, what, when, where, and how—it omitted one very important question: Why? Now you're ready to tackle that all-important question. Just as there's a motive behind every crime, there's also a "motive" behind every piece of writing.

All writing is communication: A writer writes to convey his or her thoughts to an audience (the reader—you). Just as you have something to say (a motive) when you pick up the phone to call someone, writers have something to say (a motive) when they pick up a pen or pencil to write. Where a detective might ask, "Why did the butler do it?" the reader might ask, "Why did the author write this? What idea is he or she trying to convey?" What you're really asking is, "What is the writer's main idea?"

Finding the main idea is much like finding the motive of the crime. It's the motive of the crime (the *why*) that usually determines the other factors (the *who, what, when, where,* and *how*). Similarly, in writing, the

main idea also determines the *who, what, when,* and *where* the writer will write about, as well as *how* he or she will write.

SUBJECT VS. MAIN IDEA

There's a difference between the *subject* of a piece of writing and its *main idea*. To see the difference, look again at the passage about the postal system.

Today's postal service is more efficient and reliable than ever before. Mail that used to take months to move by horse and by foot now moves around the country in days or hours by truck, train, and plane. First class mail usually moves from New York City to Los Angeles in three days or less. If your letter or package is urgent, the U.S. Postal Service offers Priority Mail and Express Mail services. Priority Mail is guaranteed to go anywhere in the U.S. in two days or less. Express Mail will get your package there overnight.

You will often see a question in the reading comprehension portion of a test that asks, in essence, "What is the main idea of this passage?"

For the passage above, you might be tempted to answer: "The post office."

But you'd be wrong.

This passage is *about* the post office, yes—but "the post office" is not the main idea of the passage. "The post office" is merely the *subject* of the passage (*who* or *what* the passage is about). The main idea must say something *about* this subject. The main idea of a text is usually an *assertion* about the subject. An assertion is a statement that requires evidence ("proof") to be accepted as true.

The main idea of a passage is an assertion about its subject, but it is something more: It is the idea that also holds together or controls the passage. The other sentences and ideas in the passage will all relate to that main idea and serve as "evidence" that the assertion is true. You might think of the main idea as a net that is cast over the other sentences. The main idea must be general enough to hold all of these ideas together.

Thus, the main idea of a passage is:

- An assertion about the subject
- The general idea that controls or holds together the paragraph or passage

Look at the postal service paragraph once more. You know what the subject is: "the post office." Now, see if you can determine the main idea. Read the passage again and look for the idea that makes an assertion about the postal service *and* holds together or controls the whole paragraph. Then answer the following question:

18. Which of the following sentences best summarizes the main idea of the passage?
   a. Express Mail is a good way to send urgent mail.
   b. Mail service today is more effective and dependable.
   c. First class mail usually takes three days or less.

Because **a** is specific—it tells us *only* about Express Mail—it cannot be the main idea. It does not encompass the rest of the sentences in the paragraph—it doesn't cover Priority Mail or first class mail. Answer **c** is also very specific. It tells us only about first class mail, so it, too, cannot be the main idea.

But **b**—"Mail service today is more effective and dependable"—*is* general enough to encompass the whole passage. And the rest of the sentences *support* the idea that this sentence asserts: Each sentence offers "proof" that the postal service today is indeed more efficient and reliable. Thus, the writer's motive is to tell us

about the efficiency and reliability of today's postal service.

TOPIC SENTENCES

You'll notice that in the paragraph about the postal service, the main idea is expressed clearly in the first sentence: "Today's postal service is more efficient and reliable than ever before." A sentence, such as this one, that clearly expresses the main idea of a paragraph or passage is often called a *topic sentence.*

In many cases, like the postal service paragraph, you will find the topic sentence at the beginning of the paragraph. You will also frequently find it at the end. Less often, but on occasion, the topic sentence may be found in the middle of the passage. Whatever the case may be, the topic sentence—like "Today's postal service is more efficient and reliable than ever before"—is an assertion, and it needs "proof." The proof is found in the facts and ideas that make up the rest of the passage. (Not all passages provide such a clear topic sentence that states the main idea. Such passages will come up later in this chapter.)

Remember that a topic sentence is a clear statement of the main idea of a passage; it must be general enough to encompass all of the ideas in that passage, and it usually makes an assertion about the subject of that passage. Knowing all that, you can answer the following question even without reading a passage.

Topic Sentence Practice 1

19. Which of the following sentences is general enough to be a topic sentence?
   a. UNIX is one of the most common computer languages.
   b. There are many different computer languages.
   c. An old computer language is BASIC.

d. Most IBM computers use OS/2.

The answer is **b**, "There are many different computer languages." Answers **a**, **c**, and **d** are all specific examples of what is said in **b**, so they are not general enough to be topic sentences.

Topic Sentence Practice 2

Now look at the following paragraph. Underline the sentence that expresses the main idea, and notice how the other sentences work to support that main idea.

Erik always played cops and robbers when he was a boy; now, he's a police officer. Suzanne always played school as a little girl; today, she is a high school math teacher. Kara always played store; today, she owns a chain of retail clothing shops. Long before they are faced with the question, "What do you want to be when you grow up?" some lucky people know exactly what they want to do with their lives.

Which sentence did you underline? You should have underlined the *last* sentence: "Long before they are faced with that question 'What do you want to be when you grow up?' some lucky people know exactly what they want to do with their lives." This sentence is a good topic sentence; it expresses the idea that holds together the whole paragraph. The first three sentences—about Erik, Suzanne, and Kara—are *specific examples* of these lucky people. Notice that this time the topic sentence is found at the *end* of the paragraph.

Topic Sentence Practice 3

Among the eight sentences below are *two* topic sentences. The other sentences are supporting sentences. Circle the two topic sentences. Then write the numbers of the supporting sentences that go with each topic sentence.

1. Furthermore, government employees receive terrific heath-care coverage.

2. Some police officer duties, like writing reports, have no risk at all.

3. For example, government employees have more paid holidays than employees of private companies.

4. Not all police duties are dangerous.

5. Others, like traffic duty, put police officers at very little risk.

6. Government employees enjoy numerous benefits.

7. Still other duties, like investigating accidents, leave officers free of danger.

8. In addition, government employees are well compensated for overtime hours.

Sentences 4 and 6 are the <u>two</u> topic sentences because both make an assertion about a general subject. The supporting sentences for topic sentence 4, "Not all police duties are dangerous," are sentences 2, 5, and 7. The supporting sentences for topic sentence 6, "Government employees enjoy numerous benefits," are the remaining sentences: 1, 3, and 8.

Here's how they look as paragraphs:

Not all police duties are dangerous. Some duties, like writing reports, have no risk at all. Others, like traffic duty, offer very little risk. Still other duties, like investigating accidents, leave officers free of danger.

Government employees enjoy numerous benefits. For example, they have more paid holidays than employees of private companies. In addition, they are well compensated for overtime hours. Furthermore, they receive terrific heath-care coverage.

You might have noticed the supporting sentences in the first paragraph about police duties begin with the following words: *some, others,* and *still other.* These words are often used to introduce examples. The second paragraph uses different words, but they have the same function: *for example, in addition,* and *furthermore.* If a sentence begins with such a word or phrase, that is a good indication it is *not* a topic sentence—because it is providing a specific example.

Here are some words and phrases often used to introduce specific examples:

for example	in particular
for instance	some
in addition	others
furthermore	

If you're having trouble finding the main idea of a paragraph, you might try eliminating the sentences that you know contain supporting evidence.

Now you can answer the last of the questions—the *why.* What is the writer's motive? What's the main idea he or she wants to convey? By finding the sentence that makes an assertion about the subject of the paragraph and that encompasses the other sentences in the paragraph, you can uncover the author's motive.

DRAWING CONCLUSIONS

Writers know that they can get an idea across to their readers without directly saying it. Instead of providing a topic sentence that expresses their main idea, many times they simply omit that sentence and instead provide a series of clues through structure and language to get their ideas across.

Finding an implied main idea is much like finding a stated main idea. Remember, a main idea is an assertion about the subject that controls or holds together all of the ideas in the passage. If the writer provides a topic sentence that states the main idea, finding the main idea is something of a process of elimination: You eliminate the sentences that aren't general enough to encompass the whole passage. But what do you do when there's no topic sentence?

You use your observations to make an inference—an inference about the main idea or point of the passage.

Finding an implied main idea requires you to use your observations to make an inference that, like a topic sentence, encompasses the whole passage. It might take a little detective work, but you can make observations that will enable you to find main ideas even when they're not explicitly stated.

Inference Practice 1

For the first example of finding an implied main idea, let's return to our friend Mr. Blank. If you remember, earlier in this chapter his apartment was robbed. Now look at a statement from the building manager in response to news of the robbery:

This is the third robbery in our building this month. Each time, the thieves have gotten past building security with almost the entire contents of the victim's apartment. Yet each time, the security officers say they have seen nothing unusual.

Now, there is no topic sentence in this paragraph, but you should be able to determine the manager's main idea from the facts he provides and from his tone. What is he suggesting?

20. Which of the following best summarizes the manager's main idea?
   a. There are too many robberies in the building.
   b. There are not enough security officers in the building.
   c. There is something wrong with the security in the building.

The correct answer is **c**. There is something wrong with the security in the building. How can you tell that this is the main idea? For one thing, it's the only one of the three choices that is general enough to serve as a "net" for the paragraph; choice **a** is implied only in the first sentence and choice **b** isn't mentioned at all. In addition, each sentence on its own suggests that security in the building has not been working properly. Furthermore, the word "yet" indicates that there is a conflict between the events that have taken place and the duties of the security officers.

Inference Practice 2

Now examine the following statement from Mr. Blank's neighbor, who was also interviewed after the robbery:

Well, Mr. Blank's a pretty carefree man. A few times I've knocked on his door and he just hollers "Come in," and I just have to push the door open because it isn't locked. He often forgets things, too, like where he parked his car or where he put his keys. One time I found him in the hall searching through his bags because he couldn't find his keys, and it turned out the door was open anyway. Sometimes I wonder how he remembers to eat, let alone to take care of his apartment.

21. What is Mr. Blank's neighbor suggesting?
   a. Mr. Blank forgets everything.

   b. Mr. Blank may have left his door open that day.
   c. Mr. Blank is too carefree for his own good.

You can attack the question this way: Which of these three statements do the sentences in the neighbor's statement support? Try a process of elimination. Do all of the sentences support choice **a**? If not, cross **a** out. Do all of the sentences support choice **b**? Choice **c**?

The correct answer is **b**. Mr. Blank may have left his door open that day. How can you tell? Because this is the only idea that all of the sentences in the neighbor's statement support. You know that Mr. Blank often doesn't lock his door when he's home; you also know that he often forgets things. Thus, the neighbor's statement contains both **a** and **c**, but neither can be the main idea because the neighbor discusses both things in combination. This combination makes it likely that Mr. Blank left his apartment door open on the day he was robbed.

Inference Practice 3

Now look at a paragraph in which the *language* the writer uses is what enables you to determine meaning. Read the following paragraph carefully and see if you can determine the implied main idea of the paragraph.

Mr. B, my manager, is six feet ten inches tall with eyes that pierce like knives and a mustache like Hitler's. He invades the office at precisely 8:00 every morning demanding this report and that report. He spends half of the day looking over my shoulder and barking orders. And whenever there's a mistake—even if it's his fault—he blames it on me.

Before you decide on the implied main idea, list your observations. What did you notice about the language in this paragraph? An example is provided to get you started.

Example: *I noticed that Mr. B's eyes are compared to knives.*

22. Which of the following best expresses the implied message of the passage?
    a. Working for Mr. B is a challenge.
    b. Working for Mr. B is like working for a tyrant.
    c. Mr. B is a terrible manager.

The correct answer is **b**, working for Mr. B is like working for a tyrant. There are many clues in the langauge of this paragraph that lead you to this inference. First, you probably noticed that Mr. B "has eyes that pierce like knives." This comparison (called a *simile*) suggests that Mr. B does not look at others very warmly; instead, his eyes stab.

Second, the description of Mr. B's mustache is a critical part of the way the author establishes the tone of this paragraph. To say that Mr. B has a mustache "like Hitler's" automatically makes us picture Mr. B as Hitler. This is a very serious comparison (also a simile). A writer wouldn't compare someone to Hitler—even on a physical level—unless he wanted to paint that person as evil.

Third, the author tells us that Mr. B "invades" the office at "precisely" 8:00 A.M. every morning. "Invade" is a key word choice. The author could have said that Mr. B "storms into" the office or "barges into" the office, but he chose the word "invades," as if Mr. B doesn't belong there or as if Mr. B is attempting to take over territory that isn't his. Furthermore, Mr. B spends the day "barking orders," and, like a tyrant, he passes the blame onto others when something goes wrong. Thus,

though answers **a** and **c** may be true—it must be a challenge to work with Mr. B, and he doesn't seem to be the best "people person"—answer **b** is the only idea that all of the sentences in the paragraph support.

Of course, this person's description of Mr. B is very subjective, using as it does the first person point of view. As an active reader, you should wonder whether everyone sees Mr. B this way or if this employee is unable to be objective about Mr. B.

Many writers use implication to convey meaning rather than directly stating their ideas. Finding the implied main idea requires a little detective work, but it is not as difficult as you may have thought.

TIPS FOR CONTINUING TO IMPROVE YOUR READING

Reading is like exercise: If you don't keep doing it, you'll get out of shape. Like muscles that grow stronger and bigger with each repetition, your reading skills will grow stronger and stronger with each text that you read. But if you stop working out, your reading comprehension muscles will deteriorate.

The following are some ways you can continue to strengthen your reading comprehension skills:

- **Read!** Read anything—books, newspapers, magazines, novels, poems. The more you read, the better. Set yourself a reading goal: one book a month, two books while you're on vacation, a half hour of reading every night before bed.
- **Discover new authors.** Check out the best-seller list and try one of the books on that list. If it's a best-seller, it's probably a book that appeals to a wide variety of readers, and chances are good that you'll like it.
- **Spend some time in bookstores.** There are bound to be books and authors out there that appeal to

some of your interests. Don't be afraid to ask a salesperson to help you: Describe your interests and your preferences in style, and he or she can help you find books you'll enjoy reading.

- **Take a course at a local college.** Most courses (other than mathematics and computer science) require a significant amount of reading, so they're a great way to sharpen your reading comprehension skills while you work towards a degree or greater understanding of a certain subject. In addition, if you are in a class, you'll have a teacher who can guide you to make sure you're correctly comprehending what you read.

- **Make reading a family project.** For example, if your children have a reading contest or a book drive, read a book for each book they read. Go with them to the library and choose a book for yourself each time you go. The more your children see you reading, the more likely they are to become interested in reading themselves, and strong reading skills are a key to success in school.

- **Join a reading group.** Most cities and towns have a club that meets every two weeks or each month to discuss a selected book. In these groups, you'll get to discuss your ideas and questions with a group of friends and associates in an informal setting. If your area doesn't have a reading group, start your own. You and your friends can take turns choosing which book you'll read and discuss.